CW01559067

797,885 Books

are available to read at

www.ForgottenBooks.com

Forgotten Books' App
Available for mobile, tablet & eReader

ISBN 978-1-330-95258-0
PIBN 10125656

This book is a reproduction of an important historical work. Forgotten Books uses state-of-the-art technology to digitally reconstruct the work, preserving the original format whilst repairing imperfections present in the aged copy. In rare cases, an imperfection in the original, such as a blemish or missing page, may be replicated in our edition. We do, however, repair the vast majority of imperfections successfully; any imperfections that remain are intentionally left to preserve the state of such historical works.

Forgotten Books is a registered trademark of FB &c Ltd.
Copyright © 2015 FB &c Ltd.
FB &c Ltd, Dalton House, 60 Windsor Avenue, London, SW19 2RR.
Company number 08720141. Registered in England and Wales.

For support please visit www.forgottenbooks.com

1 MONTH OF
FREE
READING

at
www.ForgottenBooks.com

By purchasing this book you are eligible for one month membership to ForgottenBooks.com, giving you unlimited access to our entire collection of over 700,000 titles via our web site and mobile apps.

To claim your free month visit:

www.forgottenbooks.com/free125656

* Offer is valid for 45 days from date of purchase. Terms and conditions apply.

Similar Books Are Available from
www.forgottenbooks.com

Poems
by Edgar Allan Poe

The Complete Poetical Works and Letters of John Keats
by John Keats

Erotica
by Arthur Clark Kennedy

The Complete Poetical Works of John Milton
by John Milton

One Hundred Poems of Kabir
by Kabir

The Barons' Wars, Nymphidia, and Other Poems
by Michael Drayton

A Book of English Poetry
by George Beaumont

Poems: Sonnets, Lyrics, and Miscellaneous
by Edward Blackadder

The Book of Fairy Poetry
by Dora Owen

Chinese Poems
by Charles Budd

Coleridge's The Rime of the Ancient Mariner
And Other Poems, by Samuel Taylor Coleridge

Complaints; Containing Sundrie Small Poemes of the Worlds Vanitie
Whereof the Next Page Maketh Mention, by Edmund Spenser

The Complete Poetical Works of Geoffrey Chaucer
Now First Put Into Modern English, by John S. P. Tatlock

Cursor Mundi (The Cursor of the World)
A Northumbrian Poem of the XIVth Century, by Richard Morris

The Defence of the Bride Other Poems
by Anna Katharine Green

The Divine Comedy, Vol. 1
by Dante Alighieri

The Duke of Gandia
by Algernon Charles Swinburne

Eanthe
A Tale of the Druids, and Other Poems, by Sandford Earle

The Earthly Paradise
A Poem, by William Morris

The English Poems of George Herbert
Newly Arranged in Relation to His Life, by George Herbert Palmer

A TREASURY OF BIRD POEMS

SELECTED AND EDITED BY

CHARLES HENRY POOLE, LL.D.

" O all ye fowls of the air, bless ye the Lord :
Praise Him and magnify Him for ever."

" Winged Angels of this visible world we fly
To sing God's praises in the lofty sky ;
We seek the height to praise our Lord Most High."

LONDON

SIMPKIN, MARSHALL, HAMILTON, KENT & CO. LTD.

CONTENTS

ix

PREFACE

THIS volume is, as its title declares, "A TREASURY OF BIRD POEMS." As in every Treasury there will be found things new and old, so in this poetical collection are poems of intrinsic value, bearing the hall-mark of universal approbation, others mediocre, yet which, on account of their popularity, sentimentality or even ancientness, could hardly be omitted from a work of this nature. Hence to pass over Poe's "Raven," "The Jackdaw of Rheims," or "The Rime of the Ancient Mariner," familiar as they are to most readers of English poetry, would be deemed unpardonable. Lovers of the archaic would regard the work as deficient if no mention were made of Dunbar's "Merle and Nightingale," or Chaucer's "Parliament of Birds." No test then can be laid down for the selection of poems of any anthology. The rule that must guide the compiler or editor of such a work as the present one must be the Horatian dictum—"Not to swear allegiance to any master" in the task of selection from Bianor, who wrote of birds a thousand years before Christ, to the many sweet and fresh-voiced poets of the present century who have allowed their bird-songs to be incorporated in this collection. And, although not swearing allegiance to any master, the Editor has not been *masterful*; he has profited much by the kindly assistance and encouragement of a few personal friends in producing this many-sided volume.

The work attempts to bring together poems that ought to meet acceptance. It is divided into twelve sections, and if the sad, the joyous, the religious, the lovers of classical or legendary lore, the mystic, too, and poets and naturalists find no contentment in its perusal, the Editor will be sorry indeed. It is to be hoped that the work will appeal to a wider circle—all who love the Bird Creation.

This book then makes no pretence as a text-book of any sort, be it of English literature or ornithology Its mission will be served if it appeal to and please in some degree those blest with sympathy and love and interest in the beautiful, unspoilt, undegenerate ones, the denizens of earth and sky, who wish more especially that God's earthly choir should be spared—a choir whose only remuneration is to bank with Providence and pleasure to minister to the ears of men. It tries also to appeal to those wishful of discouraging the wilful destruction of birds, who believe that, although man holds the sovereignty of the whole animal creation, he ought to use reason as to their preservation or destruction. The killing of singing-birds is rampant, especially of larks, merely to make side-dishes for fastidious epicures. Soon will their songs cease to cheer men!

The bird-catcher trapping these songsters solely to retail them as cage-birds is not so criminal as the London dealers who create an excessive demand for these "minstrels of the sky" to meet the desires of fashionable diners. Cage-birds, perhaps, have done much to brighten a "slum" home; delight children; reclaim many a hard heart; and afford an outlet for the love of many a widow and spinster, who might, instead, have bestowed their affections on less worthy objects.

By the vagaries of fashion, ladies encourage the wholesale slaughter of beautiful birds—the osprey, bird of Paradise (it is pleasing to see that it is now almost a social offence for a lady to be seen wearing this bird's plumage), lark, egret, albatross, the lyre-bird, and other avian marvels.

For what good?—simply, for the adornment of a hat! "When will heartless fashion find a heart?" and Christian *gentlewomen* discourage the wearing of feathers, in the quest of which cruelties are perpetrated which would not be tolerated in slaughter-houses. Ladies can stop this by not creating a demand

and ceasing to carry about with them relics of God's beautiful Creation.

Birds make an especial appeal to ladies. This " Treasury " affords many examples, for are they not loved by them ?   Lesbia wept over her pet sparrow ; Mrs Katharine Tynan Hinkson loved the sparrow, too ; Lady Lindsay reads from St Francis a lesson of bird-teaching, as also Miss Cicely Fox Smith and Miss Olive Katharine Parr.

Ladies and birds were ever associated with sacred and profane legend as followers of the Founder of Christianity.   A nun, Miss Ada Lovegrove, and Miss Florence Coates, have given us respectively gem-legends of Noël, Passiontide and the Resurrection.

Needless is it to say that the Editor cannot claim for this work exhaustiveness or freedom from errors. He has still in hand enough poems to form a work nearly as large as the present.   Bird lovers will do him a favour by suggestions as to new authors, poems, or unknown sources, as also the pointing out of errors which inevitably must occur in the pre-paration of a first edition of this kind.

The work is probably unique (1) on account of the number of poets (about 300) who have written on birds to be found therein ; (2) its interesting in-troduction by an idealist, who pleads for a closer sympathy between ornithologists and poets ; (3) the large number of living poets who sing of birds and who will be found dateless in the index ; and (4) its division into twelve sections illustrating how the birds stand out in poetic vision, beaming with celestial beauty and lightsomeness.

Perhaps the reader is anxious to be admitted into the " hall " of the Avian Paradise, after thus parleying with the Editor at its " gate." Remembering, however, the words of the present Dean of Durham : " That if we do not love the animal creation we shall find no entrance into those blessed fields, in which, as in the works of the old poetic painters, man strays at peace with all God's creatures under the sun," let all love the Birds, for they joined, may be, in the loneliness of expectation awaiting man's Redemption !

CHARLES HENRY POOLE.

" What can I pay thee for this noble usage,
   But grateful praise ?   So Heav'n itself is paid !"
                                                    ROWE

ACKNOWLEDGMENTS

THE Editor wishes to record his warmest thanks of appreciation of the kindness of the following Authors in placing so generously at his disposal their copyright poems—some of which were written especially for this "Treasury of Bird Poems":—A. St John Adcock, His Grace the Duke of Argyll, K.T., Rose Arresti, J. E. Bode, Rev. C. L. Brain, W. J. Courthope, Joseph Cronshaw, Mrs Augusta Hancock, Mrs Katharine Tynan Hinkson, R. M. Ingersley, Canon F. Langbridge, Lady Lindsay, Miss Ada Lovegrove, Canon H. D. Rawnsley, Miss Maud Sargent, Canon P. A. Sheehan, E. V. Palgrave Simpson, H. F. Morland Simpson, Miss Cicely Fox Smith, Rev. F. W. Orde Ward (F. Harald Williams), W. Percival Westell, F.L.S., Rev. G. R. Woodward, Arthur Wright.

The Editor has also to thank the following Publishers, Literary Executors and others for their courtesy in allowing him to use copyright poems over which they have control:—The Editor of *The Animal World* for poems by Miss Lucy Hardy, Gerald Massey, Canon Rawnsley, Rev. F. W. Orde Ward; the Editor of *The Athenæum* for Eric Mackay's poem—"The Quelétzû"; Messrs George Bell & Sons for poems, from "Poetry of America," by W. C. Bryant, W. E. Channing, G. W. Curtis, R. H. Dana, C. F. Hoffman, J. R. Lowell, C. L. Thaxter, C. Sprague; Messrs Burns & Oates and Mr and Mrs Meynell for poems by Fr. Tabb and Francis Thompson; the Editor (Orby Shipley) of "Carmina Mariana" for "Two Nightingales," by G. R. Woodward; the Editor of *The Catholic Home Journal* for a poem by Miss F. Coates; the Proprietors of *The Century Magazine* for a poem by S. H. Nichols; the Editor of *Chambers's Journal*, and the Authors —A. St John Adcock, E. W. Lummis and L. M. Watt; Messrs Chatto & Windus for permission to use Dr W. C. Bennett's "Swallow," from "Songs for Sailors," "Itylus," by A. C. Swinburne; Messrs Constable & Co. for two poems by J. Burroughs ; the Editor of *The Country-Side Monthly* for poems by Mrs Augusta Hancock, Miss M. Sargent, E. V. Palgrave Simpson ; Mr Ellis for D. G. Rossetti's sonnet " Beauty and the Bird " ; the Editor of *The Children's Encyclopædia* (Harmsworth) for some bird poems appearing in volume for 1909 ; Mr John Heywood for poem by E. Waugh ; Messrs Kegan, Paul & Co. for lines by Mrs Hamilton King ; Messrs Longmans, Green & Co. for R. Jefferies' poem, " The Chaffinch," R. L. Stevenson's " Nest Eggs," and W. Morris' lines from " Land East of the Sun " ; Mr Elkin Mathews for G. F. Bradby's " Blue Tit " ; Messrs Maclehose & Co. and Canon Rawnsley for poems contained in " Poems of Nature " ; Messrs Macmillan for some copyright verses of C. G. Rossetti ; Messrs Routledge & Sons for the " Nest Robber " from the " Shi King " ; Messrs Sampson Low & Co. for the use of verses from Canon Evans' " Songs of the Birds " ; Messrs Walter Scott & Co. for poems in " New Zealand Verse," " Painter Poets," " Sonnets of the Nineteenth Century," " Canadian Poems," " Australian Ballads," " Poems of Owen Meredith," and " Poems of Nature," by J. C. Andersen, A. Bathgate, A. Domett, A. East, J. D. Edgar, C. A. Fox, R. S. Hawker, D. Gray, Jean Inglelow, the Earl of Lytton, W. Renton, W. Sharp, J. Thomas, Lord Thurlow, C. Tennyson-Turner ; Messrs A. P. Watt & Son and Lady Betty Balfour for Lord Lytton's " Titlark's Nest."

The Editor has especially to thank Messrs Longmans, Green & Co. for information respecting the " Dying Swan," by J. E. Bode ; also the Walter Scott Publishing Co. for generously placing at the Editor's disposal Bird Poems found in their admirable series.

If by chance the Editor has infringed any copyrights, either of publishers or authors, he trusts that he will be forgiven in the name of the Birds.

INTRODUCTION

BIRDS, BARDS AND NATURALISTS

ARCHITECTURE, wood-carving, and even building are excluded from the estimate when certain birds plan their family abodes. Do not beach-loving Little Tern and cliff-seeking Guillemot treat nest-making as a wasteful habit—the outcome of an invalid's fancy, or of a diseased ambition ? Land surveying is the chief science, and judicious site-choosing the art of arts for them. They lay their eggs in an eye-baffling or inaccessible situation and assert the right of first occupation by patient sittings. Other projectors, though far from emulating the snuggeries and boudoirs of the Chaffinch and Jenny Wren, feel it becoming to co-operate with Lady Nature's gift of site and material by scratching on some piece of ground by way of receipt ; and in most cases electing to gather a few fragments of grass, sedge or twig, as a monument of gratitude. These arcadian nurseries, favoured by lapwings, curlews, snipe and others, may invite comparison with such preparatory examples of prose-industry as introductory notes, acting as a foundation on which to arrange the poems of this " Treasury," to await their fate like precious eggs—those dumb orbs trembling at the equinox of death and life. There is one foreboding. Why should unwary readers be threatened with a professedly plain composition, comparable to the simple structure of the Lapwing, or the scooped-out arena wherein the Ostrich deposits her fifteen three-pounders ? It may be pleaded that similar homes shelter the heirs of notable chieftains of the feathered clans. The egg ennobles its nest ! Confident that the songs are able to dignify their Introduction, the writer will endeavour to put together some appropriate facts and thoughts without intending to weary nature-lovers who prefer to enjoy the inner treasures of bird-poesy.

The curious and instructive features of avian annals are so numerous that only one or two historical incidents, as also a few

xix

touching principally upon the feeding, nesting and singing habits, will be selected, before concluding with an attempt to advocate a closer alliance between bards and ornithologists.

The world's oldest picture is one unearthed from a tomb in the Medum pyramid. Six geese are painted—two feeding energetically. The first individual bird mentioned in the Old Testament was Noah's honoured, but too voracious messenger— the Raven—who, even if he returned to perch on the roof of the Ark, did not re-enter his former hospice. Later on, however, as the Prophet was fed by a lineal descendant, the dark-robed penitent's reputation recovered its lustre. According to Sedulius, an early Christian poet : " He expiated on land, whatever he had perpetrated in the Flood."

In animated nature the antipathies and sympathies which amuse and amaze mankind, have given rise to so much inconclusive discussion, that I shall only take a limited view of their manifestations between Reptiles and Birds. To be enchanted by rude instrumental music is a supposed ophidian virtue. Be that as it may, the detestable habitude of devouring living feathered minstrels is a vicious corruption of the reputed taste for one of the fine arts. Retribution on the serpent tribe is forthcoming from an African falconoid—the Secretary Bird, so styled on account of a penlike array of plumes springing from the back of the head. His " secretarial " duties would, it may be imagined, consist in drawing up the wills of troublesome snakes, and rendering them effective by encompassing the death of the testators. He grimly kicks a victim forward, till its back-bone is broken in several places. Should the venomous haje-cobra succeed in planting a desperate bite near the flesh of its towering pursuer, the feathers poisoned are at once plucked out. Amiably wide of the mark, is the reprisal negotiated by a harmless colubrine (twenty inches long) found in South Africa, surnamed the Egg-eater. An egg, about the size of a hen's, is seized, but not crushed by the hard-lipped mouth incapable of retaining the slippery contents. When worked well into the gullet, the shell is broken by tooth-like projections from the flexible spine. A gold and silvery streamlet of chicken essence meanders into " the Serpentine " fertilizing his delectable domains without the preliminary disparagement of salt, or the waste hinted at by a concluding wipe on a grassy serviette.

On the other hand—an instance of sympathy—a plover, called the *trochilus* by Herodotus and Pliny, enters the crocodile's cyclopean jaws, and clears the premises of parasites. This is the " ziczac," who also warns his sleepy beast-friend of danger by screaming this alarm-cry, and dashing against the saurian's scaly face. " He is at peace with the trochilus," is the weighty deduction of Herodotus. Mutual aid societies are, however, rare between the reptilian and avian Classes, and they seem to be non-existent between the Birds and Ophidians or Snakes proper. Antipathies are rampant. An interesting example of woodland skirmishing presents itself. The Mocking Bird practises in sound what a familiar lizard achieves for colour. The Chameleon may be styled a variable animated photochrome, a travelling lantern-slide, an invisible notoriety! Nevertheless, this miracle of a colour scheming is outrivalled by the self-advertising Mocking Bird which utilises the vocal characteristics of all other animals for its own glorification, and is declared by some Americans to excel the Nightingale! They doubtless mean the Virginian species. The Black Snake is undeterred by this polyglot entertainment, from trying to despoil the nest, so the arch-mimics, scorning all possible frights and fascinations, resist and often repel the attacks by a deadlier use of their talented beaks.

The imagination and reason find endless pleasure in tracing to many unexpected nooks and corners, naïve resemblances or exemplars of our human inventions. The unity of the Creator's plan is all-pervading, minute, enduring. To suppose that man has not a faculty superior to the mere power of detecting and imitating the mechanisms and contrivances found in other terrestrial beings seems to be a mistaken notion. Yet it is probable, in view of the wonderful inventions taking their rise from exact observation, that if intending discoverers used their eyes more the brain would be wearied less. Still the mind is obliged to think deeply as well as observe. Man designs, and in a sense creates. A tragedy of Sophocles, a painting by Zeuxis are considered works of the reason and judgment. This truth Socrates carefully drew from the half unwilling heart of Aristodemus, in order to prove that the first Framer of mankind "designed their advantage when He gave them several senses by which objects are apprehended." The elements of a true theory may exist. The discovery lags, or rather is made to wait. The further the material objects, the abstract reasoner, the occasion are separated, the more overpowering becomes our sense of the infinitely perfect Prescience of the Deity, when they come together at the destined moment. The solar system moving, an apple falling, a Newton thinking, the law of gravitation, an Eternal Designer !

The task of allocating the origin of arts and inventions to their proper sources—anticipations, hints, parallels, prototypes, may be safely left to the sagacity of each theorist. The birds will plead their own view of the case in chorus, on p. 177. The tired citizen rambling through wood and field is not compelled to be too pensive. Artisans are cheered by the kindred labours of beak and claw. They are glad to forget for a few sunlit hours the responsible accumulation of organs, models and appliances packed with such crowded ease and appalling safety in their own frames. Builders watch swallows with delight, miners eagerly behold sand-martins pecking out a safe dwelling, carpenters are encouraged by the strenuous hammering and splintering of woodpeckers ; manufacturers revel in the industry of the Tailor and Weaver birds, and the thatcher gleefully draws attention to the multiplex habitation of the sociable Grosbeak, to show that his occupation will never be gone. Are all these accomplishments worthy to be raised to the status of architecture ? Ruskin lays it down that, " No art is capable of expressing thought which does not change." This dictum, if true, tends to minimise the value of complimentary tributes showered upon ingenious nest-constructors, as if they were architects, artists, sculptors, in the true and highest meaning. Excavators, weavers, cabinet-makers, decorators they may well be called. Turning to another of their gifts—singing, they may even be termed musicians by instinct and imitation capable of improvement with training. Music, however, has progressed as a fine art since Miriam sounded her " loud timbrel o'er Egypt's dark sea," but the sea-birds cry above its watery waste now, in much the same way as when they shrieked over the swaying heads of Pharaoh's soldiery.

The rounded " little cup of fate " of the Chaffinch and the fairy dome of the Long-tailed Tit are adorned with lichens, and often with the white cocoons of spiders. Do these materials attached to the webbed, felted moss, serve for concealment ? Many authorities, including Michelet, think so. How is it possible to account for the brilliant array of *confetti* which these busy workers sometimes stick on their dwellings ?   Where is the instinct for useful concealment gone ?   Mr Kay Robinson explains the anomaly by saying that it is "the dry, papery texture of the lichen, and not the protective colouring, which is the attraction."   Hence too, the *confetti* industry.   The birdies seem to have strayed from possible disguising tactics without doing much to secure a reputation for decorative skill.   Are they colour-blind or colour-crazy, or simply papery at any risk ?   What an enticing topic for professional naturalists to discuss !   Readers anxious to drink from the Pierian springs of poesie, may invoke Shake speare to charm away the difficulty.   Is it not a woodland instance of—

> "How oft the sight of means to do ill deeds
> Makes ill deeds done."

Being little skilled in bard-lore and less in bird-lore, it is not easy to feel sanguine, when about to appeal for a closer sympathy between ornithologists and poets.   The need for conciliation existing perhaps at the present time, may not be felt in the hopeful future.   Even if fated to melt away like a mirage, how refreshing it is to imagine the advent of a literary era, when every representative species of the bird-world would be accorded a meed of gratitude for their gifts to mankind and their joy-inspiring companionship !   It is needless to impress upon our bards that all unthanked songsters would be better honoured in being uplifted to sonnet or madrigal, than by being promoted from a mere variety to an established species in nomenclature.   Yet what long-slumbering periods, charged with future reproach, have not former singers spent in repeating a narrow programme ?   From the time of Homer, who declared that the string of the recovered bow of Ulysses twanged, "like the shrill swallow's cry," and Sappho, who in an extant fragment of her imaginings is found exclaiming, "Angel of the Spring, the mellow-throated nightingale "—till after the middle of the eighteenth century, favourite groups have been overlauded.   Did minstrels think by profuse persistency of praise to smother the tuneful appeal of hundreds of candidates, passed over through numberless springtides without a metrical foot of thanks ?   Even now, many birdlings of sweet bill languish, and not a few fowl of adventurous wing are exiled with a comfortless mention accompanied by a faltering adjective and a worn-out verb. Why should not the eye of bird and bard admirers be relieved with a wider range ? Every species with well-marked characteristics could be provided with a poem. Will the poetocracy of the present generation be heedless of their petitions ? Naturalists, in strenuous contrast, have been silently searching, comparing, pondering, sketching, or *vivâ voce* discussing, correcting slight errors for the sake of a new variety, and they are ever striving to obtain fresh records of notable individuals. They do not allow each other to remain the plenipotentiaries of erudition, but with a twofold interest they brave the wilds for new species, and cherish those verging to extinction. How they scan the size, the shape, the marking of eggs, considering their smooth shells as Dame Nature's bright manuscripts or autograph letters to her pupils! Bird observers add to the mass of facts for the use of their leading thinkers, who are willing to learn from their inferiors, and wait patiently—habits not congenial to the quicker impulses of the bards. There are songs innumerable to unconscionable owls and unabashed cuckoos. Where is there more than a line or two to the alert Oystercatcher ? The knightly Secretary Bird has been loaded with twenty scientific names. Has he been greeted with one cloud-piercing pæan for his redoubtable deeds ?

Bird-mounters perpetuate the memory of all kinds in their variations of plumage. They cheat the avine cemetery. A lively corncrake can quickly provide a self-made stage corpse. The taxidermist enables this schemer to sham life, when too dead to sham death. In an elegy on p. 231, the poetic tendency is disclosed. Catullus, in Byron's English, admonishes the " devouring grave," and in Mr Morland Simpson's Scots, falls foul of some " auld greedy carl," in order to console Lesbia for the demise of her favourite sparrow—probably frightened to death by Lesbia's equally pet brother. If the defunct chirruper had been sent to the local embalmer, or the more skilled Egyptian artist, it would have come back a durable memorial of affection, rivalling the sacred ibis-mummies of the Pyramids and more life-like than the fossilised remains of the archæopteryx ! It is a sign of increasing harmony and co-operation between ornithologists and poets, that the field naturalist has been saluted with a genuine tribute in the following spirited lines by Mr Gerald Bull :

" Alone he stands.   His step is firm and even ;
His hair is combed by every wind of heaven,
And shades a brow that juts above keen eyes
Well used to watching where the wonder lies
Of Nature's secret working in the tree,
The plant, the stone, the shell, the bird and bee."

There is a thrush, called the Iceland redwing, which merits a
little poetic praise, if only for having eluded the "keen eyes " of re-
search, till Mr Coburn's quick ear enabled him to discover this new
species (*Turdus coburni*), during his expedition to the North of
Iceland in 1899.   It will be better to borrow from this famous
naturalist's narrative, as given in *Country Queries*—July 1908.
" A strange song I had never before heard arrested my attention,
and after some searching I saw a thrush-like bird clinging to the
slender top twigs of a birch—as represented in the accompanying
photograph, the first ever published—and singing the most
scratchy and unmusical thrush's song I had ever heard.   When this
bird found that I was watching it, it vanished, and I searched
assiduously for it or another, but none could I find or hear until I
accidentally stumbled across a nest.   When I stooped down to
examine the young there was instantly such a chatter that the
forest appeared to be teeming with redwings. . . . When I
visited the British Museum, Dr Bowdler Sharpe at once declared
the bird to be new to science.   The Hon. Walter Rothschild also
declared it to be perfectly distinct."

This Treasury has been carefully culled from votaries of the
Muse, acclaiming their winged brethren in verse displaying various
degrees of acquaintance with their general economy.   If field
glasses could have been used by the more fancy-fed ancients, the
outlook might have been enriched.   The poems of recent times
attest that many of their authors are quietly becoming clever
observers of wild life.   Here and there among the contributors
one is agreeably surprised to see trained ornithologists roaming
around the pleasant slopes of Parnassus, as if to try the rest-cure
for weary eyes with a course of contemplation,

" By the light that never was on sea or land,
The consecration and the poet's dream."

What, in this hap, is the lot of one who enshrines his nature-
knowledge in verse ?   Some aspects of bird-life plead for this

soothing treatment, though the essential work is best done in carefully chosen prose-phrases. The master in metre and illuminative diction—the born poet, is asked to respect ornithological facts! This is just. Similarly, those initiated into the mysteries of woodland and field, will feel impelled to study the craft of versification ; and, if they wish to please as poet-naturalists, guide themselves along the intangible paths of wavy rhythm and musical cadence into the more idealistic sphere of the career of birds—their marvellous migrations, their joyous spirit, their misfortunes, their entrancing melodies, their captivating association with man. Imagination, so important in these matters, is apt to be despised instead of trained. No one will be bold enough to deny that wide-minded field naturalists, vastly superior to the examiners of dead specimens, have a peculiar claim to be listened to with respect in their own happy domain. Their eyes lovingly and faithfully turned to the ceaseless pageant of the seasons teach them that the undying poetry of the bird-world is a mystic force infusive of grandeur and gladness. Moreover, such is the exhaustless richness of Creation that we all become strongly attracted to the wonderful beings that allure us by approaching friendlike on almost every tract of land ; or elude us by diving like fishes in the yielding waters, and roaming fairylike in the unfretted highways of the sky.

> " All men are poets if they might but tell
> The dim ineffable changes which the sight
> Of natural beauty works on them."

Poets who do not intend to remain gloriously mute, assert their kinship to the birds, with generous emotion rather than calm study. Despite the hate-tipped epithets that they launch at vultures and ravens when seeking metaphors for human sins, I am inclined to think that most of the lyric band—when they unfold their ideas of a particular bird—strive to bring out its endearing qualities. Bestowing praise is their best-loved tendency. The supreme wave of the weird wand of genius when directing attention to their office transcends mere divination. It sets up a telepathy through ages and eras. Homer and Horace assure immortality to warriors celebrated in their pages. Whittier exclaims, " And Poets, garland bound, the Lords of thought draw near." The Lark is glorified as the embodiment of the witchery of their own music. The swan's body is invaded and used as a semi-detached villa for the sojourn of a departed poet's shade ; and it was fabled that the reason why a dying swan became songful, was because its whilom guest bemoaned the desolation of emigrating to some untenanted cygnet. Far from denying their little instrumental *confrères* the status of musicians, their laureates elevate them to the highest of the fine arts, and pleasingly conjure them to answer to the myrtle-sweet name of POET !

The favourite creatures, therefore, of ornithologist and bard are identical ! Is it not waste of time and thought, to seek for feebler bonds to unite these genuine admirers of the innumerable tribes of air, water, mountain and woodland ? They have already a fascinating fairyland inhabited by their bright plumaged friends, as their native haunt. " *Par nobile fratrum, et Arcades ambo.*" They are a noble pair of brothers, and both love the country with its birds. For every reader who feels the thrice-woven spell and responds to its gently uttered invitation, these words, I hope, will be happily realised :

> " Thy mind
> Shall be a mansion for all lovely forms,
> Thy memory be as a dwelling-place
> For all sweet sounds and harmonies."

C. BRAIN.

AN INVOCATION TO BIRDS

COME, all ye feathery people of mid-air,
Who sleep 'midst rocks, or on the mountain
    summits
Lie down with the wild winds ; and ye who
    build
Your homes amidst green leaves by grottoes
    cool ;
And ye who on the flat sands hoard your eggs
For suns to ripen, come '—O phœnix rare !
If death hath spared thee, or philosophic
    search
Permit thee still to own thy haunted nest,
Perfect Arabian,—lonely nightingale !
Dusk creature, who art silent all day long,
But when pale eve unseals thy clear throat,
    loosest
Thy twilight music on the dreaming boughs,
Until they waken ; and thou, cuckoo bird,
Who art the ghost of sound, having no shape
Material, but dost wander far and near,
Like untouched Echo whom the woods deny
Sight of her love,—come all to my slow charm .

Come thou, sky-climbing bird, wakener of
    morn,
Who springest like a thought unto the sun,
And from his golden floods dost gather wealth,
(Epithalamium and Pindarique song),
And with it enrich our ears ;—come all'to me,
Beneath the chamber where my lady lies,
And, in your several musics, whisper—LOVE !
                              BARRY CORNWALL.

I
BIRDS' NESTS AND NESTLINGS

" Thus yields the cedar to the axe's edge,
Whose arms gave shelter to the princely eagle."

SHAKESPEARE.

THE BIRDS

He

WHERE thou dwellest, in what grove,
Tell me, fair one, tell me, love ;
Where thou thy charming nest dost build,
O thou pride of every field !

She

Yonder stands a lonely tree ·
There I live and mourn for thee.
Morning drinks my silent tear,
And evening winds my sorrow bear.

He

O thou summer's harmony,
I have lived and mourned for thee ;
Each day I moan along the wood,
And night hath heard my sorrows loud.

She

Dost thou truly long for me ?
And am I thus sweet to thee ?
Sorrow now is at an end,
O my ·lover and my friend !

HE

Come ! on wings of joy we'll fly,
To where my bower is hung on high ;
Come, and make thy calm retreat
Among green leaves and blossoms sweet.
                              WILLIAM BLAKE.

THE LONELY BIRD

POOR bird, thy mate is far away ;
  I know it by thy song,
That fainter grows from day to day,
  Less musical and strong.
I would the fair green fields were thine,
  The woods, the hawthorn tree—
Thy cage a gilded prison is,
  But not a home for thee.

Thou wouldst not seek the greenwood shade—
  Thou couldst not find her now ;
Her low, sweet voice thou couldst not hear
  Upon the forest bough.
As much a home as those bright realms
  From which thy mate hath flown,
These prison bars, if thou must seek
  Their silent glades alone.

'Tis ever thus—the human heart
  Is like that lonely bird,
When only echoes of the past
  Among its chords are stirr'd ;

It pines away in silent grief
O'er joys long past and flown,
And then, neglected, breaks at last,—
It cannot live alone.

Poor lonely bird ! our world, like thine,
    Hath many a weary heart,
Hath many a ruin'd shrine, from which
    The shade will not depart ;
I would not bid thee seek the woods,
    For now I feel, like thee,
Without a kindred heart to love
    I could not happy be.

              J. E. CARPENTER.

THE HAPPINESS OF BIRDS

From " Emblems," Bk. V.

How happy are the Doves, that have the pow'r
    Whene'er they please, to spread their airy
        wings !
Or cloud-dividing Eagles, that can tow'r
    Above the scent of these inferior things !
How happy is the Lark, that ev'ry hour
    Leaves earth, and then for joy mounts up and
        sings !
    Had my dull soul but wings as well as they,
    How I would spring from earth, and clip away,
As wise *Astræa* did, and scorn this ball of clay !

              FRANCIS QUARLES.

THE INSTINCTIVE GENIUS OF BIRDS

I LOVE to see the little goldfinch pluck
The groundsel's feather'd seed, and twit and twit,
And soon in bower of apple-blossom perch'd,
Trim his gay suit, and pay us with a song ;
I would not hold him prisoner for the world!
   The chimney-haunting swallow, too, my eye
And ear well pleases ; I delight to see
How suddenly he skims the glassy pool,
How quaintly dips, and, with a bullet's speed,
Whisks by. I love to be awake, and hear
His morning song twitter'd to dawning day.
But most of all it wins my admiration,
To view the structure of this little work :
A bird's nest. Mark it well, within, without.
No tool had he that wrought, no knife to cut,
No nail to fix, no bodkin to insert,
No glue to join ; his little beak was all,
And yet how neatly finish'd! What nice hand,
And every implement and means of art,
And twenty years' apprenticeship to boot,
Could make me such another ? Fondly then
We boast of excellence, whose noblest skill
Instinctive genius foils.

JAMES HURDIS.

THE BIRDS IN GRAY'S ELEGY

SAVE that, from yonder ivy-mantled tower,
   The moping owl does to the moon complain
Of such as, wandering near her secret bower,
   Molest her ancient solitary reign.

Beneath those rugged elms, that yew-tree's shade,
  Where heaves the turf in many a mouldering heap,
Each in his narrow cell for ever laid,
  The rude forefathers of the hamlet sleep.

The breezy call of incense-breathing morn,
  The swallow twittering from the straw-built shed,
The cock's shrill clarion, or the echoing horn,
  No more shall rouse them from their lowly bed.
                                    THOMAS GRAY.

THE NESTS OF BIRDS

From " The Last of March "

AT distance from the water's edge,
  On hanging sallow's farthest stretch,
The moor-hen 'gins her nest of sedge,
  Safe from destroying school-boy's reach.
  Fen-sparrows chirp and fly to fetch
The wither'd reed-down rustling nigh,
  And, by the sunny side the ditch,
Prepare their dwelling warm and dry.
                                    JOHN CLARE.

A BIRD'S NEST

From " Lyra Innocentium "

BEHOLD the treasure of the nest,
  The wingèd mother's hope and pride :
See how they court her downy breast,
  How soft they slumber, side by side.

Strong is the life that nestles there,
  But into motion and delight
It may not burst, till soft as air
  It feel Love's brooding, timely might.

  .   .

Now steal once more across the lawn,
  Stoop gently through the cypress bough,
And mark which way life's feeble dawn
  Works in their little hearts, and how.

Still close and closer, as you pry,
  They nestle 'neath their mother's plume,
Or, with a faint forlorn half-cry,
  Shivering bewail her empty room.

Or haply, as the branches wave,
  The little round of tender bills
Is raised, the due repast to crave
  Of her who all their memory fills.

JOHN KEBLE.

A NEST

From " A Rosebud by my early Walk "

A ROSEBUD by my early walk,
Adown a corn-inclosèd bawk,
Sae gently bent its thorny stalk,
    All on a dewy morning.
Ere twice the shades o' dawn are fled,
In a' its crimson glory spread,
And drooping rich the dewy head,
    It scents the early morning.

Within the bush, her covert nest,
A little linnet fondly prest,
The dew sat chilly on her breast
    Sae early in the morning.
She soon shall see her tender brood,
The pride, the pleasure o' the .wood,
Amang the fresh green leaves bedewed,
    Awake the early morning.
                ROBERT BURNS.

THE CHAFFINCH'S NEST

(AT DUNNABECK)

THERE is a little cup of fate
Beside my trellised garden-gate,
A tiny cup most deftly made
With moss and lichen overlaid,
Wherein through all its strands is wove
The golden innocence of love—
A little loving-cup of life
And joy for feathered man and wife.
And therein, while the chaffinch sings,
A silent mother folds her wings,
Content to watch long hours apart
And press her jewels to her heart—
Jewels one day to find a voice   .
And bid the Junetide earth rejoice.
She knows her treasure-house shall be
Filled with new life, new song, new glee,

And roofs with her brown back the home
Against all rain and winds that come.
Bravely she sits though men pass by,
Meets questioning gaze with fearless eye ;
Unblenching though we giants stare,
Holds to ·her heaven-appointed care,
And shames us with a faith sublime
In life to be that keeps its time.
Far mightier powers than she has guessed
Bend like great angels o'er her nest ·
The sun that rolls in royal state
Is with her watch confederate ;
The punctual morn, the sequent eve,
Their spell about her casket weave,
Till sudden, with a heart aglow
A mother's triumph she shall know,
And life will fill the cup of fate
Beside my trellised garden-gate.
Ah ! would to God with such a heart
Our English mothers bore their part,
With such self-sacrificing zest
Would guard the home and keep the nest
                H. D. RAWNSLEY.

THE NEST OF THE GOLDFINCH

From " Birds of Scotland "

THE goldfinch weaves with willow-down inlaid,
And Cannach tufts, his wonderful abode ;
Sometimes suspended at the limber end
Of plane-tree spray among the broad-leaved shoots,

The tiny hammock swings to every gale.
Sometimes in closest thickets 'tis concealed,
Sometimes in hedge luxuriant, where the briar,
The bramble, and the plum-tree branch
Warp through the thorn, surmounted by the flowers
Of climbing vetch and honeysuckle wild.

JAMES GRAHAME.

THE HUMMING BIRD'S NEST

WHAT a frail house to trust with family cares,
   Hair, string, and moss in cunning complex
   twisted
Upon a branch exposed to windy airs,
   As though for nestlings danger ne'er existed !

But there the humming-bird with bravo courage,
   Lays, and broods upon her tinted eggs so slight
Within the woven cup, and for her forage
   Trusts thoughtless Nature to give food aright.

The winds may blow till like a leaf the nest
   Dances and whips upon the frolic breeze,
Yet will the fledglings thrive and take their rest
   Rocked to small sleep amid the airy seas.

The sharp-nosed fox about the wood may prowl,
   The sharp-eyed hawk peer down in search of prey,
And 'neath the.stars may hunt the sharp-billed owl,
   But still the jewelled.wee ones hide alway.

A wonder 'tis, such tiny creatures dare
  Perils so fearsome in th'unsheltered wild !
But wonder greater that small son and heir
  Survives such perils safe as eagle's child !
                STARR HOYT NICHOLS.

NESTING

(THE LARK)

I HEAR thee, hear thee, hear thee
As if earth were drawing near thee ;
And I now behold thee too
Making circlets in the blue ;
And a new song dost thou sing,
Timing to thy fluttering :
Then dead-heavy, as a stone
Shot from Etna's flaming cone,
Dropping on a land afar,
Or more like a falling star
From the sameness of the sky,
Down thou comest wearily
Only with a gradual swerve,
Cutting out a gentle curve,
Just to come upon thy feet
In amongst th'unripened wheat.
And so well I mark the place,
That I might thy cover trace,
Keeping still my eyes there resting,
Find where thou art warmly nesting.
             W. MOY THOMAS.

THE LINNET'S NEST

THE busy birds, with nice selection, cull
Soft thistle-down, gray moss, and scatter'd wool;
Far from each prying eye the nest prepare,
Form'd of warm moss, and lined with softest hair.
Week after week, regardless of her food,
Th'incumbent linnet warms her future brood,
Each spotted egg with ivory bill she turns,
Day after day with fond impatience burns;
Hears the young prisoner chirping in his cell,
And breaks in hemispheres the fragile shell.

ERASMUS DARWIN.

MAGPIE'S NEST

ON turf-reared platform, intermixt,
With clay and cross-laid sticks betwixt,
'Mid hawthorn, fir, or elm tree slung,
Is piled for the expected young,
A soft and neatly woven home;
Above of tangled thorns a dome,
Forms a sharp fence the nest about,
To keep all rash intruders out.
So, like a robber in his hold,
Or some marauding baron bold,
On coasted cliff in olden time,
They sit unblenched in state sublime,
And fortress intricately planned;
As if they felt that they whose hand

Is aimed at others, rightly deem
The hand of others aimed at them.
So there they dwell, man's dwelling nigh,
But not in man's society ;
Arabian-like : and little share
His love, nor for his hatred care.

BISHOP MANT.

THE RAVEN

From " The Penitent Raven "

THE Raven's house is built with reeds,—
Sing woe, and alas is me !
And the Raven's couch is spread with weeds,
High on the hollow tree ;
And the Raven himself, telling his beads
In penance for his past misdeeds,
Upon the top I see.

THOMAS D'ARCY McGEE.

THE TITLARK'S NEST

A Parable

WHERE o'er his azure birthplace still the smile
Of sweet Apollo kindles golden hours,
High on the white peak of a glittering isle
A ruin'd fane within a wild vine's bowers
Muffled its marble-pillar'd peristyle ;
As under curls, that clasp in frolic showers
A young queen's brow, her antique diadem's
Stern grandeur hides its immemorial gems.

The place was solitary and the fane
 Deserted save that where, in saucy scorn
Of desolation's impotent disdain,
 The revelling leaves and buds and bunches born,
From that wild vine along a roofless lane
 Of mouldering marble columns roam'd, one morn
A titlark, by past grandeur unopprest,
Had boldly built her inconspicuous nest.

ROBERT, EARL OF LYTTON.

THE THRUSH'S NEST

WITHIN a thick and spreading hawthorn bush,
That overhung a mole-hill large and round,
I heard, from morn to morn a merry Thrush
Sing hymns to sunrise, while I drank the sound
With joy—and oft, an unintruding guest,
I watched her secret toils, from day to day,
How true she warped the moss to form her nest,
And model'd it within with wood and clay.
And by and bye, like heath-bells gilt with dew,
There lay her shining eggs as bright as flowers,
Ink-spotted over shells of green and blue :
And there I witnessed, in the summer hours,
A brood of Nature's minstrels chirp and fly,
Glad as the sunshine and the laughing sky.

JOHN CLARE.

A WREN'S NEST

AMONG the dwellings framed by birds
In field or forest, with nice care,
Is none that with the little Wren's
In snugness may compare.

B

No door the tenement requires,
And seldom needs a laboured roof,
It is to the fiercest sun
Impervious and storm-proof.

So warm, so beautiful, withal,
In perfect fitness for its aim,
That to the kind by special grace
Their instinct surely came.

And when for their abodes they seek
An opportune recess,
The hermit has no finer eye
For shadowy quietness.

WILLIAM WORDSWORTH.

THE WREN'S NEST

I TOOK the wren's nest ;—
Heaven forgive me !
Its merry architects so small
Had scarcely finished their wee hall,
That, empty still and neat and fair,
Hung idly in the summer air.
The mossy walls, the dainty door,
Where Love should enter and explore,
And Love sit carolling outside ;
And Love within chirp multiplied ;
    I took the wren's nest.
    Heaven forgive me !

How many hours of happy pains
Through early frosts and April rains,

How many songs at eve and morn,
O'er springing grass and greening corn ?
What labours hard through sun and shade
Before the pretty house was made !
One little minute, only one,
And she'll fly back, and find it—gone
    I took the wren's nest :
    Bird, forgive me !

Thou and thy mate, sans let, sans fear,
Ye have before you all the year,
And every wood holds nooks for you,
In which to sing and build and woo ;
One piteous cry of birdish pain—
And ye'll begin your life again,
Forgetting quite the lost, lost home
In many a busy home to come.—
But I ?—Your wee house keep I must
Until it crumble into dust.
    I took the wren's nest
    God forgive me !
THE AUTHOR OF
" JOHN HALIFAX, GENTLEMAN."

NEST EGGS

From " A Child's Garden of Verses"

    BIRDS all the sunny day
      Flutter and quarrel
    Here in the arbour-like
      Tent of the laurel.

Here in the fork
  The brown nest is seated ;
Four little blue eggs
  The mother keeps heated.

While we stand watching her,
  Staring like gabies,
Safe in each egg are the
  Bird's little babies.

Soon the frail eggs they shall
  Chip, and upspringing
Make all the April woods
  Merry with singing.

Younger than we are,
  O children, and frailer,
Soon in blue air they'll be
  Singer and sailer. '

We, so much older,
  Taller and stronger,
We shall look down on the
  Birdies no longer.

They shall go flying
  With musical speeches
High overhead in the
  Tops of the beeches.

In spite of our wisdom
  And sensible talking,
We on our feet must go
  Plodding and walking.

ROBERT LOUIS STEVENSON.

THE NESTLING OF BIRDS

A THOUSAND bills are busy now ; the skies
Are winnow'd by a thousand fluttering wings,
While all the feather'd race their annual rites
Ardent begin, and choose where best to build,
With more than human skill ; some cautious seek
Sequester'd spots, while some, more confident,
Scarce ask a covert. Wiser, these elude
The foes that prey upon their several kinds ;
Those to the hedge repair ; with velvet down
Of budding sallows beautifully white.
The cavern-loving Wren sequester'd seeks
The verdant shelter of the hollow stump,
And with congenial moss, harmless deceit,
Constructs a safe abode. On topmost boughs
The glossy Raven, and the hoarse-voiced Crow,
Rock'd by the storm, erect their airy nests.
The Ouzel, lone frequenter of the grove
Of fragrant pines, in solemn depth of shade
Finds rest ; or 'mid the holly's shining leaves,
A simple bush the piping Thrush contents,
Though, in the woodland concert, he aloft
Trills from his spotted throat a powerful strain,
And scorns the humbler choir. The Lark too asks
A lowly dwelling, hid beneath a turf,
Or hollow, trodden by the sinking hoof :
Songster of heaven ! who to the sun such lays
Pours forth, as earth ne'er owns. Within the hedge

The Sparrow lays her sky-stain'd eggs.   The barn
With eaves o'er pendant, holds the twittering tribe;
Secret the Linnet seeks the tangled copse;
The white Owl seeks the antique ruined wall,
Fearless of rapine; or, in hollow trees,
Which age has cavern'd, safely courts repose;
The thievish Pie, in two-fold colours clad,
Roofs o'er her curious nest with firm-wreath'd twigs
And sidelong forms her cautious door; she dreads
The talon'd Kite, or pouncing Hawk; savage
Herself, with craft suspicion ever dwells.

JOHN BIDLAKE.

JAY RAIDING BLACKBIRD'S NEST

THE orchard rings

With the loud chattering of the noisy Jay,
Who, mocking up there in the cherry-tree,
(Oh! how he loves the fruit!) all creatures near,
Ventriloquial bleats, neighs, and sounds th' alarm
For all around if danger be but nigh.
Strange bird! he makes on any nest his raid
Especially the Blackbird's.   Cunning, he
(They say he's so discriminative, too,
He knows the Sunday from a common day)
Receives no mercy at the sportsman's hand,
Who, 'spite his mimicry, and loud " shay, shay,"
Straight brings him down and nails him to the
    barn,
A warning to his gay, audacious tribe.

S. W. PARTRIDGE.

NEST-ROBBING

From " The Four Bridges "

To yonder copse by moonlight I did go,
  In luxury of mischief, half afraid,
To steal the great owl's brood, her downy snow,
  Her screaming imps to seize, the while she preyed
With yellow, cruel eyes, whose radiant glare
Fell with their mother rage, I might not dare.

Panting I lay till her great fanning wings
  Troubled the dreams of rock-doves, slumbering
    nigh ;
And she and her fierce mate, like evil things,
  Skimmed the dusk fields ; then rising with a cry
Of fear, joy, triumph, darted on my prey,
And tore it from the nest and fled away.

But afterward, belated in the wood,
  I saw her moping on the rifled tree,
And my heart smote me for her, while I stood
  Awakened from my careless reverie ;
So white she looked, with moonlight round her shed,
So mother-like, she drooped and hung her head.

JEAN INGLELOW.

From " Winter Rain "

WEAVE a bower of love
  For birds to meet each other,
Weave a canopy above
  Nest and egg and mother.

CHRISTINA G. ROSSETTI.

ANGEL STAIRWAYS

From " The Foot-Path "

THE bird I list hath never come
  Within the scope of mortal ear ,
My prying step would make him dumb,
  And the fair tree, his shelter, sear.

Behind the hill, behind the sky,
  Behind my inmost thought, he sings ;
No feet avail ; to hear it nigh,
  The song itself must lend the wings.

Sing on, sweet bird, close hid, and raise
  Those angel stairways in my brain,
That climb from these low-vaulted days
  To spacious sunshines far from pain.

Sing when thou wilt, enchantment fleet,
  I leave thy covert haunt untrod,
And envy Science not her feat
  To make a twice-told tale of God.
                JAMES RUSSELL LOWELL.

II

TIMES AND SEASONS OF BIRDS

"Ye gentle Birdes   the worlds faire ornament,
And heavens glorie,   Joy may you have."
SPENSER.

THE ALMANAC

From " May Day"

I KNOW the trusty almanac
Of the punctual coming-back,
On their due days, of the birds.
I marked them yestermorn,
A flock of finches darting
Beneath the crystal arch,
Piping, as they flew, a march,—
Belike the one they used in parting
Last year from yon oak or larch ;
Dusky sparrows in a crowd,
Diving, darting, northward free,
Suddenly betook them all,
Everyone to his hole in the wall,
Or to his niche in the apple-tree.

RALPH WALDO EMERSON.

DAWN

(THE HUMMING-BIRD)

WHEN morning dawns, and the bless'd sun again
Lifts his red glories from the eastern main,
Then through our woodbines, wet with glittering
  dews,
The flower-fed Humming-bird his round pursues ;

Sips, with inserted tube, the honied blooms,
And chirps his gratitude as round he roams.
While richest roses, though in crimson dress'd,
Shrink from the splendour of his gorgeous breast ;
What heavenly tints in mingling radiance fly ;
Each rapid movement gives a different dye ;
Like scales of burnish'd gold, they dazzling show,
Now sink to shade—now like a furnace glow !

ALEXANDER WILSON.

THE BREAK AND CLOSE OF DAY

From " Morning " and " Night "

THE soften'd light,
'Twixt day and night,
That steals in beauty, through th'awakening skv ;
And o'er the lawn,
Sheds down the dawn,
As Nature brightly opes her radiant eye ;
How sweet it breaks
In myriad streaks,
Telling the earth, that glorious day is nigh

The birds' sweet lays,
From bushy sprays,
How rich they echo through the tuneful grove
The trilling lark,
Springs from the dark,

To cheer its nest-mate, from its realms above ;
  The nut-brown thrush,
  In one wild gush,
Fills the whole welkin, with its lays of love.

When Night puts on her starry robe,
  And lifts her glorious lamp on high,
When Silence reigns o'er half the globe,
  And calmness lives along the sky,—
  How sweet the holy lullaby,
That Nature deigns to breathe around,
  Soft as a mourning mother's sigh,
O'er infant hushed in sleep profound.

There is a whispering in the trees ;
  The leaves discourse like living things ;
Earth's balmy incense on the breeze,
  Is mounting on her murm'ring wings,—
  And in the grove the blackbird sings
His plaintive farewell ere to rest ;
  Whilst the rich thrush around her flings,
Her last notes as she seeks her nest.
NER GARDINER.

COCK-CROWING

FATHER of Lights ! what sunny seed,
  What glance of day hast Thou confin'd
Into this bird ? To all the breed
  This busy ray Thou hast assign'd ;
    Their magnetism works all night
    And dreams of Paradise and light.

Their eyes watch for the morning hue ;
Their little grain, expelling night,
So shines and sings, as if it knew
The path unto the house of light ·
It seems their candle, howe'er done,
Was tined[1] and lighted at the sun.
                         HENRY VAUGHAN.

THE LARK AT DAWN

From " Aubade "

THE Lark now leaves his wat'ry nest,
   And climbing shakes his dewy wings.
He takes this window for the East,
   And to implore your light he sings—
Awake ! Awake ! The morn will never rise
Till she can dress her beauty at your eyes.

The merchant bows unto the seaman's star,
   The ploughman from the sun his season takes ;
But still the lover wonders what they are
   Who look for day before his mistress wakes.
Awake ! Awake ! break thro' your veils of lawn
Then draw your curtains, and begin the Dawn.
                         SIR WILLIAM DAVENANT.

[1] Set on fire.

BIRDS AT MORN

From " The Critic"

Now has the whispering breath of gentle morn
Bid Nature's voice and Nature's beauty rise ;
While orient Phœbus, with unborrow'd hues,
Clothes the waked loveliness which all night slept
In heavenly drapery !   Darkness is fled.

Now, too, the feather'd warblers tune their notes
Around, and charm the listening grove.   The lark
The linnet ! chaffinch ! bullfinch ! goldfinch ! green-
   finch !
But O, to me no joy can they afford !
Nor rose, nor wallflower, nor smart gillyflower,
Nor polyanthus mean, nor dapper daisy,
Nor William sweet, nor marjoram—nor lark,
Linnet, nor all the finches of the grove !

RICHARD BRINSLEY SHERIDAN.

TO THE THRUSH

(DAYBREAK)

DEAR Chorister, who from those shadows sends,
   Ere that the blushing morn dare show her light,
Such sad lamenting strains, that night attends,
   (Become all ear) stars stay to hear thy plight ;
If one, whose grief even reach of thought transcends,
   Who ne'er (not in a dream) did taste delight,
May thee importune, who like case pretends,
   And seems to joy in woe, in woe's despite ;

Tell me (so may thou fortune milder try,
  And long, long sing !) for what thou thus com-
    plains,
Since winter's gone, and sun in dappled sky,
  Enamoured smiles on woods and flowery plains ?
The bird, as if my questions did her move,
  With trembling wings, sighed forth, " I love, I
    love ! "
          WILLIAM DRUMMOND OF HAWTHORNDEN.

THE BELL-BIRDS

(MID-NOON IN THE AUSTRALIAN FOREST)

A LYRE-BIRD sang a low melodious song
Far off, then ceased : a soft wind swept along
The lofty gums and breathless died away :
And Silence woke and knew her dream was day.

     .   .   .   .

Hush, from the trackless depths comes what sweet
  sound
Ineffable ?   Do spirits underground
In hollow caverns ring phantasmal chimes
For elfin deaths in fairy sunless climes—
Or does some sad aërial spirit high
In serene air suspend the listening sky
With sweet remember'd music of joy-bells
Changing for death ? Hush, how it swells and swells
Still sweet and low and sad—as tho' the peal
Were chimed in forest depths where never steal
Sounds from the world beyond, and where no noise
Breaks ever the long dream.   It is the voice

Of the mysterious bird whose bell-like note
Chimes thro' the Austral noon as church-bells float
O'er lonely slopes and pastures far at home.
Sometimes but once it sang, as when the foam
On northern seas sleeps on the ebbing tide
And scarcely stirs the Inchcape's sounding side
To one faint clang : then ceased : then once again
Tolled out with silver sweetness its part pain,
Part reverie over some beloved thing.
At last it too was still, recovering
Some dream to brood upon with voiceless peace.

WILLIAM SHARP.

IN THE SHADOWS

Now, while the long-delaying ash assumes
   The delicate April green, and, loud and clear,
Through the cool, yellow, mellow twilight glooms
   The thrush's song enchants the captive ear ;
Now, while a shower is pleasant in the falling,
   Stirring the still perfume that wakes around ;
Now that doves mourn, and from the distance
     calling,
   The cuckoo answers with a sovereign sound,—
Come, with thy native heart, O true and tried ;
   But leave all books ; for what with converse high,
Flavoured with Attic wit, the time shall glide
   On smoothly, as a river floweth by,
     Or as on stately pinion, through the gray
     Evening, the culver cuts his liquid way.

DAVID GRAY.

OWL-LIGHT

COME out and hear the owls shout
In the still and dewy night-hour ;
The moon a fading white flower
Hangs low, with mists about.

Like pale moths, along the hedge
Withering bindweed lies ;
Night looks in with hollow eyes,
Dim at the window-ledge.

With weird shriek, the hunting bird
Flits sorrowfully by ;
Mournful woods against the sky
Are full of griefs unheard.

Trancèd scents of dying flowers
In Summer's requiem wreath ;
Not a breath—but damp of death,
And sea tolling the hours.

ROSE ARRESTI.

THE THRUSH'S SONG

(IN THE GLOAMING)

SWEET Mavis ! at this cool delicious hour
Of gloaming, when a pensive quietness
Hushes the odorous air,—with what a power
Of impulse unsubdued dost thou express

Thyself a spirit ! While the silver dew
Holy as manna on the meadow falls,
Thy song's impassioned clarity, trembling through
This omnipresent stillness, disenthrals
The soul to adoration. First I heard
A low thick lubric gurgle, soft as love,
Yet sad as memory, through the silence poured
Like starlight. But the mood intenser grows,
Precipitate rapture quickens, move on move
Lucidly linked together, till the close.   ·

DAVID GRAY.

TO THE NIGHTINGALE

O NIGHTINGALE, that on yon bloomy spray
  Warblest at eve, when all the woods are still ;
  Thou with fresh hope the lover's heart dost
    fill,
  While the jolly hours lead on propitious May.
Thy liquid notes that close the eye of day,
  First heard before the shallow cuckoo's bill,
  Portend success in love ; O, if Jove's will
  Have linked that amorous power to thy soft
    lay,
Now timely sing, ere the rude bird of hate
  Foretell my hopeless doom in some grove nigh :
  As thou from year to year hast sung too late
For my relief, yet hadst no reason why :
  Whether the Muse, or Love, call thee his mate,
  Both them I serve, and of their train am I.

JOHN MILTON.

TWILIGHT AND THE MAKO-MAKO

NIGHT on the forest is falling,
  Slowly the day leaves the hill,
Birds from the coverts are calling,
  Calling in tinkle and trill :

Medley of harmony ringing,
  Musical, mellow and chiming ;
Night-airs a-quiver with singing,—
  Jangle of sweetness and riming !

Twilight is gone from the hill,
  Dark are the woods to the moon ;
All the sweet voices are still,
  Darkness has come too soon.—

One lone bird forgets
  That the white moon is climbing ;
While over a hill a star sets,
  It is chiming and chiming :—

Bell-birds, softer than bells,
  Bell-bird, ever in tune,
What god in your bosom dwells ?—
What passion your bosom swells
  As you chime to the climbing moon ?

JOHANNES C. ANDERSEN.

THE NIGHT-BIRD

(A Myth)

A-floating, a-floating,
Across the sleeping sea,
All night I heard a singing bird
Upon the topmost tree.

" Oh came you off the Isles of Greece,
Or off the banks of Seine ;
Or off some tree in forests free,
Which fringe the western main ? "

" I came not off the old world
Nor yet from off the new—
But I am one of the birds of God
Which sing the whole night through."

" Oh sing and wake the dawning—
Oh whistle for the wind ;
The night is long, the current strong,
My boat it lags behind."

" The current sweeps the old world,
The current sweeps the new ;
The wind will blow, the dawn will glow,
Ere thou hast sailed them through."

CHARLES KINGSLEY.

THE NIGHT-SONG OF THE CURLEWS

A lonely road in the Northern land,
A mountainous country, bleak and grand ;
The lonely road by the haunted mere,
The tarn that all but the curlews fear.

As daylight slowly fades to night
They skim the lake in the mystic light
Of the moon, as it slowly mounts the skies.
Then from the mere come plaintive cries !

Is it the shriek of a spectre dread,
Wraith of a murdered man long dead ?
No !—'Tis not from a phantom throng ;
'Tis only the lonely curlews' song.

R. M. INGERSLEY.

BIRDS IN MAY

From " Poet and Anchorite "

IN pairing-time, we know, the bird
Kindles to its deepmost splendour,
    And the tender
  Voice is tenderest in its throat ·
Were its love, for ever nigh it,
    Never by it,
  It might keep a vernal note,
The crocean and amethystine
    In their pristine
  Lustre linger on its coat.
Therefore must my song-bower lone be
    That my tone be
  Fresh with dewy pain alway ;
She, who scorns my dearest care ta'en,
    An uncertain
  Shadow of the sprite of May.

FRANCIS THOMPSON.

THE RAINY SEASON

A Translation of Vergil's " Georgics," i. 373-389

WET weather seldom hurts the most unwise,
So plain the signs, such prophets are the skies ·
The wary crane foresees it first, and sails
Above the storm, and leaves the lowly vales;
.   .   .
The swallow skims the river's watery face,
The frogs renew the croaks of their loquacious race.

Besides, the several sorts of watery fowls,
That swim the seas, or haunt the standing pools;
The swans that sail along the silver flood,
And dive with stretching necks to search their food,
Then lave their back with sprinkling dews in vain,
And stem the stream to meet the promised rain.
The crow, with clamorous cries, the shower demands,
And single stalks along the desert sands.

JOHN DRYDEN.

ST VALENTINE'S DAY

(THE NIGHTINGALE)

O NIGHTINGALE! thou surely art
A creature of a " fiery heart ":—
These notes of thine—they pierce and pierce;
Tumultuous harmony and fierce!
Thou sing'st as if the god of wine
Had helped thee to a Valentine;

A song in mockery and despite
Of shades, and dews, and silent night ;
And steady bliss, and all the loves
Now sleeping in their peaceful groves.
WILLIAM WORDSWORTH.

A MAY-DAY REVERIE

MERRY birds are mating
'Mid the hawthorn trees,
Pliant branches flushed with green
Nod before the breeze.

Pipits in the dizzy heights
Soar and poise and tremble ;
Minstrels these of sheer delight ;
Feathered choir assemble.

Hark ! the warbler in the copse,
List ! the sparrow cheeping,
Con the wee wren on its nest,
Male bird vigil keeping.

Honey bee upon the wing
Hovers o'er a wild flower,
Gathering nectar while it may,
'Mid the glistening rain-shower.

Now Philomel starts his song,
Wondrous and God-given,
How exultant are the notes,
Fit for saints in Heaven.

Pretty wild flowers deck the earth,
  Meadows starred with golden ;
Birds and beasts and wildlings all
  Love-tokens beholden.

Hearken to the cuckoo's call,
  Note ! the swallow's twitter ;
Watch the bats towards gloaming hour,
  As they chant and flitter.

Merle and mavis tune their lutes,
  Scream, and then take cover ;
Larks descend from ether blue,
  And sink among the clover.

Rooks are busy in the trees ;
  Whitethroats call and chatter ;
Robin comes from grassy mead ;
  Squirrels dart and scatter.

Fish are leaping in the stream,
  See their shadows darken ;
Sedge-bird sings from osier bed,
  Sit ye down and hearken.

Bluebells peep from leafy dell ;
  Gay the lords and ladies '
Yaffle laughs and wryneck shouts,
  He the cuckoo's page is.

Thus we pass the sunlit hours
  'Mid the May-time glory,
Seeking to enrich the mind,
  From Nature's wondrous story.
                W. PERCIVAL WESTELL.

DESCRIPTION OF SPRING

THE soote[1] season, that bud and bloom furth brings,
With green hath clad the hill and eke the vale,
The nightingale with feathers new she sings ;
The turtle to her make[2] hath told her tale.
Summer is come, for every spray now springs,
The hart hath hung his old head on the pale ;
The buck in brake his winter coat he flings ;
The fishes flete[3] with new repairèd scale ;
The adder all her slough away she slings[4] ; .
The swift swallow pursueth the flies smale[5] ;
The busy bee her honey now she mings.[6]
Winter is worn that was the flowers' bale,
   And thus I see among these pleasant things
   Each care decays, and yet my sorrow springs.
EARL OF SURREY.

THE SPRING.

Now that the winter's gone, the earth has lost
Her snow-white robes ; and now no more the frost
Candies the grass, or casts an icy cream
Upon the silver lake or crystal stream.

But the warm sun thaws the benumbèd earth,
And makes it tender ; gives a second birth
To the dead swallows ; wakes in hollow tree
The drowsy cuckoo and the humble-bee.

[1] sweet.   [2] mate.   [3] float.
[4] flings off, casts off.   [5] small.   [6] mixes.

Now do a choir of chirping minstrels bring
In triumph to the world the youthful spring :
The valleys, hills, and woods in rich array,
Welcome the coming of the longed-for May.
THOMAS CAREW.

TO THE THRUSH

OH ! herald of the Spring ! while yet
No hare-bell scents the woodland lane,
Nor starwort fair, nor violet,
Braves the bleak gust, and driving rain
'Tis thine, as through the copses rude
Some pensive wanderer sighs along,
To soothe him with thy cheerful song,
And tell of Hope and Fortitude.

For thee, then, may the hawthorn bush,
The elder, and the spindle-tree,
With all their various berries blush,
And the blue sloe abound for thee !
For thee the coral holly glow,
Its arm'd and glossy leaves among ;
And many a branchèd oak be hung
With the pellucid mistletoe.

Still may thy nest, with lichen lin'd,
Be hidden from the invading jay ;
Nor truant boy its covert find,
To bear thy callow young away.

So thou precursor still of good,
Oh ! herald of approaching Spring !
Shalt to the pensive wanderer sing,
Thy song of Hope and Fortitude !
                    MRS CHARLOTTE SMITH.

A THRUSH IN SPRING

AWAKE and weary at the dawn of day
  I heard thy music ringing thro' the hush ,
  It made a hundred morning memories rush
To give me back mine old life passed away—
A little boy at prime in garden play
  I paused to wonder listening by the bush,
  A youth, at early school, I heard the thrush,
And dropped my task, enchanted by her lay.

But most I well remember how that voice
    Throbbed in mine ears upon my wedding morn,
      Bidding me rise my well-beloved to greet ;
      And now in thy sweet tones as sad as sweet
    I feel such sympathy for souls forlorn
That thro' my tears I hearken, and rejoice.
                    H. D. RAWNSLEY.

SPRING

THEN bursts the song from every leafy glade,
The yielding season's bridal serenade ;
Then flash the wings, returning Summer calls
Through the deep arches of her forest halls,—

The bluebird, breathing from his azure plumes
The fragrance borrowed where the myrtle blooms ;
The thrush, poor wanderer, dropping meekly down,
Clad in his remnant of autumnal brown ;
The oriole, drifting like a flake of fire,
Rent by a whirlwind from a blazing spire ;
The robin, jerking his spasmodic throat,
Repeats, imperious, his *staccato* note ;
The crack-brained bobolink courts his crazy mate,
Poised on a bulrush tipsy with his weight ;
Nay, in his cage the lone canary sings,
Feels the soft air, and spreads his idle wings.

OLIVER WENDELL HOLMES.

SWEET SPRING

SPRING, the sweet Spring, is the year's pleasant king ;
Then blooms each thing, then maids dance in a ring,
Cold doth not sting, the pretty birds do sing—
  Cuckoo, jug-jug, pu-we, to-witta-woo !

The palm and may make country houses gay,
Lambs frisk and play, the shepherds pipe all day,
And we hear aye birds tune this merry lay—
  Cuckoo, jug-jug, pu-we, to-witta-woo !

The fields breathe sweet, the daisies kiss our feet,
Young lovers meet, old wives a-sunning sit,
In every street these tunes our ears do greet—
  Cuckoo, jug-jug, pu-we, to-witta-woo !
    Spring, the sweet Spring !

THOMAS NASHE.

A QUERY TO THE BIRDS BEFORE SPRING'S RETURN

From " Hymn to Spring "

——Ye sweet Birds,
Were you asleep through all the wintry hours,
Beneath the waters, or in mossy caves ?
There are, 'tis said, birds that pursue the spring,
Where'er she flies, or else in deathlike sleep
Abide her annual reign, when forth they come
With freshened plumage and enraptured song,
As ye do now, unwearied choristers,
Till the land ring with joy.

        JOHN WILSON ("Christopher North").

A WELCOME TO SPRING

WHAT bird does sing, yet so does wail ?
O 'tis the ravish'd nightingale.
" Jug, jug, jug, jug, tereu ! " she cries,
And still her woes at midnight rise.
Brave prick-song ! " Who is't now we hear ? "
None but the lark so shrill and clear ;
Now at Heaven's gate she claps her wings,
The morn not waking till she sings !
Hark ! Hark ! With what a pretty throat
Poor Robin Redbreast tunes his note !
Hark ! how the jolly cuckoos sing—
Cuckoo ! to welcome in the Spring !
Cuckoo ! to welcome in the Spring !

        JOHN LYLY.

THE EARLY BLUE-BIRD

BLUE-BIRD ! on yon leafless tree,
Dost thou carol thus to me,
" Spring is coming ! Spring is here ! "
Say'st thou so, my birdie dear ?
What is that, in misty shroud,
Stealing from the darken'd cloud ?
Lo ! the snow-flakes' gathering mound
Settles o'er the whitened ground,
Yet thou singest, blithe and clear,
" Spring is coming ! Spring is here ! "

Strik'st thou not too bold a strain ?
Winds are piping o'er the plain ;
Clouds are sweeping o'er the sky
With a black and threatening eye ;
Urchins, by the frozen rill,
Wrap their mantles closer still ;
Yon poor man, with doublet old,
Doth he shiver. at the cold ?
Hath he not a nose of blue ?
Tell me, birdling, tell me true.

Spring's a maid of mirth and glee,
Rosy wreaths and revelry :
Hast thou wooed some wingèd love
To a nest in verdant grove ?
Sung to her of greenwood bower,
Sunny skies that never lower ?
Lured her with thy promise fair
Of a lot that knows no care ?

Pr'ythee, bird, in coat of blue,
Though a lover, tell her true.
Ask her if, when storms are long
She can sing a cheerful song ?
When the rude winds rock the tree,
If she'll closer cling to thee ?
Then the blasts that sweep the sky,
Unappalled shall pass thee by ;
Though thy curtained chamber show
Siftings of untimely snow,
Warm and glad thy heart shall be,
Love shall make it Spring for thee.
LYDIA HUNTLY SIGOURNEY.

LINES ON A CUCKOO

HAIL to thee, shouting Cuckoo ! in mv youth
  Thou wert long time, the Ariel of my hope,
The marvel of a summer ! it did soothe
  To listen to thee on some sunny slope,
  Where the high oaks forbade an ampler scope
Than of the blue skies upward,—and to sit
  Canopied, in the gladdening horoscope,
Which thou, my planet, flung—a pleasant fit,
Long time my hours endear'd, my kindling fancy
    smit.

And thus I love thee still—thy monotone,
  The selfsame transport flashes through my frame,
And when thy voice, sweet sibyl, all is flown,
  My eager ear, I cannot choose but blame.

O may the world these feelings never tame !
If age o'er me her silver tresses spread,
   I still would call thee by a lover's name,
And deem the spirit of delight unfled,
Nor bear, though gray without, a heart to nature
     dead !

JEREMIAH HOLME WIFFEN.

TO THE CUCKOO

O BLITHE new-comer ! I have heard,
   I hear thee, and rejoice ;
O cuckoo ! shall I call thee bird,
   Or but a wandering voice ?
While I am lying on the grass,
   Thy twofold shout I hear,
That seems to fill the air's whole space,
   As loud far off as near.
Though babbling only to the vale
   Of sunshine and of flowers,
Thou bringest unto me a tale
   Of visionary hours.
Thrice welcome, darling of the spring !
   Even yet thou art to me
No bird ; but an invisible thing,
   A voice, a mystery.
The same which in my schoolboy days
   I listen'd to ; that cry
Which made me look a thousand ways
   In bush, and tree, and sky.

To seek thee did I often rove
  Through woods and on the green ;
And thou wert still a hope, a love ;
  Still long'd for, never seen !
And I can listen to thee yet ;
  Can lie upon the plain,
And listen till I do beget
  That golden time again.
O blessèd bird ! the earth we pace
  Again appears to be
An unsubstantial, faëry place,
  That is fit home for thee.
                    WILLIAM WORDSWORTH.

HOME THOUGHTS FROM ABROAD

OH, to be in England
Now that April's there,
And whoever wakes in England
Sees, some morning, unaware,
That the lowest boughs and the brushwood sheaf,
Round the elm-tree bole are in tiny leaf,
While the chaffinch sings on the orchard bough
In England—now !

And after April, when May follows,
And the whitethroat builds, and all the swallows !
Hark, where my blossomed pear-tree in the hedge
Leans to the field and scatters on the clover
Blossoms and dewdrops—at the bent-spray's edge—
That's the wise thrush ; he sings each song twice over,

Lest you should think he never could recapture
The first fine careless rapture !
And though the fields look rough with hoarv dew,
All will be gay when noontide wakes anew
The buttercups, the little children's dower
—Far brighter than this gaudy melon-flower !
ROBERT BROWNING.

PACK, CLOUDS, AWAY
(THE BIRDS' GOOD-MORROW FROM A LOVER)
PACK, clouds, away, and welcome day,
    With night we banish sorrow ;
Sweet air, blow soft ; mount, larks, aloft,
    To give my Love good-morrow !
Wings from the wind to please her mind,
    Notes from the lark I'll borrow ;
Bird, prune thy wing ; nightingale, sing,
    To give my Love good-morrow !
        To give my Love good-morrow,
        Notes from them both I'll borrow.
Wake from thy nest, robin redbreast ;
    Sing, birds, in every furrow ;
And from each hill let music shrill
    Give my fair Love good-morrow.
Blackbird and thrush in every bush,   ,
    Stare, linnet, and cock-sparrow ;
You pretty elves, among yourselves,
    Sing my fair Love good-morrow.
        To give my Love good-morrow,
        Sing, birds, in every furrow !
            THOMAS HEYWOOD.

TO A NIGHTINGALE

These lines were included in Shakespeare's " Passionate Pilgrim "

As it fell upon a day
In the merry month of May,
Sitting in a pleasant shade
Which a grove of myrtles made,
Beasts did leap, and birds did sing,
Trees did grow, and plants did spring ;
Every thing did banish moan,
Save the nightingale alone :
She, poor bird, as all forlorn,
Lean'd her breast up-till a thorn,
And there sung the dolefull'st ditty,
That to hear it was great pity :
" Fie, fie, fie," now would she cry ;
" Tereu, tereu ! " by and by ;
That to hear her so complain,
Scarce I could from tears refrain ;
For her griefs, so lively shown,
Made me think upon mine own,
Ah, thought I, thou mourn'st in vain
None takes pity on thy pain :
Senseless trees they cannot hear thee ;
Ruthless beasts they will not cheer thee
King Pandion he is dead ;
All thy friends are lapp'd in lead ;

All thy fellow birds do sing,
Careless of thy sorrowing.
Even so, poor bird, like thee,
None alive will pity me.
RICHARD BARNEFIELD.

THE WREN

A LOVELY morn, so still, so very still!
It hardly seems a growing day of spring,
Though all the odorous buds are blossoming,
And the small matin birds were glad and shrill;
Some hours ago; but now the woodland rill
Murmurs along, the only vocal thing,
Save when the wee wren flits with stealthy wing
And cons by fits and bits her evening trill.
HARTLEY COLERIDGE.

THE SWALLOW

WHITE-THROATED herald of the coming May,
It joys me much to see thee here again;
Once more shalt thou, sweet bird, at dawn of day,
Chase my dull slumbers with thy cheerful strain.
Thy patient labours at my window pane,
With placid morning thoughts my breast shall fill,
And I shall quit my bed,
Full fraught in heart and head,
With soothing trust in God, and unto all goodwill.
THOMAS SMIBERT.

THE FIRST OF APRIL

(SWALLOW AND ROOK)

THE Swallow for a moment seen,
Skims in haste the village green ;
From the grey moor, on feeble wing,
The screaming plover idly spring ;
The butterfly, gay-painted, soon,
Explores awhile the tepid noon,
And fondly trusts its tender dyes
To fickle suns and flattering skies.

Where in venerable rows
Widely waving oaks inclose
The moat of yonder antique hall,
Swarm the Rooks with clamorous call ,
And to the toils of nature true,
Wreathe their capacious nests anew.
                              THOMAS WARTON.

NO NIGHTINGALES

How glorious were the nightingales last night,
'Neath the dim, April, warm, half moonlit sky
As from wood-choirs and temples of delight,
The dewy stream-side grass, the black-thorn nigh,
                    They poured their melody !

Indeed ! I heard it not ! I looked around,
And deemed that night and silence had their fill ·
From forest, fallow, distant lane, no sound,
Save the dull dronings of the water mill :
            The Nightingales were still.

O dull of ear to hear ! but mark thou this
My ears were sharpened by a bed of pain ;
Thus, out of sorrow, God works often bliss,
And that flits by, and this shall still remain ·
            The Nightingales no strain !

But *sursum corda* ! may it not be so,
That these sweet strains on Jordan's further side,
Unheard by souls who only this world know,
May yet to them not wholly be denied
            Who drink the cup of woe ?
                        J. M. NEALE.

THE SWALLOW'S COMING

SWALLOW, Swallow, hither wing,
Hither, Swallow, bringing Spring ;
From the lake hath gone the Teal,
    Fled the Widgeon from the stream ;
Now no more our bursting woods
    Hear the swooping Merlin's scream.
Come, thou dawn of summer, come,
    Hither leaves and shadows bringing,
Bladed furrows—nested eaves,—
    Sweetest songs the South is singing,
Bringing violets, bringing Spring,
Hither, Swallow, hither wing.

Swallow, Swallow, hither wing,
Dearest playmate of the spring ;
Come—the celandine no more
  Dreads the gusty wrath of March,
Golden tasselled is the birch,—
  Emerald fringes have the larch.
Come, thou news of Summer, come,
  Trills and hedgerow twitterings bringing,
Quivering mountings of the Lark,—
  Shrillest songs the Ousel singing ;
Snowing orchards, flight of spring,
Hither, Swallow, hither wing.
                    WILLIAM COX BENNETT.

TO ALAUDA, THE HERALD OF SPRING

HARK ! to the joyous lark !
  On buoyant wing,
Voicing his raptured lays—
  Pæans of Spring.

Pearl of the feathered race ;
  Prince of the air ;
Full-throated Alauda ;
  Songster so fair.

Cleaving the ether blue,
  I hear thee sing
Love-songs of welcome
  For earth's blossoming.

Bird of the meadowland ;
  Speck of the sky ;
Earth's gay ambassador,
  Soaring on high.

Snow, wind and rain may come,
  Naught dost thou care ;
Still soar and sing aloud,
  Prince of the air.

Spirit of blithesomeness,
  Happy and gay !
Love-flights of gladsomeness,
  Day after day.

Why dost thou scorn the ground ?
  Why mount the cloud ?
Sending back lullabies,
  Rich, long, and loud.

Joy-bird of early spring ;
  Compass in feathers ;
Head to the breeze thou soarest
  High in all weathers.

Bird-sprite of lilting lay ;
  Laureate of glee :
Lone minstrel of the air,
  Happy and free.

Sing thou again to me,
  Through rain or shine,
Shimmering bridal-songs ;
  Minstrel divine !

Brown bird of Happy-land,
   Sing, ever sing—
Call earth from her slumber,
   Thou herald of spring.
         W. PERCIVAL WESTELL.

SUMMER

(BIRDS IN SUMMER)

How pleasant the life of a bird must be,
Flitting about in each leafy tree ;
In the leafy trees, so broad and tall,
Like a green and beautiful palace-hall,
With its airy chambers, light and boon,
That open to sun, and stars, and moon !
That open upon the bright blue sky,
And the frolicsome winds as they wander by.

They have left their nests in the forest bough ;
Those homes of delight they need not now ;
And the young and the old they wander out,
And traverse their green world round about "
And hark ! at the top of this leafy hall,
How one to the other they lovingly call ;
" Come up, come up ! " they seem to say,
" Where the topmost twigs in the breezes sway."

" Come up, come up, for the world is fair,
Where the merry leaves dance in the summer air ! "
And the birds below give back the cry :
" We come, we come, to the branches high ! "

How pleasant the life of a bird must be,
Flitting about in a leafy tree ;
And away through the air what joy to go,
And to look on the bright green earth below.

How pleasant the life of a bird must be
Wherever it listeth, there to flee ;
To go, when a joyful fancy calls,
Dashing adown 'mong the waterfalls,
Then wheeling about with its mates at play,
Above and below, and among the spray,
Hither and thither, with screams as wild,
As the laughing mirth of a rosy child !

How pleasant the life of a bird must be,
Skimming about on the breezy sea,
Cresting the billows like silvery foam,
And then wheeling away to its cliff-built home
What joy it must be to sail upborne
By a strong free wing, through the rosy morn,
To meet the young sun face to face,
And pierce like a shaft the boundless space

What joy it must be, like a living breeze,
To flutter about 'mong the flowering trees ;
Lightly to soar, and to see beneath
The wastes of the blossoming purple heath,
And the yellow furze, like fields of gold
That gladden some fairy regions old !
On mountain tops, on the billowy sea,
On the leafy stems of the forest tree,
How pleasant the life of a bird must be !

MARY HOWITT.

SUMMER

WIDE o'er the winding umbrage of the floods,
Like vivid blossoms glowing from afar,
Thick-swarm the brighter birds. For Nature's
    hand,
That with a sportive vanity has deck'd
The plumy nations, there her gayest hues
Profusely pours. But, if she bids them shine,
Array'd in all the beauteous beams of day,
Yet frugal still, she humbles them in song.
Nor envy we the gaudy robes they lent
Proud Montezuma's realm, whose legions cast
A boundless radiance, waving on the sun,
While Philomel is ours ; while in our shades,
Through the soft silence of the listening night,
The sober-suited songstress trills her lay.

JAMES THOMSON.

SKYLARK

WINGED seraph of the Summer heaven,
    Whose wondrous rapture, wild and long,
A hundred bards in vain have striven
    To prison in a song !

How can they tell, with all their art,
    What passions make thy glad throat swell,
That, throbbing at thy fiery heart,
    Thou feel'st but canst not tell ?

How can we picture in our dreams
 The joys that thro' thy pæan glow,
That joy that soars so high it seems
 About to break in woe ?

Sing on, wild bird, thy wild glad song,
 That fills our eyes with sudden tears,
While back upon the fancy throng
 Memories of vanished years !

Sing on, sing on, for ever free !
 We cannot know what thou dost sing,
And better it should ever be
 An undiscovered thing.

CICELY FOX SMITH.

MY THRUSH

ALL through the sultry days of June,
From morning blithe to golden noon,
 Until the star of evening climbs
The gray-blue East, a world too soon,
 There sings a Thrush amid the limes.

God's poet, hid in foliage green,
Sings endless songs himself unseen ;
 Right seldom come his silent times.
Linger, ye summer hours serene !
 Sing on, dear Thrush, amid the limes

Nor from these confines wander out,
Where with old gun, bucolic lout
 Commits all day his murderous crimes
Though cherries ripe are sweet, no doubt,
 Sweeter thy song amid the limes.

May I not dream God sends thee there,
Thou mellow angel of the air,
   Even to rebuke my earthlier rhymes
With music's soul, all praise and prayer ?
   Is that thy lesson in the limes ?

Closer to God art thou than I :
His minstrel thou, whose brown wings fly
   Through silent æther's summer climes.
Ah, never may thy music die !
   Sing on, dear Thrush, amid the limes !
                    MORTIMER COLLINS.

A GOOD BYE TO SUMMER

GOOD-BYE, good-bye to Summer !
   For Summer's nearly done ;
The garden smiling faintly,
   Cool breezes in the sun ;
Our thrushes now are silent,
   Our swallows flown away,—
But Robin's here, in coat of brown,
   With ruddy breast-knot gay.
      Robin, Robin Redbreast,
         O Robin dear !
      Robin singing sweetly
         In the falling of the year.

Bright yellow, red, and orange,
   The leaves come down in hosts ;
The trees are Indian Princes,
   But soon they'll turn to ghosts ;

The scanty pears and apples
  Hang russet on the bough ;
It's autumn, autumn, autumn late,
  'Twill soon be winter now.
    Robin, Robin Redbreast,
      O Robin dear !
    And welaway ! my Robin, Robin,
      For pinching days are near.
The fireside for the cricket,
  The wheat-stack for the mouse,
When trembling night-winds whistle
  And moan all round the house ;
The frosty ways like iron,
  The branches plumed with snow—
Alas ! in winter, dead and dark,
  Where can poor Robin go ?
    Robin, Robin Redbreast,
      O Robin dear !
    And a crumb of bread for Robin,
      His little heart to cheer.
          WILLIAM ALLINGHAM.

AUTUMN

STERN Time hath banished with a frown
  The Summer, now grown wan and old ;
In grief the woodlands lay adown
  Their crowns of gold.
No more the copses echo round
  With stockdove's moan and woodwren's lay ;
To gladden distant shores with sound
  They wing their way.

The wild winds shudder thro' the trees,
  Where late the redstart's carol rang ;
The torn nests wanton with the breeze
  Where sweet birds sang.

The sere, sad leaves, their glory done,
  Fall from the bough to meet the wave ;
The stream they shadowed from the sun
  Gives them a grave.

Cicely Fox Smith.

THE HAWK IN AUTUMN

Farewell, sweet Summer, and thy fading flowers
Farewell, sweet Summer, and thy woodland songs
No woodland note is heard, save where the hawk,
High from her eyry, skims in circling flight,
With all her clamorous young, first venturing forth
On untried wing. At distance far, the sound
Alarms the barn-door flock, the fearful dam
Calls in her brood beneath her ruffling plumes ;
With crowding feet they stand, and frequent peep
Through the half-open'd wing. The partridge quakes
Among the rustling corn. Ye gentle tribes,
Think not your deadliest foe is now at hand.
To man, bird, beast, *man* is the deadliest foe.

James Grahame.

AUTUMN BIRDS

WHEN Autumn scatters his departing gleams,
Warn'd of approaching Winter, gather'd, play
The swallow-people ; and toss'd wide around,
O'er the calm sky, in convolution swift,
The feather'd eddy floats : rejoicing once,
Ere to their wintry slumbers they retire ;
In clusters clung, beneath the mouldering bank,
And where, unpierc'd by frost, the cavern sweats.
Or rather into warmer climes convey'd,
With other kindred birds of season, there
They twitter cheerful, till the vernal months
Invite them welcome back : for, thronging, now
Innumerous wings are in commotion all.
  Where the Rhine loses his majestic force
In Belgian plains, won from the raging deep,
By diligence amazing, and the strong
Unconquerable hand of Liberty,
The stork-assembly meets ; for many a day,
Consulting deep, and various, ere they take
Their arduous voyage through the liquid sky ·
And now their route design'd, their leaders chose,
Their tribes adjusted, clean'd their vigorous wings ;
And many a circle, many a short essay,
Wheel'd round and round, in congregation full
The figur'd flight ascends ; and, riding high
The aërial billows, mixes with the clouds.
  Or where the Northern ocean, in vast whirls,
Boils round the naked melancholy isles
Of farthest Thulè, and the Atlantic surge

Pours in among the stormy Hebrides ;
Who can recount what transmigrations there
Are annual made ? What nations come and go ?
And how the living clouds on clouds arise ?
Infinite wings ! till all the plume-dark air,
And rude resounding shore are one wild cry.

Haply some widow'd songster pours his plaint,
Far, in faint warblings, through the tawny copse ;
While congregated thrushes, linnets, larks,
And each wild throat, whose artless strains so late
Swell'd all the music of the swarming shades,
Robb'd of their tuneful souls, now shivering sit
On the dead tree, a dull despondent flock ;
With not a brightness waving o'er their plumes,
And nought save chattering discord in their note.
O let not, aim'd from some inhuman eye,
The gun, the music of the coming year
Destroy ; and harmless, unsuspecting harm,
Lay the weak tribes, a miserable prey,
In mingled murder, fluttering on the ground !

JAMES THOMSON.

OCTOBER—THE PLOVER

WHEN Autumn winds are chanting
The roses' funeral strain,
And falling leaves are whirling
Through field, and wood, and lane,
We hear 'mid dreary marshlands
The plovers' weird refrain.

No bird sings in the woodlands,
But o'er the woodland wide,
And where the lonely saltings
Stretch far beside the tide,
And 'mid the swaying grasses
The piping plover hide.

All day above the marshes
They wheel in restless flight,
Their glossy plumage gleaming
In green and black and white,
Their plaintive notes re-echo
Upon the silent night.

MAUD E. SARGENT.

WINTER

But chief the plumy race,
The tenants of the sky, its changes speak.
Retiring from the downs, where all day long
They pick'd their scanty fare, a blackening train
Of clamorous rooks thick urge their weary flight,
And seek the closing shelter of the grove.
Assiduous, in his bower, the wailing owl
Plies his sad song. The cormorant on high
Wheels from the deep, and screams along the land.
Loud shrieks the soaring hern; and with wild wing
The circling sea-fowl cleave the flaky clouds.

One alone,
The redbreast, sacred to the household gods,
Wisely regardful of the embroiling sky,

In joyless fields and thorny thickets, leaves
His shivering mates, and pays to trusted man
His annual visit.   Half-afraid, he first
Against the window beats ; then, brisk, alights
On the warm hearth ; then, hopping o'er the floor,
Eyes all the smiling family askance,
And pecks, and starts, and wonders where he is ;
Till more familiar grown, the table-crumbs
Attract his slender feet.

JAMES THOMSON.

THE MISSEL THRUSH

WHO fears the storms of winter, the frost upon the
   pane,
When missel-thrush is singing his spring-song once
   again ;
Who heeds the stinging hailstorm, the heap'd-up
   clouds behind
While lilt of sudden sweetness comes ringing down the
   wind ?

Who mourns 'mid barren branches, who sighs 'neath
   skies of grey
While missel-thrush flutes clearly that Spring's not
   far away ?
Who misses Autumn red-gold, her leaves of changing
   hue,
When snowdrops soon shall tinkle their joybells in
   the dew ?

Who hears your wild sweet singing and goes un-
    heeding by
My silv'ry-throated songster beneath grey Winter's
    sky,
Who hears nor longs to thank you for sweetness of
    your song,
That brings new hope, new gladness, that lifts the
    year along ?

                                        AUGUSTA HANCOCK.

TO THE OWL

SAD bird of night, what sorrows call thee forth,
    Tò vent thy plaints thus in the midnight hour ?
Is it some blast that gathers in the north,
    Threatening to nip the verdure of thy bower ?

Is it, sad owl, that Autumn strips the shade,
    And leaves thee here, unshelter'd and forlorn ?
Or fear that Winter will thy nest invade ?
    Or friendless melancholy bids thee mourn ?

Shut out, lone bird, from all the feather'd train,
    To tell thy sorrows to the unheeding gloom ;
No friend to pity when thou dost complain,
    Grief all thy thought, and solitude thy home.

Sing on, sad mourner ! I will bless thy strain,
    And pleased in sorrow listen to thy song :
Sing on, sad mourner ! to the night complain ;
    While the lone echo wafts thy notes along.

Is beauty less, when down the glowing cheek,
    Sad, piteous tears, in native sorrows fall ?
Less kind the heart when anguish bids it break ?
    Less happy he who lists to pity's call ?

Ah, no, sad owl ! nor is thy voice less sweet,
    That sadness tunes it, and that grief is there ;
That Spring's gay notes, unskill'd, thou canst repeat ;
    That sorrow bids thee to the gloom repair.

Nor that the treble songsters of the day
    Are quite estranged, sad bird of night ! from thee,
Nor that the thrush deserts the evening spray,
    When darkness calls thee from thy reverie.

From some old tower, thy melancholy dome,
    While the gray walls, and desert solitudes,
Return each note, responsive to the gloom
    Of ivied coverts and surrounding woods.

There hooting, I will list more pleased to thee
    Than ever lover to the nightingale ;
Or drooping wretch, oppress'd with misery,
    Lending his ear to some condoling tale.

                                        ROBERT BURNS.

THE ROBIN REDBREAST

WHEN the winter wind whistles around my lone cot,
And my holiday friends have my mansion forgot,
Though a lonely poor being, still do not I pine,
While my poor Robin Redbreast forsakes not my
    shrine.

He comes with the morning, he hops on my arm,
For he knows 'tis too gentle to do him a harm
And in gratitude ever beguiles with a lay
The soul-sick'ning thoughts of a bleak Winter's day.

What, though he may leave me, when Spring again
    smiles,
To waste the sweet Summer in love's little wiles,
Yet will he remember his fosterer long,
And greet her each morning with one little song.

And when the rude blast shall again strip the trees,
And plenty no longer shall fly on the breeze,
Oh ! then he'll return to his Helena kind,
And repose in her breast from the rude northern wind.

My sweet little Robin's no holiday guest,
He'll never forget his poor Helena's breast ;
But will strive to repay, by his generous song,
Her love, and her cares, in the winter day long.

HENRY KIRKE WHITE.

TO MY ROBIN REDBREAST

From " The Captive Chief "

Now keenly blows the northern blast ;
Like winter hail the leaves fall fast,
And my pet Robin's come at last
    To our old thorn ;
With warbling throat and eye upcast
    He greets the morn ;

Like some true friend you come to cheer,
When all around is dark and drear,
And oh ! what friend to me more dear
        Than your sweet sel' ?
Your mellow voice falls on my ear
        Like some sweet spell.

Oft at the gloaming's pensive hour,
When clouds above me darkly lower,
I've sought a seat in some lone bower,
        With heart opprest ;
You soothed me with your magic power,
        And calmed my breast,

When Morning dons her sober gray
To usher in the coming day,
And Phœbus shines with sickly ray
        On all around ;
No warblers greet him from the spray
        With joyous sound.

But you, sweet Bird, unlike the throng,
Salute him with a joyous song.
When heavy rains and sleet prolong
        The dreary day ;
You chant to him your evening song
        Upon the spray.

JAMES THOMSON.

A CHRISTMAS CAROL

IT chanced upon the merry merry Christmas eve,
  I went sighing past the church across the moorland
    dreary—
"Oh! never sin and want and woe this earth will leave,
  And the bells but mock the wailing round, they
    sing so cheery.
How long, O Lord! how long before Thou come again?
  Still in cellar, and in garret, and on moorland
    dreary,
The orphans moan, and widows weep, and poor men
    toil in vain,
  Till earth is sick of hope deferred, though Christmas
    bells be cheery."

Then arose a joyous clamour from the wild-fowl on
    the mere,
  Beneath the stars, across the snow, like clear bells
    ringing,
And a voice within cried—"Listen—Christmas
    carols even here,
  Though thou be dumb, yet o'er their work the
    stars and snows are singing.
Blind! I live, I love, I reign; and all the nations
    through,
  With the thunder of my judgments even now are
    ringing.
Do thou fulfil thy work but as yon wild-fowl do,
  Thou wilt heed no less the wailing, yet hear
    through it angels singing."

CHARLES KINGSLEY.

A WELCOME TO THE NEW YEAR

Sound the flute !
Now 'tis mute ;
Birds delight,
Day and night,
Nightingale,
In the dale,
Lark in sky—
Merrily,
Merrily, merrily, to welcome in the Year.

Little boy
Full of joy ;
Little girl
Sweet and small ;
Cock does crow,
So do you ;
Merry voice,
Infant noise ;
Merrily, merrily, to welcome in the Year.

Little lamb,
Here I am ;
Come and lick
My white neck ;
Let me pull
Your soft wool ;
Let me kiss
Your soft face ;
Merrily, merrily, we welcome in the Year.
                                    William Blake.

BIRD MUSICIANS AND THEIR MUSIC

" But all those little birds, whose notes
    Sweetly the list'ning ear enthral,
    To the clear waters' murmuring fall,
Accord their disagreeing throats."
SHERBURNE.

THE MUSICIANS OF THE GROVE

THE lily-handed morne
Saw Phœbus stealing dewe from Ceres' corne.
The mounting Lark (daie's herauld) got on wing,
Bidding each bird chuse out his bough and sing.
The lofty treble sung the little Wren ;
Robin the meane, that best of all loves men :
The Nightingale the tenor ; and the Thrush,
The counter-tenor, sweetly in a bush ;
And that the musicke might be full in parts,
Birds from the groves flew with right willing harts ;
But (as it seem'd) they thought (as do the swaines,
Which tune their pipes on sack'd Hibernia's plaines)
There should some droaning part be, therefore will'd
Some bird to flie into a neighbouring field,
In embassie unto the king of bees,
To aid his partners on the flowres and trees ;
Who condescending gladly flew along
To beare the base to his well-tunèd song.
The Crow was willing they should be beholding
For his deep voyce, but, being hoarse with scolding,
He thus lends aide : upon an oake doth climbe,
And nodding with his head, so keepeth time.
O true delight, enharboring the brests
Of those sweet creatures with the plumy crests.
Had Nature unto man such simpl'esse given,
He would, like birds, be farre more neere to Heaven.

WILLIAM BROWNE.

THE SONG OF BIRDS

WHEN Phœbus lifts his head out of the Winter's
    wave,
No sooner does the earth her flowery bosom brave,
At such time as the year brings on the pleasant spring,
But " hunts up " to the morn the feather'd sylvans
    sing ;
And in the lower grove, as on the rising knoll,
Upon the highest spray of every mounting pole
Those quiristers are perched, with many a speckled
    breast.
Then from her burnished gate the goodly glittering
    East
Gilds every lofty top, which late the humorous
    night
Bespangled had with pearl to please the morning's
    sight :
On which the mirthful quires, with their clear open
    throats,
Unto the joyful morn so strain their warbling notes,
That hills and valleys ring, and even the echoing air
Seems all composed of sounds, about them every-
    where.
The throstle with shrill sharps, as purposely he song
T'awake the listless sun, or chiding that so long
He was in coming forth, that should the thickets
    thrill :
The woosel near at hand, that hath a golden bill,
As nature him had marked of purpose to let see
That from all other birds his tunes should different be,

For with their vocal sounds they sing to pleasant
    May :
Upon his dulcet pipe the merle doth only play,
When, in the lower brake, the nightingale hard by
In such lamenting strains the joyful hours doth
    ply,
As though the other birds she to her tunes would
    draw ;
And, but that Nature (by her all-constraining law)
Each bird to her own kind this season doth invite,
They else, alone to hear that charmer of the night,
(The more to use their ears) their voices sure would
    spare
That moduleth her tunes so admirably rare,
As man to set in parts at first had learned of her.
To Philomel, the next the linnet we prefer
And by that warbling bird, the wood-lark, place we
    then
The reed-sparrow, the nope, the redbreast, and the
    wren.
The yellow-pate,which, though she hurt the blooming
    tree,
Yet scarce hath any bird a finer pipe than she.
And of these chaunting fowls, the goldfinch not
    behind,
That hath so many sorts descending from her kind.
The tydy from her notes as delicate as they,
The laughing hecco, then the counterfeiting jay ;
The softer with the shrill (some hid among the
    leaves,
Some in the taller trees, some in the lower greaves)

Thus sing away the morn, until the mounting sun
Through thick exhalèd fogs his golden head hath run,
And through the twisted tops of our close covert creeps,
To kiss the gentle shade, the while that sweetly sleeps.
                                    MICHAEL DRAYTON.

A QUIRE OF BIRDS

You, winged quiristers, that dwell
    In woods, and there maintain a quire,
Whose music doth all art excel,
    Nought can we emulate, but admire.
You, living galleys of the air,
    That through the strongest tempests slide ;
And, by your wanton flight, who dare
    The fury of the winds divide :
Praise Him, and in this harmony and love,
Let your soft quire contend with that above.
                                    THOMAS STANLEY.

THE MAJOR AND MINOR NOTES OF BIRDS

A BIRD sang sweet and strong
    In the top of the highest tree ;
He sang—" I pour out my soul in song
    For the summer that soon shall be."

But deep in the shady wood
    Another bird sang—" I pour
My soul on the solemn solitude
    For the springs that return no more."
                                    GEORGE WILLIAM CURTIS.

LINES WRITTEN IN EARLY SPRING

I HEARD a thousand blended notes,
While in a grove I sate reclined,
In that sweet mood when pleasant thoughts
Bring sad thoughts to the mind.

To her fair works did Nature link
The human soul that through me ran ;
And much it grieved my heart to think
What man has made of man.

Through primrose tufts, in that sweet bower,
The periwinkle trailed its wreaths ;
And 'tis my faith that every flower
Enjoys the air it breathes.

The birds around me hopp'd and play'd ;
Their thoughts I cannot measure ;
But the least motion which they made,
It seem'd a thrill of pleasure.

The budding twigs spread out their fan,
To catch the breezy air ;
And I must think, do all I can,
That there was pleasure there.

From Heaven if this belief be sent,
If such be Nature's holy plan,
Have I not reason to lament
What man has made of man ?

WILLIAM WORDSWORTH.

MUSIC'S DUEL

Now westward Sol had spent the richest beams
Of Noon's high glory, when, hard by the streams
Of Tiber, on the scene of a green plat,
Under protection of an oak, there sat
A sweet lute's-master, in whose gentle airs
He lost the day's heat, and his own hot cares.
   Close in the covert of the leaves there stood
A Nightingale, come from the neighb'ring wood,
(The sweet inhabitant of each glad tree,
Their Muse, their Syren—harmless Syren she!)
There stood she list'ning, and did entertain
The music's soft report, and mould the same
In her own murmurs, that whatever mood
His curious fingers lent, her voice made good.
The man perceived his rival and her art ;
Disposed to give the light-foot lady sport,
Awakes his lute, and 'gainst the fight to come
Informs it, in a sweet præludium
Of closer strains, and, ere the war begin,
He lightly skirmishes on ev'ry string
Charged with a flying touch ; and straightway she
Carves out her dainty voice as readily,
Into a thousand sweet distinguish'd tones,
And reckons up in soft divisions
Quick volumes of wild notes, to let him know,
By that shrill taste, she could do something too.
   His nimble hands' instinct then taught each string
A cap'ring cheerfulness, and made them sing

To their own dance ; now negligently rash
He throws his arm, and with a long-drawn dash
Blends all together ; then distinctly trips
From this to that, then quick returning skips
And snatches this again, and pauses there.
She measures everv measure, ev'rywhere
Meets art with art ; sometimes, as if in doubt,
Not perfect yet, and fearing to be out,
Trails her plain ditty in one long-spun note,
Through the sleek passage of her open throat,
A clear unwrinkled song ; then doth she point it
With tender accents, and severely joint it
By short diminutives, that being rear'd
In controverting warbles ev'nly shared,
With her sweet self she wrangles.   He, amazed
That from so small a channel should be raised
The torrent of a voice whose melody
Could melt into such sweet variety,
Strains higher yet, that tickled with rare art
The tattling strings (each breathing in his part)
Most kindly do fall out ; the grumbling base
In surly groans disdains the treble's grace ;
The high-perch'd treble chirps at this, and chides,
Until his finger (Moderator) hides
And closes the sweet quarrel, rousing all,
Hoarse, shrill, at once ; as when the trumpets call
Hot Mars to th' harvest of death's field, and woo
Men's hearts into their hands ; this lesson too
She gives him back ; her supple breast thrills out
Sharp airs, and staggers in a warbling doubt
Of dallying sweetness, hovers o'er her skill,

And folds in wav'd notes with a trembling bill
The pliant series of her slipp'ry song ;
Then starts she suddenly into a throng
Of short thick sobs, whose thundering volleys float,
And roll themselves over her lubric throat
In panting murmurs, 'still'd out of her breast,
That ever-bubbling spring, the sugar'd nest
Of her delicious soul, that there does lie
Bathing in streams of liquid melody ;
Music's best seed-plot ; when in ripen'd airs
A golden-headed harvest fairly rears
His honey-dropping tops, plough'd by her breath,
Which there reciprocally laboureth
In that sweet soil ; it seems a holy choir
Founded to th' name of great Apollo's lyre ;
Whose silver-roof rings with the sprightly notes
Of sweet-lipp'd angel-imps, that swill their throats
In cream of morning Helicon, and then
Prefer soft anthems to the ears of men,
To woo them from their beds, still murmuring
That men can sleep while they their matins sing
(Most divine service) whose so early lay
Prevents the eyelids of the blushing day !
There might you hear her kindle her soft voice
In the close murmur of a sparkling noise,
And lay the ground-work of her hopeful song,
Still keeping in the forward stream, so long,
Till a sweet whirlwind (striving to get out)
Heaves her soft bosom, wanders round about,
And makes a pretty earthquake in her breast,
Till the fledged notes at length forsake their nest,

Flutt'ring in wanton shoals, and to the sky,
Wing'd with their own wild echoes, prattling fly.
She opes the floodgate, and lets loose a tide
Of streaming sweetness, which in state doth ride
On the waved back of every swelling strain,
Rising and falling in a pompous train ;
And while she thus discharges a shrill peal
Of flashing airs, she qualifies their zeal
With the cool epode of a graver note,
Thus high, thus low, as if her silver throat
Would reach the brazen voice of War's hoarse bird ;
Her little soul is ravish'd, and so pour'd
Into loose ecstasies, that she is placed
Above herself, Music's enthusiast.

    Shame now and anger mixed a double stain
In the Musician's face ; " Yet once again
(Mistress) I come ; now reach a strain, my lute,
Above her mock, or be for ever mute ;
Or tune a song of victory to me,
Or to thyself sing thine own obsequy " ;
So said, his hands sprightly as fire he flings,
And with a quav'ring coyness tastes the strings
The sweet-lipp'd sisters, musically frighted,
Singing their fears, are fearfully delighted
Trembling as when Apollo's golden hairs
Are fann'd and frizzled in the wanton airs
Of his own breath : which married to his lyre
Doth tune the spheres, and makes Heaven's self
   look higher.
From this to that, from that to this, he flies,
Feels Music's pulse in all her arteries ;

Caught in a net which there Apollo spreads,
His fingers struggle with the vocal threads.
Following those little rills, he sinks into
A sea of Helicon ; his hand does go
Those   parts   of   sweetness,   which   with   nectar
    drop,
Softer than that which pants in Hebe's cup.
The humorous strings expound his learnèd touch
By various glosses ; now they seem to grutch,
And murmur in a buzzing din, then gingle
In shrill-tongued accents, striving to be single ;
Ev'ry smooth turn, ev'ry delicious stroke
Gives life to some new grace ; thus doth h'invoke
Sweetness by all her names ; thus, bravely thus,
(Fraught with a fury so harmonious)
The Lute's light genius now does proudly rise,
Heaved on the surges of swoll'n rhapsodies,
Whose flourish (meteor-like) doth curl the air
With flash of high-born fancies ; here and there
Dancing in lofty measures, and anon
Creeps on the soft touch of a tender tone,
Whose trembling murmurs melting in wild airs
Runs to and fro, complaining his sweet cares,
Because those precious mysteries that dwell
In Music's ravish'd soul he dares not tell,
But whisper to the world : thus do they vary
Each string his note, as if they meant to carry
Their Master's blest soul (snatch'd out at his ears
By a strong ecstasy) through all the spheres
Of Music's heaven ; and seat it there on high
In th'empyrean of pure harmony.

At length (after so long, so loud a strife
Of all the strings, still breathing the best life
Of blest variety, attending on
His fingers' fairest revolution,
In many a sweet rise, many as sweet a fall)
A full-mouth'd diapason swallows all.

This done, he lists what she would say to this,
And she (although her breath's late exercise
Had dealt too roughly with her tender throat),
Yet summons all her sweet powers for a note.
Alas ! in vain ! for while (sweet soul !) she tries
To measure all those wild diversities
Of chatt'ring strings, by the small size of one
Poor simple voice, raised in a natural tone,
She fails, and failing grieves, and grieving dies.
She dies ; and leaves her life, the Victor's prize,
Falling upon his lute : O, fit to have
(That lived so sweetly) dead, so sweet a grave !

RICHARD CRASHAW.

THE WARBLING OF BLACKBIRDS

WHEN I hear the waters fretting,
When I see the chestnut letting
All her lovely blossom falter down, I think, " Alas
    the day ! "
Once with magical sweet singing,
Blackbirds set the woodland ringing,
That awakes no more while April hours wear them-
    selves away.

In our hearts fair hope lay smiling,
Sweet as air and all beguiling ;
And there hung a mist of bluebells on the slope and
down the dell ;
And we talked of joy and splendour
That the years unborn would render,
And the blackbirds helped us with the story, for
they knew it well.
Piping, fluting, " Bees are humming,
April's here, and summer's coming ;
Don't forget us when you walk, a man with men, in
pride and joy ;
Think on us in alleys shady,
When you step a graceful lady ;
For no fairer day have we to hope for, little girl
and boy.
" Laugh and play, O lisping waters,
Lull our downy sons and daughters ;
Come, O wind, and rock their leafy cradle in thy
wanderings coy ;
When they wake we'll end the measure
With a wild sweet cry of pleasure,
And a ' Hey down derry, let's be merry ! little
girl and boy ! ' "

JEAN INGELOW.

THE WILD MELODY OF THE THRUSH

DEAR, dear, dear
Is the rocky glen.
Far away, far away, far away
The haunts of men.

Here shall we dwell in love
With the lark and the dove,
Cuckoo and cornrail ;
Feast on the banded snail,
    Worm and gilded fly ;
Drink of the crystal rill
Winding adown the hill,
    Never to dry.

With glee, with glee, with glee,
    Cheer up, cheer up, cheer up, here
Nothing to harm us, then sing merrily,
    Sing to the lov'd ones whose nest is near—
    Qui, qui, qui, kweeu quip,
    Tiurru, tiurru, chipiwi,
    Too-tee, too-tee, chiu choo,
    Chirri, chirri, chooee,
    Quiu, qui, qui.

W. Macgillivray.

THE ROBIN REDBREASTS' CHORUS

There is an English belief, that when a sick person is about to depart,
a chorus of Robin Redbreasts raise their plaintive songs near the
house of death.

The summer sweets had passed away, with many
a heart-throb sore,
For warning voices said that she would ne'er see
summer more ;
But still I hoped—'gainst hope itself—and at the
autumn-tide,
With joy I marked returning strength, while watch-
ing by her side.

But dreary winter and his blasts came with re-
doubled gloom,
With trembling hands the Christmas boughs I
hung around the room ;
For gone the warmth of autumn days—her life
was on the wane :
Those Christmas boughs at Candlemas I took not
down again !

One day a Robin Redbreast came unto the casement
near,
She loved its soft and plaintive note, which few
unmoved can hear ;
But on each sad successive day this redbreast ceased
not bringing
Other Robins, till a chorus full and rich was singing.

Then, then I knew that death was nigh, and slowly
stalking on ;
I gazed with speechless agony on our belovèd one ;
No tearful eye, no fluttering mien, such sorrow durst
betray—
We tried to soothe each parting pang of Nature's
last decay.

The blessed Sabbath morning came, the last she
ever saw ;
And I had read of Jesus' love, of God's eternal law,
Amid the distant silver chime of Sunday bells sweet
ringing—
Amid a chorus rich and full of Robin Redbreasts
singing !

The grass waves high, the fields are green, which
  skirt the churchyard side,
Where charnel vaults with massive walls their
  slumbering inmates hide ;
The ancient trees cast shadows broad, the sparkling
  waters leap,
And still the Redbreast sings around her long and
  dreamless sleep.

C. A. M. W.

A TUNEFUL ROBIN

This poem was written by the Rev. S. Love, Fellow of Balliol College,
Oxford, and minor canon of Bristol Cathedral, where a Robin had
taken up its abode for fifteen years, and during the time of divine
service it usually perched on one of the pinnacles of the great
organ, and accompanied it with its harmonious melody.

SWEET social bird ! whose soft harmonious lays
Swell the glad song of thy Creator's praise,
Say art thou conscious of approaching ills ?
Fell winter's storms—the pointed blast that kills !
Shunn'st thou the savage North's unpitying breath
Or cruel man's more latent snares of death ?
Here dwell secure ; here, with incessant note,
Pour the soft music of thy trembling throat.
Here, gentle bird, a sure asylum find,
Nor dread the chilling frost, nor boist'rous wind.
No hostile tyrant of the feathered race,
Shall dare invade thee in this hallow'd place ;
Nor, while he sails the liquid air along,
Check the shrill numbers of thy cheerful song.
No cautious gunner, whose unerring sight
Stops the swift eagle in his rapid flight,

Shall here disturb my lovely songster's rest,
Nor wound the plumage of his crimson breast.
The truant school-boy, who, in wanton play,
With viscid lime involves the treach'rous spray,
In vain shall spread the wily snare for thee,
Alike secure thy life and liberty.
Peace then, sweet warbler, to thy flutt'ring heart,
Defy the rage of hawks, and toils of art ;
Now shake thy downy plumes, now gladlier pay
Thy grateful tribute to each rising day ;
While crowds below their willing voices raise,
To sing with holy zeal Jehovah's praise,
Thou, perched on high, shalt hear th' adoring throng,
Catch the warm strains, and aid the sacred song,
Increase the solemn chorus, and inspire
Each tongue with music and each heart with fire.

S. LOVE.

TO THE ROBIN IN WOODCHESTER CHURCH

Strangely enough, the wish in the last two lines has been fulfilled,
for the bird was found dead on the sanctuary step, some time after
the poem had been written.

BIRD ! what strange companion calls thee thus to
  dwell 'mid walls of stone,
Thus to leave thy feathered mates, and live thy
  brief bird-life alone ?

Is a roof, however lofty, fairer than the fair blue
  sky ?
Is the arching column dearer than the hillside to
  thine eye ?

Is a polished wooden rafter better than a swaying
bough ?
Is the ruddy lamplight brighter than the sunlight to
thee now ?

When thou perchest, strangely often, on the imaged
Saviour's Hand,
Does an old tradition haunt thee from the far-off
Holy Land

Telling how another robin from His bleeding Hands
and Feet
Strove to draw the nails : and Jesus, to reward its
action sweet,

Bade its breast remain encrimsoned with the precious
ruby Flood ?
Knowest thou thy race since then has borne the
branding of His Blood ?

Why when perching on the altar dost thou sing thy
sweetest lay ?
Art thou conscious of a List'ner, dwelling there the
livelong day ?

But alas ! thou canst not answer and our questions
are in vain ;
Dead leaves only break the stillness, rustling down
like summer rain.

Still, *we* know of One who listens, silent from His
  earthly throne,
And we know thy song must please Him, dwelling
  there too oft alone.

May'st thou spend thy life, then, singing, singing as
  the days go by,
And when all thy songs are ended, lie thee down near
  Him to die.

OLIVE K. PARR.

IV

THE WOODLAND AND ITS PEOPLE

" Louder seems each bird
    In the brightening branches heard
Still to speak some ever more delightful word."
                                    SWINBURNE.

WOODLAND SCENERY

From " The Vision of Delight "

How is't each bough a several music yields ?
The lusty throstle, early nightingale,
Accord in tune, though vary in their tale ;
The chirping swallow call'd forth by the sun,
And crested lark doth his division run ?
The yellow bees the air with murmur fill,
The finches carol, and the turtles bill ?
Whose power is this ? what god ?

BEN JONSON.

WOODLAND WARBLERS

WITHOUT Thy aid, without Thy gladsome beams,
The tribes of woodland warblers would remain
Mute on the bending branches, nor recite
The praise of Him, who, ere He formed their Lord,
Their voices tun'd to transport, wing'd their flight,
And bade them call for nurture, and receive ;
And lo ! they call ; the blackbird and the thrush,
The woodlark and the redbreast jointly call ;
He hears and feeds their feather'd families,
He feeds his sweet musicians,—nor neglects
Th'invoking ravens in the greenwood wide ;
And tho' their throats' coarse rattling hurt the ear,
They mean it all for musick ; thanks and praise
They mean, and leave ingratitude to man.

CHRISTOPHER SMART.

THE FOREST

CLOSE in the bosom of a bended hill,
  Of fair and fruitful trees a forest stood ;
Balm, myrtle, bdellium from their bark distil ;
  Ray, smilax, myrtle (Cupid's arrow-wood,)
Grew there ; and cypress with his kiss-sky tops,
And Ferrea's tree, whence pure rose-water drops.

The golden bee, buzzing with tinsel wings,
  Sucked amber honey from the silken flower ;
The dove sad love-groans on her sackbut sings,
  The throstle whistles from his oaken tower ;
And sporting lay the nymphs of woods and hills,
On beds of heart's-ease, rue, and daffodils.

EDWARD FAIRFAX.

THE WOODLANDS AT DAYBREAK

HIS task had Giles, in fields remote from home ;
Oft has he wish'd the rosy morn to come :
And when at daybreak summon'd from his bed,
Light as the lark that carol'd o'er his head ;

His own shrill matin join'd the various notes
Of Nature's music, from a thousand throats ·
The blackbird strove with emulation sweet,
And echo answer'd from her close retreat ;
The sporting white-throat on some twig's end borne,
Pour'd hymns to freedom and the rising morn ;

Stopp'd in her song, perchance, the starting thrush
Shook a white shower from the black-thorn bush,
Where dewdrops thick as early blossoms hung,
And trembled as the minstrel sweetly sung ·
Across his path, in either grove to hide,
The timid rabbit scouted by his side ;
Or bold cock pheasant stalk'd along the road,
Whose gold and purple tints alternate glow'd.

ROBERT BLOOMFIELD.

RECOLLECTIONS OF BIRDS AFTER A RAMBLE

THE rosy day was sweet and young,
    The clod-brown lark that hail'd the morn
Had just her summer anthem sung,
    And trembling dropped into the corn ;
The dew-rais'd flower was perk and proud,
    The butterfly around it play'd.;
The sky's blue clear, save woolly cloud
    That pass'd the sun without a shade.

Brazen magpies, fond of clack,
    Full of insolence and pride,
Chattering on the donkey's back
    Perch'd, and pull'd his shaggy hide ;
Odd crows settled on the path,
    Dames from milking trotting home
Said the sign foreboded wrath,
    And shook their heads at ills to come.

Sweet the birds did chant their songs,
   Blackbird, linnet, lark, and thrush ;
Music from a many tongues
   Melted from each dripping bush ˙
Deafen'd echo, on the plain,
   As the sunbeams broke the cloud,
Scarce could help repeat the strain,
   Nature's anthem flow'd so loud.
                              JOHN CLARE.

A MORNING RAMBLE IN SPRING

From " The Complaint of the Black Knight "

I ROSE anon, and thought I wouldé gone
Into the woods, to hear the birdis sing,
When that the misty vapour was agone,
And cleare and faire was the morrowing ;
The dew, also, like silver in shining,
Upon the leaves, as any baume sweet.

And in I went to hear the birdis' song,
Which on the branches, both in plain and vale,
So loudly y-sang, that all the wood y-rang,
Like as it should shiver in pieces smale ;
And as me thoughten that the nightingale
With so great might her voice began out-wrest,
Right as her heart for love would all to-brest.[1]
                              GEOFFREY CHAUCER.

[1] break.

THE NATURALIST'S SUMMER-EVENING WALK

WHEN day, declining, sheds a milder gleam,
What time the May-fly haunts the pool or stream ;
When the still Owl skims round the grassy mead,
What time the timorous Hare limps forth to feed ;
Then be the time to steal adown the dale,
And listen to the vagrant Cuckoo's tale ;
To hear the clamorous Curlew call his mate,
Or the soft Quail his tender pain relate ;
To see the Swallow sweep the darkening plain,
Belated, to support her infant train ;
To mark the Swift in rapid giddy ring
Dash round the steeple, unsubdued of wing ·
Amusive birds ! say where your hid retreat
When the frost rages and the tempests beat ;
Whence your return, by such nice instinct led,
When Spring, soft season, lifts her bloomy head ?
Such baffled searches mock man's prying pride,
The God of Nature is your secret guide !
 While deepening shades obscure the face of day,
To yonder bench leaf-sheltered let us stray,
Till blended objects fail the swimming sight,
And all the fading landscape sinks in night ;
To hear the drowsy Dor come brushing by
With buzzing wing, or the shrill Cricket cry ;
To see the feeding Bat glance through the wood ;
To catch the distant falling of the flood ;
While o'er the cliff th'awakened Churn-owl hung
Through the still gloom protracts his chattering song ;

While high in air, and poised upon his wings,
Unseen the soft enamour'd Wood-lark sings :
These, Nature's works, the curious mind employ,
Inspire a soothing, melancholy joy.
                              GILBERT WHITE.

BIRDS AND A LOVER

WITHIN a budding grove,
In April's ear sang every bird his best,
But not a song to pleasure my unrest,
Or touch the tears unwept of bitter love.
Some spoke, methought, with pity, some as if in jest.
          To every word
          Of every bird
I listened, and replied as it behove.
     Screamed Chaffinch, " Sweet, sweet, sweet !
O bring my pretty love to meet me here ! "
" Chaffinch," quoth I, " be dumb awhile, in fear
Thy darling prove no better than a cheat ;
And never come, or fly when wintry days appear."
          Yet from a twig
          With voice so big
The little fowl his utterance did repeat.
     Then I, " The man forlorn
Hears Earth send up a foolish noise aloft."
" And what'll *he* do ? What'll *he* do l '" scoffed
The Blackbird, standing in an ancient thorn ;
Then spread his sooty wings, and flitted to the croft
          With crackling laugh :
          Whom I, being half
Enraged, called after, giving back his scorn.

Worse mocked the Thrush, " Die ! die !
O could he do it ! could he do it ? Nay !
Be quick ! be quick ! Here, here, here ! " (went
 his lay)
" Take heed ! take heed ! " then, " Why ? why ?
 why ? why ? why ?
See-ee now ! See-ee now ! (he drawled) Back ι
 back ! back ! R-r-r-run away ι "
 " O Thrush, be still ι
 Or, at thy will,
Seek some less sad interpreter than I ι "

" Air, air ! blue air and white !
Whither I flee, whither, O whither, O whither
 I flee ! "
(Thus the Lark hurried, mounting from the lea)
" Hills, countries, many waters glittering bright,
Whither I see, whither I see ! deeper, deeper,
 deeper, whither I see, see, see ι "
 " Gay Lark," I said,
 " The song that's bred
In happy nest may well to heaven make flight."

" There's something, something sad,
I half remember "—piped a broken strain.
Well sung, sweet Robin ! Robin sung again,
"Spring's opening cheerily, cheerily ! be we glad ! "
Which moved, I wist not why, me melancholy mad,
 Till now, grown meek,
 With wetted cheek,
Most comforting and gentle thoughts I had.
WILLIAM ALLINGHAM.

QUATRAINS

THE PHŒNIX

WHEN Adam ate of that forbidden food,
  Sole bird that shared not in his sin was I ;
And so my life is evermore renewed,
  And I among the dying never die.

THE PELICAN

I am the bird that from my bleeding breast,
  Draw the dear stream that nourishes my brood,
And feebly unto men His love attest,
  True Pelican, that feeds them with His blood.

THE HALCYON

For twice seven days, in winter's middle rage,
  The winds are hushed, the billows are at rest ;
Heaven all for me their fury doth assuage,
  While I am brooding o'er my fluctuant nest.

THE COCK

What time an ass with horrid bray you hear,
  Believe he sees a wicked sprite at hand ;
But when I make my carol loud and clear,
  Know that an angel doth before me stand.

THE PEACOCK

I, glorying in my tail's extended pride,
  See my foul legs, and then I shriek outright ;
So shrieks a human soul, that has descried
  Its baseness 'mid vainglorious self-delight.

THE EAGLE

I no degenerate progeny will raise,
  But try my callow offspring, which will look
In the sun's eye with peremptory gaze,
  Nor other nurslings in my nest will brook.

THE NIGHTINGALE

Leaning my bosom on a pointed thorn,
  I bleed, and bleeding sing my sweetest strain ;
For sweetest songs of saddest hearts are born,
  And who may here dissever love and pain ?

ARCHBISHOP TRENCH.

A RIME ABOUT BIRDS

I SAID to the little Swallow :
  " Who'll follow ?
Out of thy nest in the eaves
Under the ivy leaves !
  Yet my thought flies swifter than thou
My thought has a softer nest,
Where it folds its wing to rest,
In a pure-hearted woman's breast ;
  While its sky is her cloudless brow."
    Swallow—swallow,
    Who'll follow ?

I said to the brown, brown Thrush ·
  " Hush, hush !
Through the wood's full strains I hear
Thy monotone deep and clear,
  Like a sound amid sounds most fine ;

And so, though the whole world sung
To my love with eloquent tongue,
However their voices rung,
    She would pause and listen to mine."
    Brown, brown thrush,
    Hush—hush !

I said to the Nightingale :
    " Hail, all hail !
Pierce with thy trill the dark,
Like a glittering music-spark,
    When the earth grows pale and dumb ;
But mine be a song more rare,
To startle the sleeping air,
And to the dull world declare
    Love sings amid darkest gloom."
    Nightingale,
    Hail, all hail !

I said to the sky-poised Lark ·
    " Hark—hark !
Thy note is more loud and free,
Because there lies safe for thee
    A little nest on the ground.
And I, when strong-winged I rise
To chant out sweet melodies,
Shall know there are home-lit eyes
    Watching me soar, sun crowned."
    Poet—lark,
    Hark—hark !
                                ANON.

THE CONVERSATION OF BIRDS

" Who," says the writer of " The Five Windows of the Soul," " can watch a pair of crows about their nest without seeing that they are expressing sentiments and desires to each other? I am not a crow, but I can often tell how a crow feels, and what it is about by the tone of its caw. So could Vergil, if we may judge by that beautiful passage in the *Georgics*, i. 410-414."

THE ravens then repeat their smooth clear notes
Thrice or once more, with hushed, contracted
  throats ;
Oft, perched aloft, they rustle 'mong the leaves,
I know not what new joy their heart receives,—
Gladdened, perchance, they view the home-sweet
  bowers,
And tell their nestlings of the bygone showers.

TRANS. by C. L. B.

JAY'S SCREAM

HE who makes his native wood
Resound his screaming, harsh and crude,
Continuously the season through,
Though scarce his painted wing you'll view,
With sable barr'd and white and grey,
And varied crest, the lively Jay.

BISHOP MANT.

WHAT THE BIRDS SAY

Answer to a Child's Question

Do you ask what the birds say ? The sparrow, the
  dove,
The linnet, and thrush, say, " I love, and I love ! "
In the Winter they're silent—the wind is so strong ;
What it says I don't know, but it sings a loud song.

But green leaves, and blossoms, and sunny warm
  weather,
And singing, and loving—all come back together.
But the lark is so brimful of gladness and love,
The green fields below him, the blue sky above,
That he sings, and he sings, and for ever sings he—
" I love my Love, and my Love loves me ! "
                    SAMUEL TAYLOR COLERIDGE.

TO A LADY—ON THE LANGUAGE OF
BIRDS

COME then, Dione, let us range the grove,
The science of the feather'd choirs explore ·
Hear linnets argue, larks descant of love,
And blame the gloom of solitude no more.

My doubt subsides—'tis no Italian song,
Nor senseless ditty, cheers the vernal tree
Ah ! who that hears Dione's tuneful tongue,
Shall doubt that music may with sense agree ?

And come, my muse ! that lov'st the sylvan shade,
Evolve the mazes, and the mist dispel ;
Translate the song ; convince my doubting maid
No solemn dervise can explain so well—

Pensive beneath the twilight shades I sate,
The slave of hopeless vows and cold disdain !
When Philomel address'd his mournful mate,
And thus I construed the mellifluent strain.

" Sing on, my bird ! the liquid notes prolong ;
At every note a lover sheds his tear ;
Sing on, my bird !—'tis Damon hears thy song,
Nor doubt to gain applause, when lovers hear.

" He the sad source of our complaining knows ;
A foe to Tereus and to lawless love,
He mourns the story of our ancient woes ;
Ah ! could our music his complaint remove !

" Yon plains are governed by a peerless maid ;
And see ! pale Cynthia mounts the vaulted sky ;
A train of lovers court the chequer'd shade ·
Sing on, my bird ! and hear thy mate's reply.

" Erewhile no shepherd to these woods retired,
No lover bless'd the glow-worm's pallid ray ;
But ill-starr'd birds, that, listening, not admired ;
Or listening, envied our superior lay.

" Cheer'd by the sun, the vassals of his power, ·
Let such by day unite their joining strains !
But let us choose the calm, the silent hour,
Nor want fit audience while Dione reigns."

WILLIAM SHENSTONE.

THE CALLING OF THE BIRDS

HAVE you heard the seagull calling, the seagull out
  at sea ?
And sorry is its voice, though its wings are wide and
  free !

Though the wind blows to the land, and the waves
    laugh on the strand,
  There are tears, there are tears in the calling of
    the sea.

The waters of the wide lough are racing cheerily ·
  The white waves leap and lighten for joy of open
    sea :
The clouds pass over lightly, and the sun glints on it
    brightly,
  And the strong ships spread their wings out and
    sail for open sea.

Have you heard the curlew calling, the curlew on the
    hill ?
  And sorry is its voice o'er the moorland floating
    shrill
Though the day is fair and fine, and the breeze a
    draught of wine,
  There are tears, there are tears in the calling on the
    hill.

The sun is shining fair,—is shining on the hill,
  On the cabin by the bog, and the water lying
    still,
On the heather blooming sweet, and the gold-green
    windy wheat,
  And the brown bog and the turf stack and the
    purple on the hill.

CICELY FOX SMITH.

VOICES OF BIRDS

A LITTLE sparrow twittered near my door,
  And to my ear
The meaning clearer came than e'er before,
  And brought me cheer.

" Not one of us without our Father's care
  Falls to the Earth ;
Why doubt His fonder care for you, who are
  Of far more worth ? "

A soaring eagle in his lofty flight
  Gave me a thought,
Which to my weak and faltering soul, a bright,
  Fresh courage brought.

" Know ye not, they that wait upon the Lord
  Strength shall renew ?
Shall mount on wings as eagles ? This His Word
  Has promised you."

Thus humble sparrow and the prouder bird
  Sweet comfort give ;
And I, reminded of God's faithful Word,
  More trusting live.

And throughout nature's varied forms of life,
  Where'er I look,
I find them all with references rife
  To that dear Book ;

As though this earth companion volume were
   To sacred page,
Where man beholds the illustration fair
   From age to age.
                              ANNIE E. POULSSON.

THE BIRDS' CALL TO A LOVER

Written for his own Wedding Morn

WAKE now, my love, awake ; for it is time ;
The rosy morn long since left Tithon's bed,
All ready to her silver coach to climb ;
And Phœbus 'gins to show his glorious head.
Hark ! how the cheerful birds do chant their lays
And carol of Love's praise.
The merry lark her matins sings aloft ;
The thrush replies ; the mavis descant plays
   The ouzel shrills ; the ruddock warbles soft ·
So goodly all agree, with sweet consent,
To this day's merriment :
   Ah ! my dear love, why do ye sleep thus long,
   When meeter were that ye should now awake,
   T'await the coming of your joyous make¹ ;
   And hearken to the birds' love-learnèd song,
The dewy leaves among !
For they of joy and pleasance to you sing,
That all the woods them answer, and their echo ring.
                              EDMUND SPENSER.

¹ mate.

THE MESSAGE

YE little birds that sit and sing
  Amidst the shady valleys,
And see how Phillis sweetly walks
  Within her garden-alleys :
Go, pretty birds, about her bower ;
Sing, pretty birds, she may not lower
Ah me ! methinks I see her frown !
  Ye pretty wantons, warble.

Go tell her through your chirping bills,
  As you by me are bidden,
To her is only known my love,
  Which from the world is hidden.
Go, pretty birds, and tell her so :
See that your notes strain not too low,
For still methinks I see her frown !
  Ye pretty wantons, warble.

Go tune your voices' harmony,
  And sing, I am her lover ;
Strain loud and sweet, that every note
  With sweet content may move her ·
And she that hath the sweetest voice,
Tell her I will not change my choice :
Yet still methinks I see her frown !
  Ye pretty wantons, warble.

O fly! make haste! see, see she falls
  Into a pretty slumber,
Sing round about her rosy bed
  That waking she may wonder ·
Say to her, 'tis her lover true
That sendeth love to you, to you!
And when you hear her kind reply,
  Return with pleasant warblings.
           THOMAS HEYWOOD.

THE CRIES OF BIRDS

COME, sweet ones, come to the fields with me,
I hear the hum of the honey-bee,
I hear the call of the gray cuckoo,
I hear the note of the shrill curlew;
I hear the cry of the hunting hawk,
The sound of the dove in our 'customed walk,
The song of the lark, the tongue of the rill
The shepherds' shout on the pasture hill.
My sweet ones, all come forth and play,
The air is balm, and I smell new hay.
           ALLAN CUNNINGHAM.

V

SONNETS AND SONGS OF BIRDS

" The birds sing many a lovely lay
Of God's high praise and of their sweet love-tune."
SPENSER.

THE SONG OF A MAIDEN AND A BIRD

*From a MS. in possession of the Editor of this Treasury,
who edited the Poet's " Fragmenta," 1886*

A WEE bird came beside me,
  And sang so low and sad—
I marvelled what did grieve her,
  When all the earth was glad.

" Now tell me, gentle birdie,
  What thing does grieve thee so—
The earth is full of music,
  Why art thou full of woe ? "

" My heart is full of sadness,
  My notes are shaped in pain,
For sorrow that my mother
  Will ne'er come back again."

Away then flew the birdie—
  And I sing on the strain,
For sorrow that my mother
  Will ne'er come back again.
                    EDWIN ROPER MARTIN.

WHAT IS POESIE ?

LISTEN by moonlight to the Nightingale,
As he pours forth his loud, clear, luscious notes ;
Singing his solitary love-lorn tale :
At early morn the Lark to heaven floats,
And Thrush and Blackbird tuneful swell their
    throats,
Trilling rich harmony :—the woodlands ring,
With myriad music—which delight denotes ;—
How joyfully each chorister doth sing !
Each note is Poesie, sweet Nature's offering.

T. J. OUSELEY.

SONG

From " The Two Noble Kinsmen "

ALL dear Nature's children sweet,
Lie 'fore bride and bridegroom's feet,
    Blessing their sense ;
Not an angel of the air,
Bird melodious or bird fair,
    Be absent hence !

The crow, the slanderous cuckoo, nor
The boding raven, nor chough hoar,
    Nor chatt'ring pie,
May on our bridehouse perch or sing,
Or with them any discord bring,
    But from it fly !

BEAUMONT AND FLETCHER.

IMITATION OF CHAFFINCH SONG

SUMMER saw our brave attacks, pecking plum and
cherry !
All among the wheaten stacks, was not Autumn
merry ?
Winter showed its tempest wracks,—weary changes,
very !
Now with Spring-time on our˙ backs, care and cold
we bury !

CHORUS OF MALE CHAFFINCHES ˙

Pipe a choice and cheerful tune ! your fear eschew !
Sweet Love reviews his chaffinch levy !—
Chatter, chatter, choose and chase ! Sweet chit !
Come chatter with me ! Chase me, Chevy !

Chaffinches in flocks are gay, during winter dreary,
Two are company to-day ! each one with his deary :
Where shall be our nesting, say ?   O let no man hear
ye !
Chicks shall cheep 'mid lichens grey, in the warm nest
cheery !

CHORUS ˙

Pipe a choice and cheerful tune ! your fear eschew !
Sweet Love reviews his chaffinch levy !—
Chatter, chatter, choose and chase ! Sweet chit !
Come chatter with me ! Chase me, Chevy !
                    THE DUKE OF ARGYLL.

A BLACKBIRD'S SONG

THE Sun had chased the winter snow,
 And kindly loosed the frost-bound soil ;
The melting streams began to flow
 And ploughmen urged their annual toil.

'Twas then amidst the vernal throng,
 Whom nature wakes to mirth and love,
A BLACKBIRD raised his amorous song,
 And thus it echoed through the grove.

" O ! fairest of the feathered train,
 For whom I sing, for whom I burn ;
Attend with pity to my strain,
 And grant my love a kind return.

" See, see the winter storms are flown,
 And Zephyrs gently fan the air !
Let us the genial influence own !
 Let us the vernal pastime share.

" The raven plumes his jetty wing,
 To please his croaking paramour ;
The larks responsive love-tales sing,
 And tell their passion as they soar.

" But, trust me, Love, the raven's wing,
 Is not to be compared with mine ;
Nor can the lark so sweetly sing
 As I, who strength with sweetness join.

" I'll lead thee to the clearest rill,
  Whose streams among the pebbles stray ;
There will we sit and sip our fill,
  Or on the flowery border play.

" To get thee food, I'll range the fields,
  And cull the best of every kind ;
Whatever nature's bounty yields,
  Or love's assiduous care can find.

" And when my lovely mate would stray,
  To taste the summer sweets at large,
At home I'll wait the livelong day,
  And tend at home our infant charge."
                              RICHARD JAGO.

THE MESSENGER OF SPRING

THE merry Cuckow, messenger of Spring,
His trompet shrill hath thrice already sounded,
That warnes al lovers wayt upon their king,
Who now is comming forth with girland crowned.
With noyse whereof the quyre of Byrds resounded,
Their anthemes sweet, devized of loves prayse,
That all the woods theyr ecchoes back rebounded,
As if they knew the meaning of their layes.
But 'mongst them all, which did Love's honor rayse,
No word was heard of her that most it ought ;
But she his precept proudly disobayes,
And doth his ydle message set at nought.
    Therefore, O Love, unlesse she turne to thee,
    Ere Cuckow end, let her a rebell be !
                              EDMUND SPENSER.

THE SONG OF THE FAIRIES

From " Midsummer-Night's Dream "

You spotted snakes with double tongue,
Thorny hedgehogs, be not seen ;
Newts and blind-worms, do no wrong,
Come not near our fairy queen.
Philomel, with melody,
Sing in our sweet lullaby ;

Lulla, lulla, lullaby, lulla, lulla, lullaby ·
    Never harm,
    Nor spell nor charm,
Come our lovely lady nigh ;
So good night, with lullaby.

Weaving spiders, come not here.
    Hence, you long-legg'd spinners, hence
Beetles black, approach not near ;
    Worm nor snail, do no offence.
Philomel, with melody,
Sing in our sweet lullaby ;
Lulla, lulla, lullaby, lulla, lulla, lullaby.
                          WILLIAM SHAKESPEARE.

SONG

From " Zapolya," ii. 2

A sunny shaft did I behold,
    From sky to earth it slanted :
And poised therein a bird so bold—
    Sweet bird, thou wert enchanted !

He sunk, he rose, he twinkled, he trolled
Within that shaft of sunny mist ;
His eyes of fire, his beak of gold,
All else of amethyst !

And thus he sang : " Adieu ! adieu !
Love's dreams prove seldom true.
The blossoms they make no delay :
The sparkling dew-drops will not stay
Sweet month of May,
We must away ;
Far, far away !
To-day ! to-day ! "
SAMUEL TAYLOR COLERIDGE.

DOVE

I HAD a dove and the sweet dove died ;
And I have thought it died of grieving ·
O, what could it grieve for ?   Its feet were tied,
With a silken thread of my own hand's weaving ;
Sweet little red feet ! why should you die—
Why should you leave me, sweet bird ! Why ?
You liv'd alone in the forest-tree,
Why, pretty thing ! Would you not live with me ?
I kiss'd you oft and gave you white peas ;
Why not live sweetly, as in the green trees ?
JOHN KEATS.

THE SONG OF THE TURTLE-DOVE

From " Britannia's Pastorals "

ALL hush'd and silent as the mid of night ;
No chatt'ring pie, nor crow appear'd in sight ;
But further in I heard the turtle-dove
Singing sad dirges on her lifeless love.
Birds that compassion from the rocks could bring,
Had only license in that place to sing :
Whose doleful notes the melancholy cat
Close in a hollow tree sat wond'ring at.

WILLIAM BROWNE.

SONG

From " Cymbeline "

HARK, hark ! the lark at heaven's gate sings,
    And Phœbus 'gins arise,
His steeds to water at those springs
    On chaliced flowers that lies ;
And winking Mary-buds begin
    To ope their golden eyes :
With every thing that pretty is,
    My lady sweet, arise ·
        Arise, arise.

WILLIAM SHAKESPEARE

SONNET TO THE MOCKING BIRD

WINGED mimic of the woods, thou motley fool
Who shall thy gay buffoonery describe ?
Thine ever ready notes of ridicule
Pursue thy fellows still with jest and jibe ·
Wit, sophist, songster, Yorick of thy tribe,
Thou sportive satirist of Nature's school ;
To thee the palm of scoffing we ascribe,
Arch-mocker and mad abbot of misrule.

ROBERT WILDE.

SONNETS TO THE NIGHTINGALE

" A ROSE by any other name would smell as sweet "—
A Nightingale, by any other name,
His ear-entrancing love-notes would repeat,
  Notes that no charm but love fulfill'd could
  tame,
When o'er his nested mate and chirping young,
His silence watches of his instinct sprung.
Thy ev'ry name is, like thyself, a spell ;
  A keynote typing how thy tunes prevail ;
Sweet Bulbul—once, Aèdon—Philomel—
Luscinia—Rossignol—our Nightingale.
Sing on, rare bird ! at evening's fragrant hour,
  Till all the echoes all thy strains prolong ;
Thy magic modulations have the power
  To recreate my soul as with a bath of song.

They call thee sad,—but sadness such as thine
To Sorrow's self were exquisite relief :
They say thou griev'st,—then grief is half divine
Warbled by thee—the very joy of grief.
What time thy plainings melt upon mine ear,
　And, on night's solitude, their changes pour,
My own past griefs in Mem'ry's glass appear,
　And my lost lov'd ones live—to die once more,—
Once more my utter anguish to renew,
　My desolation, and my blank dismay,
　So deeply loved, so lovable were they,
So truly portions of ourselves they grew ;
But, as I writhe in earth-regarding woe,
My tones, no more depress'd, now high and heav'n-
　ward flow.

At once I mount on faith's sustaining wing,
　My thoughts expanding, and my soul elate ;
Fond visions, now, their consolation bring,
　And give me glimpses of the golden gate
Thro' which those lov'd ones, rob'd in white appear,
　And look so happy in the perfect ranks,
My grief is turu'd to gladness, in the tear,
　Which, for their early bliss, gives God my thanks.
Thus, thus, Enchanter ! from thy loftier strains,
　I draw a solace nothing can dispel ;
Forget my losses in my lov'd ones' gains,
　And taste a peace surpassing words to tell ;
Night, and the stars, responsive, as mine ears,
Thy melodies entwine with music of the spheres.

JACOB JONES.

THE OWL

Song from " Love's Labour's Lost "

WINTER

WHEN icicles hang by the wall
   And Dick the shepherd blows his nail
And Tom bears logs into the hall
   And milk comes frozen home in pail,
When blood is nipp'd and ways be foul,
Then nightly sings the staring owl,
               Tu-whit ;
Tu-who, a merry note,
While greasy Joan doth keel the pot.

When all aloud the wind doth blow,
   And coughing drowns the parson's saw
And birds sit brooding in the snow
   And Marian's nose looks red and raw,
When roasted crabs hiss in the bowl,
Then nightly sings the staring owl,
               Tu-whit ;
Tu-who, a merry note,
While greasy Joan doth keel the pot.

WILLIAM SHAKESPEARE.

THE OWL-SONG

From " Kenilworth "

OF all the birds on bush or tree,
   Commend me to the owl,
Since he may best ensample be
   To those the cup that trowl.

For when the sun hath left the west,
He chooses the tree that he loves the best,
And he whoops out his song, and he laughs at his
    jest ;
Then, though hours be late, and weather foul,
We'll drink to the health of the bonny, bonny owl.

The lark is but a bumpkin fowl,
    He sleeps in his nest till morn ;
But my blessing upon the jolly owl,
    That all night blows his horn.
Then up with your cup till you stagger in speech,
And match me this catch, till you swagger and
    screech,
And drink till you wink, my merry men each ;
For, though hours be late, and weather be foul,
We'll drink to the health of the bonny, bonny owl.
                                SIR WALTER SCOTT.

SONG—" THE OWL "

1

WHEN cats run home and light is come,
    And dew is cold upon the ground,
And the far-off stream is dumb,
    And the whirring sail goes round,
    And the whirring sail goes round ;
        Alone and warming his five wits,
        The white owl in the belfry sits.

II

When merry milkmaids click the latch,
　And rarely smells the new-mown hay,
And the cock hath sung beneath the thatch
　Twice or thrice his roundelay,
　Twice or thrice his roundelay ;
　　Alone and warming his five wits,
　　The white owl in the belfry sits.
ALFRED, LORD TENNYSON.

SECOND SONG

TO THE SAME

I

THY tuwhits are lull'd, I wot,
　Thy tuwhoos of yesternight,
Which upon the dark afloat,
　So took echo with delight,
　So took echo with delight,
　　That her voice untuneful grown,
　　Wears all day a fainter tone.

II

I would mock thy chaunt anew ;
　But I cannot mimick it ;
Not a whit of thy tuwhoo,
　Thee to woo to thy tuwhit,
　Thee to woo to thy tuwhit,
　　With a lengthen'd loud halloo,
　　Tuwhoo, tuwhit, tuwhit, tuwhoo-o-o.
ALFRED, LORD TENNYSON.

THE WATER-OUSEL'S SONG

Whitter! whitter! where the water
  Leaps among the rocks,
And the din of the linn
  Swelling thunder mocks,
Cheerily and merrily
  I sing my roundelay,
Whitter! whitter! bright or bitter
  Be the winter day!

Whitter! whitter! down the water
  Speeding with the stream,
Snow around wraps the ground
  In a silent dream!
Wood or hill, all are still,
  Birds as mute as clay,
Whitter! whitter! what is fitter
  For a winter day?

Whitter! whitter! in the water
  Busily I ply;
Ice and snow come and go,
  Not a care have I,
Mountain waters flee their fetters,
  So I feed and play,
Whitter! whitter! pitter! pitter!
  All the winter day.

Whitter! whitter! o'er the water
  Still and smooth and deep,
Round the pool, clear and cool,
  Where the shadows sleep,

Snowy breast, shadow-kissed,
 Whirring on its way,
Whitter! whitter! titter! titter!
 Ho! the winter day!

Whitter! whitter! through the water,
 By the miller's wheel,
Where the strong water's song
 Rings a merry peal;
Wet or dry, what care I,
 Sporting in the spray?
Whitter! whitter! twitter! twitter!
 Flies the winter day.

Whitter! whitter! with the water
 Where the burnies run,
'Mong the hills, where the rills,
 Dance into the sun,
In the nooks, where the brooks
 Ripple on for aye,
Whitter! whitter! bright or bitter
 Be the winter day!

J. H. P.

ON THE WING

ONCE in a dream (for once I dreamed of you)
We stood together in an open field ;
Above   our   heads   two   swift-winged   pigeons
    wheeled,
Sporting at ease and courting full in view.
When loftier still a broadening darkness flew,
    Down-swooping, and a ravenous hawk revealed ;
    Too weak to fight, too fond to fly, they yield ;
So farewell life and love and pleasures new.
Then as their plumes fell fluttering to the ground,
    Their snow-white plumage flecked with crimson
        drops,
    I wept, and thought I turned towards you to
        weep :
But you were gone ; while rustling hedgerow tops
Bent in a wind which bore to me a sound
    Of far-off piteous bleat of lambs and sheep.
                            CHRISTINA G. ROSSETTI.

TO THE ROBIN

SWEET singer of the sweet sad days,
    Thy requiem for the Summer dead
Rings clearly through the golden haze,
    While o'er thy head
The sere leaves, with a gentle sigh,
Float softly down to earth to die,
    Gold, brown, and red.

And is thy song all sadness ? Nay!
Thy little heart full well doth know
That where the sere leaf breaks away,
   The bud doth show ;
Sure promise of another Spring,
When thy glad song with love will ring,
   Sweet, clear, and low.

ARTHUR WRIGHT.

THE ROBIN AND THE THRUSH

A MODEST little Robin perch'd
   Close by a stately Thrush,
To talk matters over in
   A green old holly bush.
The Thrush was vain, and pride arose
   Within his speckl'd breast,
Whilst Rob in meekness slowly preen'd
   His little crimson vest.

" I wonder," said the sprightly Thrush,
   " Why you have ceas'd to sing ;
You once were wont to trill your lay,
   And make the hedgerows ring.
It cannot be domestic care
   That rankles in your breast,
Your little mate is strong and well,
   Your brood have left the nest.

" You sweetly sang in early spring,
   Through May and sunny June ;
Each treble note that left your throat
   Vied with the lark at noon.

Then why so sad and silent now,
    The summer's not yet o'er,
Come, Robin, raise your song of praise,
    And warble through your score.

" There's music sweet in wood and glen,
    The lark trills in the sky ;
The brooklet chants a sweet refrain,
    Whilst gliding gently by.
The Blackbird's voice in cadence sweet
    Sounds like an ancient lute ;
Dame Nature claims our summer song
    Whilst you, alas ! are mute."

" Just bide your time," the Robin said,
    " I'm resting for a while ;
The time will come when you'll be dumb
    Then I'll sing out in style.
When east winds blow, and winter's snow
    Come with the frost and rime ;
When folk are sad and poorly clad,
    Then comes my singing time.

"God sent you here to sing and cheer
    'Mid spring and summer flowers.
And God sent me to sing with glee
    In winter's lonesome hours.
So pipe your song whilst days are long,
    And when you cease to sing,
I'll trill my lay and trust I may
    Link winter into spring."
                        JOSEPH CRONSHAW.

SWALLOW SONG

From " The Princess "

O SWALLOW, Swallow, flying, flying South,
Fly to her, and fall upon her gilded eaves,
And tell her, tell her, what I tell to thee.

O tell her, Swallow, thou that knowest each,
That bright and fierce and fickle is the South,
And dark and true and tender is the North.

O Swallow, Swallow, if I could follow, and light
Upon her lattice, I would pipe and trill,
And cheep and twitter twenty million loves.

O were I thou that she might take me in,
And lay me on her bosom, and her heart
Would rock the snowy cradle till I died.

Why lingereth she to clothe her heart with love,
Delaying as the tender ash delays
To clothe herself, when all the woods are green ?

O tell her, Swallow, that thy brood is flown
Say to her, I do but wanton in the South,
But in the North long since my nest is made.

O tell her, brief is life but love is long,
And brief the sun of summer in the North,
And brief the moon of beauty in the South.

O Swallow, flying from the golden woods,
Fly to her, and pipe and woo her, and make her
    mine,
And tell her, tell her, that I follow thee.

ALFRED, LORD TENNYSON.

SONNET TO THE SWALLOW TRIBE

WHITE-BOSOMED strangers, wandering tribe, that
    bring
News to our isle, of pleasant summer weather ;
From what far shore did ye set out together,
To show us your red beak, and purple wing ?
I guess 'tis pleasant for ye, feathered people,
When winds are still, and evening waxes dim,
To wheel and frolic round the silent steeple,
Or down the stream, or o'er the lake to skim.
Pr'ythee, dear bird, indulge me in my whim ;
Come, cease your twittering play, and tell me where
Ye live when ye're at home, and all about it,
And how such tiny things as you are, dare
(For I, my summer friends, do somewhat doubt it)
Trust your frail wings to the wide fields of air.

By THE AUTHOR OF " SOLITARY WALKS
THROUGH MANY LANDS."

LINES ON HEARING A THRUSH SING IN A MORNING WALK IN JANUARY

SING on, sweet Thrush, upon the leafless bough ;
    Sing on, sweet bird, I listen to thy strain :
    See aged Winter, 'mid his surly reign,
At thy blithe carol clears his furrowed brow.

So in lone Poverty's dominion drear,
    Sits meek Content with light unanxious heart ;
    Welcomes the rapid moments, bids them part,
Nor asks if they bring aught to hope or fear.

I thank Thee, Author of this opening day !
Thou whose bright sun now gilds yon orient skies !
Riches denied, Thy boon was purer joys,
What wealth could never give nor take away !
Yet come, thou child of Poverty and Care ;
The mite high Heav'n bestow'd, that mite with
    thee I'll share.

ROBERT BURNS.

SONG OF THE WHITETHROAT

THE Autumn leaf was brown and sere,
    And dreary look'd the clouded sky ;
The stream that used to run so clear,
    With troubled waters hurried by.
        The warblers gone,
        We heard alone
    The robin's wintry song ;
Save when the plaintive woodlark's note
Did softly on the still air float,
        With cadence long.

We little loved a scene so cold,
    Its falling leaves and piercing wind ;
Away we flew on pinions bold,
    Far o'er the foaming waves to find
        Some gentle clime,
        Where rolling time
    No chilling change would bring ;
Where we might rest beneath the shade,
By never-fading foliage made,
        Our weary wing.

And thus with restless wing we flew
  Through many a clime and region fair ;
Till from our isle the breezes blew
  And told us Spring was smiling there.
    The wild bird's strain
    Was heard again
  Beneath the opening bough ;
The hawthorn in the well-known vale
Its scented tresses to the gale
    Was waving now.

W. E. Evans.

THE YELLOW-HAMMER'S SONG

Out on the waste, a little lonely bird, I flit and I
  sing ·
My breast is yellow as sunshine, and light as the
  wind my wing.

The golden gorse me shelters, in the tufted grass
  is my nest,
And *sweet, sweet, sweet the world*, though the wind
  blow east or west.

The harebells chime their music, the canna floats
  white in the breeze,
But as for me, I flit to and fro and I sing at my ease.

When the thyme is dripping with dew, and the hill
  wind beareth along
The pungent scent of the gale, loudly I sing my
  morning song.

When the sun beats on the gorse, the broom, and
the budding heather,
I flit from spray to spray and my song is of the
golden weather.

When the moor-fowl sink to their rest, and the
sky is soft rose red,
I sing of the crescent-moon and the single star
overhead.

Out on the waste, out on the waste, I flit all day as
I sing,
*Sweet, sweet, sweet is the world—dear world, how
beautiful everything !*

Only a little lonely bird that loved the moorland
waste,
And little perhaps of the joy of the world is that
which I taste,

But out on the wild free moorlands, on the gold
gorse-boughs I swing,
And *sweet, sweet, sweet the world ; oh sweet, ah sweet !*
the song that I sing.

WILLIAM SHARP.

SONG OF THE YELLOW-HAMMER

You oft have heard the nightingale
    At midnight's silent hour,
When pouring out her plaintive tale
    Within the hazel bower ;
How sweet doth she her love-tale tell,
With pensive grace that suits the hour so well !

You've heard the blackbird's song at dawn
On the morning breezes float,
And the skylark, springing from the lawn,
Send forth his joyous note ;
Well may those notes of pleasure sound,
When day comes forth to shed its gladness round.

You've heard at eve the sedge-bird sing,
The willow boughs among,
And the woodlark give on gentle wing
Her melancholy song ;
For they their lonely vigils keep ;
And softly sing the silent eve to sleep.

But no glad tale of praise is told,
When noon is shining bright,
And all the earth's array'd in gold
Beneath the glorious light ;
When each glad bird hath, in its mirth,
Fed on the fulness of the teeming earth.

Each bird, now day is at its height,
Flies off on careless wing,
And in the depth of their delight
They all forget to sing.
My lowly note is left alone,
To break the stillness of the golden noon.

W. E. EVANS.

VI
BIRDS IN CAPTIVITY

" How are we fettered and caged
Within our dark prison-house !
We are made to look for a loving plan."

TO MY CANARY IN HIS CAGE

SING away, ay, sing away,
  Bonnie little bird !
Sing, with patient soul and gay,
Though a woodland roundelay
  You have never heard ;
Though your life from youth to age
Passes in a narrow cage.

Near the window wild birds fly,
  Trees and flowers are round :
Fair things everywhere you spy
Through the glass-pane's mystery—
  Your horizon's bound :
Nothing hinders your desire
But a little gilded wire.

Like a human soul you seem,
  Shut in golden bars ;
Placed amid earth's sunshine-stream,
Singing to the morning-beam,
  Dreaming 'neath the stars :
Seeing all life's pleasures clear—
But they never can come near !

Never !—Sing, bird-poet mine,
  As most poets do—
Guessing with an instinct fine
Of some happiness divine
  Which they never knew
Lonely in a prison bright,
Hymning for the world's delight.

Yet, my birdie, you're content
  In your tiny cage ;
Not a carol thence is sent
But for happiness is meant—
  Wisdom sweet and sage !
Teaching the true poet's part
Is to sing with merry heart.

So, lie down thou peevish pen !
  Eyes, smile off all tears ;
And, my wee bird, sing again ;
I'll translate your song to men
  In these coming years :
Howsoe'er thy lot's assigned,
Bear it with a cheerful mind.

THE AUTHOR OF
" JOHN HALIFAX, GENTLEMAN."

IMPRISONED LOYALTY

(Said to have been written by Sir Roger L'Estrange while in prison
on account of his loyalty to Charles I.)

HAVE you not seen the nightingale
  A prisoner like, coop'd in a cage,
How doth she chant her wonted tale,
  In that her narrow hermitage !
Even then her charming melody doth prove
That all her bars are trees, her cage a grove.

I am that bird whom they combine
  Thus to deprive of liberty ;
But though they do my corpse confine,
  Yet maugre hate, my soul is free ;
And, though immur'd, yet can I chirp and sing
Disgrace to rebels, glory to my king.

CAPTIVE BIRDS

From " Spring "

BE not the Muse asham'd, here to bemoan
Her brothers of the grove, by tyrant Man
Inhuman caught, and in the narrow cage
From liberty confin'd, and boundless air.
Dull are the pretty slaves, their plumage dull,
Ragged, and all its brightening lustre lost ;
Nor is that sprightly wildness in their notes,
Which, clear and vigorous, warbles from the beech.
O then, ye friends of love and love-taught song,
Spare the soft tribes, this barbarous art forbear ;
If on your bosom innocence can win,
Music engage, or piety persuade.

But let not chief the nightingale lament
Her ruin'd care, too delicately fram'd
To brook the harsh confinement of the cage.
Oft when, returning with her loaded bill,
The astonish'd mother finds a vacant nest,
By the hard hand of unrelenting clowns
Robb'd, to the ground the vain provision falls ;
Her pinions ruffle, and low-drooping scarce
Can bear the mourner to the poplar shade ;
Where, all abandon'd to despair, she sings
Her sorrows through the night ; and on the bough,
Sole-sitting, still at every dying fall
Takes up again her lamentable strain
Of winding woe ; till wide around the woods
Sigh to her song, and with her wail resound.

JAMES THOMSON.

SONG OF THE CAPTIVE LARK

'Tis merry morn—the sun hath shed
His light upon the mountain head.
The golden dews are sparkling now
On heath and hill, on flower and bough ;
And many a happy song is heard
From every gay rejoicing bird :
But never more, alas ! shall I
Soar up and sing in yonder sky.

Through these harsh wires I glimpse in vain,
The ray that once awoke my strain ;
In pain, while coop'd, I fret and pine,
My useless wings their strength decline.
Sad is my fate to see the stars
Pass one by one before my bars ;
And know, when dawn returneth, I
No more may sing in yonder sky.

Oh, barbarous you, who still can bear
This mournful doom to bid me share—
To see me droop and sadden on
With wishful eye, from dawn to dawn ;
Beating my little breast in woe,
'Gainst these dread wires that vex me so
And my glad passage still deny
To soar and sing in yonder sky.

Oh, let me fly—fly up once more,
How would my wing delighted soar,
What rapture would my song declare,
Pour'd out upon the sunny air :
Oh, let me hence depart ! in vain
I try to breathe one gladsome strain ·
In this dark den, I pine, I die ;
Oh, let me fly to yonder sky !

JOHN LOGAN.

TO A CAPTIVE THRUSH

SPECKLED, mellow-throated Thrush,
While thy partner patient sits
On her blue eggs in the bush,
Forgetful thou of traps and nets
Pourest forth thy wondrous song,
All day long.

All day long thou pourest forth
Mellow notes in cadence rare ;
Be the wind or south or north,
Thou carolest and dost not care,
Scarcely taking time to eat—
Sweet, O Sweet.

Was it not a sin, a crime,
To capture and to pen thee in
A narrow cage for all thy time,
Lodge thee 'mid the city's din,
Far from love and liberty
Dear to thee ?

Were I in thy place, I'd die ;
Yes, I'd die before I'd sing
To a jailer ; nay, not I,
I would eat the food they'd bring,
Just, my vocal friend, as thou
        Eatest now.

Life is dear to slave or free,
Life than liberty's more dear ;
Shall I then find fault with thee
For partaking of the cheer
That thy masters to thee bring ?
        No ; I'd sing—

I'd sing, as thou art doing now,
Perhaps not quite so merrily,
But as well as I know how ;
For alas ! I am not free.
Freedom ne'er shall I know more.
        Ah ! Lenore !

Ah ! Lenore ! thou fickle maid !
Thou my heart hast captive ta'en
And prisoned it in utter shade
Where it must aye remain,
If thou wilt not set it free
        By loving me.
                    ANON.

THE LARK IN LONDON

LISTEN, my little one ! it is the lark,
Captured and blinded, singing in the dark.
His nest-mate and his younglings all are dead.
Their feathers flutter on some foolish head.
Of some lost Paradise, poor bird he sings,
Which for a moment back his vision brings ;
Wide fields of morning, woods and waterfall ·
A world of boundless freedom over all.
He sings of that great glory far away;
He sings his fervid life out, day by day ;
Imprisoned in an area underground,
He seems as if all Heaven were listening round.
He soars in spirit still divinely strong,
And spends each heart-beat in a wave of song,
Trying to make a little heaven here
For others, he who has lost his own; poor dear
As if with floods of music he would drown
The dire, discordant roar of London town

GERALD MASSEY.

THE CAGED BIRD

OH, who would keep a little bird confined,
When cowslip bells are nodding in the wind;
When every hedge as with " good morrow " rings,
And, heard from wood to coombe the blackbird sings.
Oh who would keep a little bird confined
In his cold wiry prison ?—Let him fly,
And hear him sing · " How sweet is liberty ! "

WILLIAM LISLE BOWLES.

AUGURIES OF INNOCENCE

1

A Robin Redbreast in a cage
Puts all Heaven in a rage.

2

A dove-house filled with doves and pigeons
Shudders Hell through all its regions.

6

A skylark wounded on the wing
Doth make a cherub cease to sing.

7

A game-cock clipped and armed for fight
Does the rising sun affright.

12

The owl that calls upon the night
Speaks the unbeliever's fright.

13

He who shall hurt the little wren
Shall never be beloved by men.

51

The emmet's inch and eagle's mile
Make lame philosophy to smile.

WILLIAM BLAKE.

ON A GOLDFINCH STARVED TO DEATH IN HIS CAGE

TIME was when I was free as air,
The thistle's downy seed my fare,
  My drink the morning dew ;
I perch'd at will on every spray,
My form genteel, my plumage gay,
  My strains for ever new.

But gaudy plumage, sprightly strain,
And form genteel were all in vain,
  And of a transient date ;
For caught and caged, and starved to death,
In dying sighs my little breath
  Soon pass'd the wiry gate.

Thanks, gentle swain, for all my woes,
And thanks for this effectual close
  And cure of every ill ;
More cruelty could none express ;
And I, if you had shewn me less,
  Had been your prisoner still.

                    WILLIAM COWPER.

BEAUTY AND THE BIRD

SHE fluted with her mouth as when one sips,
  And gently waved her golden head, inclin'd
  Outside his cage close to the window blind ;
Till her fond bird, with little turns and dips,

Piped low to her of sweet companionships.
And when he made an end some seed took she
And fed him from her tongue, which rosily
Peeped as a piercing bud between her lips.

And like the child in Chaucer, on whose tongue
  The Blessed Mary laid, when he was dead,
A grain,—who straightway praised her name in song:
  Even so, when she, a little lightly red
Now turned on me and laughed, I heard the throng
  Of inner voices praise her golden head.
                    DANTE GABRIEL ROSSETTI.

THE SONNET

From " Cithara Mea "

I PUT my trembling bird with down-drooped wing
  Within a golden cage that hung before
  The Muse's temple ; closed the clanging door,
And stept aside, silent, and wondering
Whether the captive minstrel soul would sing,
  She whose aspiring fancy fain would soar
  To the far Pisgah heights whose altars bore
Traces of the lordliest poets' ministering.

And, lo ! the rough-hewn prison bars did glow
  Into a golden lyre serenely strung,
And o'er their quivering chords did sweetly flow
  The wavelets of an echo, swiftly sprung
From the imprisoned rage, the frenzied glow,
  For here hath Milton, here hath Petrarch sung.
                    P. A. SHEEHAN.

THE BIRDS' PROCLAMATION

From " Epirrema "

HANDSOME bounties have been offered of a talent
for his head
Likewise, with respect to Tyrants (Tyrants that are
gone and dead)
Bounties of a talent each, for all that can be killed
or caught
With a zealous emulation, we, the Birds, have also
thought
Just and proper, to proclaim, from this time forth,
that we withdraw
From Philocrates, the fowler, the protection of the
law :
Furthermore, we fix a price, for bringing him alive
or dead,
Four, if he's secured alive ; a single talent for his
head :
He, that Ortolans and Quails to market has pre-
sumed to bring ;
And the Sparrows six a penny, tied together in a
string,
With a wicked art retaining, sundry Doves in his
employ,
Fastened, with their feet in fetters, forced to serve
for a decoy ;
Farther, we declare and publish our command to
men below,
All the Birds you keep in prison, to release, and let
them go,

We shall, else, revenge ourselves, and we shall teach
the tyrants yet,　　　　　　　　　　　　　`
How to chirp and dance in fetters, in the tangles of
a net.

ARISTOPHANES' " Aves."

Translated by JOHN HOOKHAM FRERE.

ON SEEING A BIRD CATCHER

HEALTH in his rags, Content upon his face,
He goes th'enslaver of a feather'd race :
And cunning snares, warm hearts, lithe warblers,
take ;
The one to sing for sport, the other, break.

ELIZA COOK.

VII
BIRD ELEGIES AND MEMORIAL LINES

" But beauty and worth can no privilege claim
    When Death wings his pitiless dart ;
Sweet bird ! shall the language of sorrow exclaim,
    Too soon it has pierced thy heart."

MANN.

THE BIRDS' LAMENT OVER THE DEATH OF
" BION "

The Poet calls Lord Rochester " Bion "

YE gentle swans, that haunt the brooks and springs,
Pine with sad grief, and droop your sickly wings :
In doleful notes the heavy loss bewail,
Such as you sing at your own funeral,
Such as you sung when your lov'd Orpheus fell.
Tell it to all the rivers, hills, and plains,
Tell it to all the British nymphs and swains,
And bid them too the dismal tidings spread
Of Bion's fate, of England's Orpheus dead.
   Come all ye Muses, come, adorn the shepherd's
     hearse
   With never-fading garlands, never-dying verse.

  .   .   -

Ne'er did the dolphins on the lonely shore
In such loud plaints utter their grief before ·
Never in such sad notes did Philomel
To the relenting rocks her sorrow tell ·
Ne'er in the beach did poor Alcyone
So weep, when she her floating lover saw ·
Nor that dead lover, to a sea-fowl turn'd,
Upon those waves, where he was drown'd, so
   mourn'd
Nor did the bird of Memnon with such grief
Bedew those ashes, which late gave him life

As they did now with vying grief bewail,
As they did all lament dear Bion's fall.
  Come all ye Muses, come, adorn the shepherd's
    hearse
  With never-fading garlands, never-dying verse.

In every wood, in every tree and bush,
The lark, the linnet, nightingale, and thrush,
And all the feather'd choir, that us'd to throng
In list'ning flocks to learn his well-tun'd song ·
Now each in the sad concert bear a part,
And with kind notes repay their teacher's art :
Ye turtles too (I charge you) here assist,
Let not your murmurs in the crowd be missed ·
To the dear swain do not ungrateful prove,
That taught you how to sing and how to love.
  Come all ye Muses, come, adorn the shepherd's
    hearse
  With never-fading garlands, never-dying verse.
                                — JOHN OLDHAM.

LINES WRITTEN IN MEMORY OF A FAVOURITE BIRD

I TAUGHT my gay and beauteous bird some words of
    love to prize,
And fancied meaning beamed within his dark and
    lustrous eyes ;
I taught him fond and winning ways he never knew
    before—
Ah ! how the sweet one fluttering gained his rare and
    dainty lore.

That bird was strangely dear to me ; and when I
mused alone,
His thrilling cadence seemed to mourn some loved
and absent one.
But at the holy sunset hour he nestled in my breast,
And understood of all sweet birds I loved my own
the best !

In solitude and loneliness the human heart must
cling
And rest on something—though it be a dumb and
soulless thing.
When summer roses fade away, 'tis sad to see them
die,
But far more sad it was to hear my gentle bird's
last sigh.

And all beneath a white rose-tree I laid his little
head—
The tree he loved to nestle on now shades his grassy
bed ;
And when at eve these buds are gemmed with dew-
drops soft and cool,
Amid them falls a tear for thee, my bright, my
beautiful !

C. A. M. W.

ON THE DEATH OF MRS THROCKMORTON'S BULLFINCH

YE Nymphs, if e'er your eyes were red
With tears o'er hapless favourites shed,
   Oh, share Maria's grief !
Her favourite, even in his cage,
(What will not hunger's cruel rage ?)
   Assassinated by a thief.

Where Rhenus strays his vines among,
The egg was laid from which he sprung ;
   And though by nature mute,
Or only with a whistle bless'd,
Well-taught, he all the sounds express'd
   Of flageolet or flute.

The honours of his ebon poll
Were brighter than the sleekest mole,
   His bosom of the hue
With which Aurora decks the skies,
When piping winds shall soon arise
   To sweep away the dew.

Above, below, in all the house,
Dire foe alike of bird and mouse,
   No cat had leave to dwell ;
And Bully's cage supported stood
On props of smoothest-shaven wood,
   Large-built and latticed well.

Well lattic'd—but the grate, alas !
Not rough with wire of steel or brass,
    For Bully's plumage sake,
But smooth with wands from Ouse's side,
With which, when neatly peel'd and dried,
    The swains their baskets make.

Night veil'd the pole ; all seem'd secure ;
When, led by instinct sharp and sure,
    Subsistence to provide,
A beast forth sallied on the scout,
Long-back'd, long-tail'd, with whisker'd snout,
    And badger-colour'd hide.

He, entering at the study door,
Its ample area 'gan explore ;
    And something in the wind
Conjectur'd, sniffing round and round,
Better than all the books he found,
    Food chiefly for the mind.

Just then, by adverse fate impress'd,
A dream disturb'd poor Bully's rest ;
    In sleep he seem'd to view
A rat fast clinging to the cage,
And screaming at the sad presage,
    Awoke and found it true.

For, aided both by ear and scent
Right to his mark the monster went,—
    Ah ! Muse ! forbear to speak
Minute the horrors that ensued ;
His teeth were strong, the cage was wood,—
    He left poor Bully's beak.

Oh, had he made that too his prey !
That beak, whence issued many a lay
    Of such mellifluous tone,
Might have repaid him well, I wote
For silencing so sweet a throat,
    Fast stuck within his own.

Maria weeps,—the Muses mourn,—
So, when, by Bacchanalians torn,
    On Thracian Hebrus' side,
The tree-enchanter Orpheus fell,
His head alone remained to tell
    The cruel death he died.
                            WILLIAM COWPER.

THE DIRGE OF THE DIPPER

RARE optimist ! when earth is drear,
Thou chantest forth a ditty clear ·
    When troubles lower,
Within the fort of thy small breast
No wavering thought can long find rest,
    No meanness cower.

Fay of the brook and rocky height !
A torrent's roar is thy delight,
    Thy young ones' charm ;
A moss-wove tent protects them all,
Oft curtained by a waterfall
    To screen from harm.

Long may thy dipping cleverness
Rob moor and upland wilderness
    Of half their gloom
Far from thy nest that wretch begone,
Who, heedless, seeks to hasten on
    An ouzel's doom !

But now, alas ! I see thee dead,
Sore-bitten by the viewless lead ;
    A mournful thing !
Perhaps the last piping of thy joys
Made signal for the baleful noise,
    And fiery sting.

How well was used thy life's short breath,
And well thy plumes become thy death,
    Meek on the sod—
A shadowy pall around thee thrown,
In front, a pure white veil is shown
    Designed by God ;

And ev'n the fringe of dusky red
Matches the wound by which life fled
    From every limb.
Bereft of thee, the streamlet's notes
Grow sad, and from its murmur floats
    Thy funeral hymn.

                            C. L. BRAIN.

FALCON, EAGLE, VULTURE AND WILD SWAN

MARS ! my brave bird, and I have killed thee, then,
Thou wast the truest servant—fed me, loved,
When all the world had left me ?—Never more
Shalt thou and I in mimic battle play,
Nor thou pretend to die (to die, alas !)
And with thy quaint and frolic tricks delight
Thy master in his solitude.   No more,
No more, old Mars ! (thou wast the god of birds)
Shalt thou rise fiercely on thy plumed wing,
And hunt the air for plunder : thou couldst ride,
None better, on the fierce and mountain winds,
When birds of lesser courage droop'd.   I've seen
Thee scare the wandering Eagle on his way,
(For all the wild tribes of these circling woods
Knew thee, and shunn'd thy beak), and thro' the air
Float like a hovering tempest feared by all.
Have I not known thee bring the Wild Swan down
For me, thy cruel master : ay, and stop
The screaming Vulture in the middle air,
And mar his scarlet plumage—all for me,
Who killed thee, murdered thee, poor bird ; for thou
Wast worthy of humanity ; and I
Feel, with these shaking hands, as I had done
A crime against my race.

                                        BARRY CORNWALL.

ON THE DEATH OF A LINNET

BENEATH this fragrant woodbine's shade
A little songster's bones are laid ;
Who, ever innocent and gay,
Felt all his hours glide smooth away ;
No guilty passion tore his breast,
No dream of greatness broke his rest ;
He with a cheerful, patient mind
Played well that part the gods assigned ;
Nor matters it, when this be done,
How soon the thread of life is spun !
   Ye warbling tenants of the grove,
Approach this spot and mark your love,
Light hovering round on airy wing
Soft notes of plaintive friendship sing.
   So may no prying eye pervade
The hedge-rows, where your young are laid,
Nor cruel hand of wanton boy
Your dwellings plunder or destroy :
Far may you bend your flight from where
The artful fowler spreads his snare,
And live from ev'ry danger free,
Enjoying still sweet liberty !

GEORGE KEATE.

THE BURIAL OF THE LINNET

FOUND in the garden dead in his beauty—
Oh, that a linnet should die in the spring !
Bury him, comrades, in pitiful duty,
Muffle the dinner bell, solemnly ring.

Bury him kindly, up in the corner ;
Bird, beast, and goldfish are sepulchred there.
Bid the.black kitten march as chief mourner,
Waving her tail like a plume in the air.

Bury him nobly—next to the donkey ;
Fetch the old banner, and wave it about ;
Bury him deeply—think of the monkey,
Shallow his grave, and the dogs get him out.

Bury him softly—white wool around him,
Kiss his poor feathers—the first kiss and last ;
Tell his poor widow kind friends have found him
Plant his poor grave with whatever grows fast.

Farewell, sweet singer ! dead in thy beauty,
Silent through summer, though other birds sing.
Bury him, comrades, in pitiful duty,
Muffle the dinner-bell, mournfully ring.

                                        Mrs Ewing.

AN EPITAPH ON A ROBIN REDBREAST

Tread lightly here, for here, 'tis said,
    When piping winds are hush'd around,
    A small note wakes from underground
Where now his tiny bones are laid.

No more in lone and leafless groves,
    With ruffled wing and faded breast,
His friendless, homeless spirit roves ;
    —Gone to the world where birds are blest !

Where never cat glides o'er the green,
Or school-boy's giant form is seen ;
But Love, and Joy, and smiling Spring
Inspire their little souls to sing.

SAMUEL ROGERS.

THE DIRGE OF THE SWAN

So down the silver streams of Eridan,[1]
On either side banked with a lily wall,
Whiter than both, rides the triumphant swan,
And sings his dirge, and prophesies his fall,
Diving into his watery funeral !
But Eridan to Cedron[2] must submit
His flowery shore ; nor can he envy it,
If, when Apollo sings, his swans do silent sit.

That heavenly voice I more delight to hear
Than gentle airs to breathe ; or swelling waves
Against the sounding rocks their bosoms tear ;
Or whistling reeds that rutty Jordan laves
And with their verdure his white head embraves ;
To chide the winds ; or having bees that fly
About the laughing blossoms of sallowy,
Rocking asleep the idle grooms that lazy lie.

GILES FLETCHER.

[1] The River Po.   [2] See Mark xiv. 26 ; John xviii. 1.

THE DEATH-SONG OF THE SWAN ;
OR,
THE HOPE OF THE WISEST OF THE HEATHEN

The following lines were suggested to the author by a passage in the Ballad of " Arion." There is something in the passage of the Phaedo of Plato which gave rise to them, where Socrates accuses the vulgar herd of going so far in their fear of death as even to " bely the swans, and say that their last song arises from grief and is a dirge of death," whereas he says that " it is a song of joy because they are going to the God whose servants they are," and " because being prophetic and knowing the good things which shall be theirs in Hades, they rejoice and sing more then than at any former time."

ON glassy stream, by greenwood bower,
    His voice was rarely heard
Why sings he thus in dying hour
    Yon fair majestic bird ?
There's many a pleasant sight on earth
    Although they last not long ·
Nor marvel I that thoughts of mirth
    Should issue forth in song.
Nay, Sorrow's self, while hope remains,
    Beneath the twilight dim
May chant her own half-soothing strains,
    A dirge-entangled hymn.
But when from all that's bright and fair
    Unwillingly we go,
From genial haunts of upper air
    To darksome shades below,—
Where ghastly spectres glimmering pale
    The gray marsh wander o'er,
And ceaseless drones the voice of wail
    On bleak Cocytus' shore,—

To blank despair, in face of death,
  No tuneful strains belong,
And strangely sounds a dying breath
  E'en in a mournful song.
And therefore, till some wiser word
  The secret shall avow,
I marvel much the silent bird
  Should break his silence now.

There's many a pleasant sight on earth
  But, ah ! they last not long :
And meagre is the mingled mirth
  That swells a mortal song.
And Sorrow, who with pensive note
  Woos back the fleeting bliss,
Could never tune her parchèd throat
  To sound so clear as this.
How liquid, yet how sweet the strain
  It charms the listening air ;
There's not an under-note of pain,
  No muffled discord there.
For joy, for joy, the creature sings !
  Of Phœbus' train is he ;
The oarage of his stately wings
  Expects a nobler sea.
By Phœbus taught of things to come,
  The prophet songster knows
The glories of the happier home
  To which through death he goes.
Ecstatic thoughts of joy and love
  His snowy bosom thrill ;

Sweet echoes of glad songs above
  His tuneful accents fill.

He leaves the glassy streams of earth,
  He leaves her greenwood bowers
For clearer springs of heavenly birth,
  For bright eternal flowers.
He goes to join his Master dear,
  The God he served below,
The Lord of Light, the Minstrel-Seer,
  Him of the silver bow.
He goes where love attunes each word,
  Joy brightens every brow,—
I marvel not the silent bird
  Should break his silence now.

We too, my friend, whose spirits rise
  To loftier flights than they,
Who to be prudent, sober, wise,
  Or guess or learn the way ;
To whom, though pent in fleshly cage,
  The pitying Gods have given
Faint echoes of a nobler age,
  Dim memories of heaven ;—
If from our bodies' clinging stain
  We cleanse our soul alway,
And while on earth we yet remain
  Soar nearer heaven each day,
A surer hope than bird or beast
  Methinks may claim to know,
That, from our prison-house released,
  We too shall homeward go,

Unto a brighter earth and sky,
  More liquid streams and seas ;
And (thought more cheering and more high !)
  To better hearts than these !

Good men, whose souls were purged below
  We trust that home shall share ;
But Gods, all perfect Gods, we *know*
  Shall be our patrons there.
There wisdom, virtue, all things good,
  Whose shadows here we see,
Like trees in some translucent flood
  Reflected distantly,
In bright reality confessed
  Before our face shall glow—
Oh ! perfect vision of the blest,—
  Who would not sing to go ?

                        J. E. BODE.

THE DYING SWAN

I

THE plain was grassy, wild and bare,
Wide, wild, and open to the air,
Which had built up everywhere
  An under-roof of doleful gray.
With an inner voice the river ran,
Adown it floated a dying swan,
  And loudly did lament.
  It was the middle of the day.
Ever the weary wind went on,
  And took the reed-tops as it went.

II

Some blue peaks in the distance rose,
And white against the cold-white sky,
Shone out their crowning snows.
   One willow over the river wept,
And shook the wave as the wind did sigh ;
Above in the wind was the swallow,
   Chasing itself at its own wild will,
   And far thro' the marish green and still
   The tangled water-courses slept,
Shot over with purple, and green, and yellow.

III

The wild swan's death-hymn took the soul
Of that waste place with joy
Hidden in sorrow : at first to the ear
The warble was low, and full and clear ;
And floating about the under-sky,
Prevailing in weakness, the coronach stole
Sometimes afar, and sometimes anear ;
But anon her awful jubilant voice,
With a music strange and manifold,
Flow'd forth on a carol free and bold ;
As when a mighty people rejoice
With shawms, and with cymbals, and harps of gold,
And the tumult of their acclaim is roll'd
Thro' the open gates of the city afar,
To the shepherd who watcheth the evening star.
And the creeping mosses and clambering weeds,
And the willow-branches hoar and dank,

And the wavy swell of the soughing reeds,
And the wave-worn horns of the echoing bank,
And the silvery marish-flowers that throng
The desolate creeks and pools among,
Were flooded over with eddying song.
                    ALFRED, LORD TENNYSON.

ROBIN REDBREAST

Verse from an old Ballad

THUS wander'd these poor innocents,
    Till death did end their grief ;
In one another's armes they dyed,
    As wanting due relief :
No burial this pretty pair
    Of any man receives,
Till Robin-redbreast piously
    Did cover them with leaves.
                            ANON.

A DIRGE

CALL for the robin-redbreast and the wren,
Since o'er shady groves they hover
And with leaves and flowers do cover
The friendless bodies of unburied men.
Call unto his funeral dole
The ant, the field-mouse, and the mole
To rear him hillocks that shall keep him warm
And (when gay tombs are robb'd) sustain no harm ;
But keep the wolf far thence, that's foe to men.
For with his nails he'll dig them up again.
                            JOHN WEBSTER.

TO THE NIGHTINGALE AND ROBIN REDBREAST

WHEN I departed am, ring thou my knell,
Thou pittiful, and pretty Philomel :
And when I'm laid out for a corse ; then be
Thou Sexton (Redbreast) for to cover me.

ROBERT HERRICK.

THE ROBIN REDBREAST

From " The Christian Year "

SWEET messenger of " calm decay,"
Saluting sorrow as ye may,
As one still bent to find or make the best,
In thee, and in this quiet mead
The lesson of sweet peace I read,
Rather in all to be resign'd than blest."

JOHN KEBLE.

VIII

HABITS, PLUMAGE, AND MEETING
PLACES OF BIRDS

" Tribes of the air ! whose favoured race
   May wander through the realms of space,
      Free guests of earth and sky ;
   In form, in plumage, and in song
   What gifts of nature mark your throng
      With bright variety."

MRS HEMANS.

CHORUS OF BIRDS

WE wish to declare how the Birds of the air all high
Institutions designed,
And holding in awe, art, science, and law, delivered
the same to mankind.
To begin with : of old Man went naked and cold
whenever it pelted or froze,
Till we showed him how feathers were proof against
weathers ; with that he bethought him of hose.
And next it was plain that he in the rain was forced to
sit dripping and blind,
While the reed-warbler swung in a nest with her
young, deep-sheltered and warm from the wind.
So our homes in the boughs made him think of the
house ; and the swallow, to help him invent,
Revealed the best way to economise clay, and bricks
to combine with cement.
The knowledge withal of the carpenter's awl is
drawn from the nuthatch's bill,
And the sand-marten's pains in the hazel-clad lanes
instructed the mason to drill.
Is there one of the arts more dear to men's hearts, to
the bird's inspiration they owe it,
For the nightingale first sweet music rehearsed,
prima donna, composer, and poet.
The owl's dark retreats showed sages the sweets of
brooding to spin or unravel
Fine webs in one's brain, philosophical, vain,—the
swallows the pleasures of travel,

Who chirped in such strain of Greece, Italy, Spain,
    and Egypt, that men, when they heard,
Were mad to fly forth from their nests in the north,
    and follow the tail of the bird.
Besides, it is true to our wisdom is due the knowledge
    of sciences all,
And chiefly those rare Metaphysics of air men
    Meteorology call.
For, indeed, it is said a kingfisher when dead has
    his science alive in him still ;
And, hung up, he will show how the wind means
    to blow, and turn to the point with his bill.
And men in their words acknowledge the birds' erudi-
    tion in weather and star ;
For they say, " 'Twill be dry—the swallow is high " ;
    or, " Rain—for the chough is afar."
'Twas the rooks who taught men vast pamphlets
    to pen upon Social Compact and Law,
And Parliaments hold, as themselves did of old,
    exclaiming " Hear, hear," for " Caw, caw ! "
When they build, if one steal, so great is their zeal
    for justice, that all, at a pinch,
Without legal test will demolish his nest, and hence is
    the trial by Lynch.
And whence arose love ?   Go ask of the dove, or
    behold how the titmouse, unresting,
Still early and late ever sings by his mate, to lighten
    her labours of nesting.
Their bonds never gall, though the leaves shoot and
    fall, and the seasons roll round in their course,

For their Marriage each year grows more lovely and
dear, and they know not decrees of Divorce.
That these things are Truth we have learned from
our youth, for our hearts to our customs incline,
As the rivers that roll from the fount of our soul,
immortal, unchanging, divine.
Man, simple and old, in his ages of gold, derived
from our teaching true light,
And deemed it his praise in his ancestors' ways to
govern his footsteps aright.
But the fountain of woes, Philosophy, rose, and what
betwixt Reason and Whim,
He has splintered our rules into sections and schools,
so the world is made bitter for him.
But the birds, since on earth they discovered the
worth of their souls, and resolved, with a vow,
No custom to change for a new or a strange have
attained unto Paradise now.

WILLIAM JOHN COURTHOPE.

PAIRING TIME ANTICIPATED

(A FABLE)

I SHALL not ask Jean Jacques Rousseau
If birds confabulate or no ;
'Tis clear that they were always able
To hold discourse at least in fable ;
And even the child that knows no better
Than to interpret the letter,
A story of a cock and bull,
Must have a most uncommon skull

It chanc'd then on a winter's day,
But warm and bright and calm as May,
The birds, conceiving a design
To forestall sweet St Valentine,
In many an orchard, copse and grove,
Assembled on affairs of love,
And with much twitter and much chatter,
Began to agitate the matter.
At length a Bullfinch who could boast
More years and wisdom than the most,
Entreated, opening wide his beak,
A moment's liberty to speak ;
And silence publicly enjoined,
Deliver'd briefly thus his mind ·
   " My friends ! be cautious how you treat
The subject upon which we meet ;
I fear we shall have winter yet."
A Finch whose tongue knew no control,
With golden wing, and satin poll,
A last year's bird, who ne'er had tried
What marriage means, thus pert replied
" Methinks the gentleman," quoth she,
" Opposite in the apple-tree,
By his good will would keep us single
Till yonder heaven and earth shall mingle,
Or (which is likelier to befall)
Till death exterminate us all.
I'll marry without more ado,
My dear Dick Redcap, what say you ? "
   Dick heard, and tweedling, ogling, bridling,
Turning short round, strutting and sideling,

Attested, glad, his approbation
Of an immediate conjugation.
Their sentiments so well express'd
Influenc'd mightily the rest,
All pair'd, and each pair built a nest.
  But though the birds were thus in haste,
The leaves came on not quite so fast,
And Destiny, that sometimes bears
An aspect stern on man's affairs,
Not altogether smil'd on theirs.
The wind, of late breath'd gently forth,
Now shifted east, and east by north ;
Bare trees and shrubs but ill, you know,
Could shelter them from rain or snow,
Stepping into their nests they paddled,
Themselves were chill'd, their eggs were addled ;
Soon every father bird and mother,
Grew quarrelsome, and peck'd each other,
Parted without the least regret,
Except that they had ever met,
And learn'd in future to be wiser,
Than to neglect a good adviser.

MORAL

Misses ! the tale that I relate
This lesson seems to carry—
Choose not only a proper mate,
But proper time to marry.

WILLIAM COWPER.

THE PARLIAMENT OF BIRDS

" In a land upon a hill of flowers
Was set the noble goddess Nature ;
Of branches were her halls and her bowers,
Wrought after her craft and her measure."
*Here met the birds on St Valentine's day to choose
their mates. The goddess Nature presided and arranged
them in four divisions—*
" That is to say, the fowls of rapine
Were highest set, and then fowles small,
That eat as Nature would incline,
As worms, or thing of which I tell no tale ·
But waterfowl sat lowest in the vale,
And fowl that live by seed sat on the green,
And that so numerous that wonder was to see."

*The poet has given us a gem which in its entirety
is of the greatest interest to the student of English,
but its length, archaisms, grammar, etc., fall not
within the scope of this work, but no Treasury of
Bird Poems would be in any measure complete,
if it did not contain a reference to this poem, which
has been carefully edited by Dr Sweet. Chaucer
enumerates the birds assembled, each with significant
epithet—the royal eagle, the gerfalcon, the hardy
sparrow-hawk, the meek-eyed dove, the jealous swan,
the death-boding owl, the jangling pie, the false lap-
wing, the tame ruddock, the sparrow—Venus' son, the
wedded turtle, the unkind cuckoo. And there are
many others, too, which as the poet sings—*

" Men might in that place assembled find
Before the noble goddess Nature."
GEOFFREY CHAUCER.

A TOWN MEETING

From " The Birds of Killingworth "

IT was the season, when through all the land
The merle and mavis build, and building sing
Those lovely lyrics, written by his hand,
    Whom Saxon Cædmon calls the Blithe-heart King;
When on the boughs the purple buds expand,
    The banners of the vanguard of the Spring,
And rivulets, rejoicing, rush and leap,
And wave their fluttering signals from the steep.

The robin and the blue-bird, piping loud,
    Filled all the blossoming orchards with their glee;
The sparrows chirped as if they still were proud
    Their race in Holy Writ should mentioned be;
And hungry crows assembled in a crowd,
    Clamoured their piteous prayer incessantly,
Knowing who hears the raven's cry, and said ·
" Give us, O Lord, this day our daily bread ! "

Across the Sound the birds of passage sailed,
    Speaking some unknown language strange and
    sweet
Of tropic isle remote, and passing hailed
    The village with the cheers of all their fleet;

Or, quarrelling together, laughed and railed
  Like foreign sailors, landed in the street
Of seaport town, and with outlandish noise
Of oaths and gibberish frightening girls and boys.

Thus came the jocund Spring in Killingworth,
  In fabulous days, some hundred years ago ;
And thrifty farmers, as they tilled the earth,
  Heard with alarm the cawing of the crow,
That mingled with the universal mirth,
    Cassandra-like, prognosticating woe ;
They shook their heads, and doomed with dreadful
    words
To swift destruction the whole race of birds.

And a town-meeting was convened straightway
  To set a price upon the guilty heads
Of these marauders, who, in lieu of pay,
  Levied black-mail upon the garden beds
And corn-fields, and beheld without dismay
  The awful scarecrow, with his fluttering shreds ;
The skeleton that waited at their feast,
Whereby their sinful pleasure was increased.

      .   .   .

Ill fared it with the birds, both great and small ;
  Hardly a friend in all that crowd they found,
But enemies enough, who every one
Charged them with all the crimes beneath the sun.

When they had ended, from his place apart,
  Rose the Preceptor, to redress the wrong.

" Plato, anticipating the Reviewers,
    From his Republic banished without pity
The Poets ; in this little town of yours,
    You put to death, by means of a Committee,
The ballad-singers and the Troubadours,
    The street-musicians of the heavenly city,
The birds—who make sweet music for us all
In our dark hours, as David did for Saul.

" The thrush that carols at the dawn of day
    From the green steeples of the piny wood ;
The oriole in the elm ; the noisy jay,
    Jargoning like a foreigner at his food ;
The blue-bird balanced on some topmost spray,
    Flooding with melody the neighbourhood ;
Linnet and meadow-lark, and all the throng
That dwell in nests, and have the gift of song.

" You slay them all ! and wherefore ? for the gain
    Of a scant handful more or less of wheat,
Or rye, or barley, or some other grain,
    Scratched up at random by industrious feet,
Searching for worm or weevil after rain !
    Or a few cherries, that are not so sweet
As are the songs these uninvited guests
Sing at their feast with comfortable breasts.

" Do you ne'er think what wondrous beings these ?
    Do you ne'er think who made them, and who
        taught
The dialect they speak, where melodies
·   Alone are the interpreters of thought ?

Whose household words are songs in many keys,
    Sweeter than instrument of man e'er caught !
Whose habitations in the tree-tops even
    Are half-way houses on the road to heaven !
" Think, every morning when the sun peeps through
    The dim, leaf-latticed windows of the grove,
How jubilant the happy birds renew
    Their old, melodious madrigals of love !
And when you think of this, remember too
    'Tis always morning somewhere, and above
The awakening continents, from shore to shore,
Somewhere the birds are singing evermore.
" Think of your woods and orchards without birds !
    Of empty nests that cling to boughs and beams
As in an idiot's brain remembered words
    Hang empty 'mid the cobwebs of his dreams !
            .   .   .
Is this more pleasant to you than the whir
    Of meadow-lark, and her sweet roundelay,
Or twitter of little field-fares, as you take ;
    Your nooning in the shade of bush and brake ?
" You call them thieves and pillagers ; but know
    They are the wingèd wardens of your farms,
Who from the cornfields drive the insidious foe,
    And from your harvests keep a hundred harms ;
Even the blackest of them all, the crow,
    Renders good service as your man-at-arms,
Crushing the beetle in his coat of mail,
And crying havoc on the slug and snail."
    .   .   .   .   .

The birds were doomed ; and, as the record shows,
A bounty offered for the heads of crows.

.   .   .

And so the dreadful massacre began ;
   O'er fields and orchards, and o'er woodland crests,
The ceaseless fusillade of terror ran,
   Dead fell the birds, with blood-stains on their
      breasts,
Or wounded crept away from sight of man,
   While the young died of famine in their nests ;
A slaughter to be told in groans, not words,
The very St Bartholomew of Birds !

         .   .   .

But the next Spring a stranger sight was seen,
   A sight that never yet by bard was sung,
As great a wonder as it would have been
   If some dumb animal had found a tongue !
A wagon, overarched with evergreen,
   Upon whose boughs were wicker cages hung,
All full of singing birds, came down the street,
Filling the air with music wild and sweet.

From all the country round these birds were brought,
   By order of the town, with anxious quest,
And, loosened from their wicker prisons, sought
   In woods and fields the places they loved best,
Singing loud canticles, which many thought
   Were satires to the authorities addressed,
While others, listening in green lanes, averred
Such lovely music never had been heard !

But blither still and louder carolled they
  Upon the morrow, for they seemed to know
It was the fair Almira's wedding-day,
  And everywhere, around, above, below,
When the Preceptor bore his bride away,
  Their songs burst forth in joyous overflow,
And a new heaven bent over a new earth
Amid the sunny farms of Killingworth.
              HENRY WADSWORTH LONGFELLOW.

THE EAGLE AND THE ASSEMBLY OF BIRDS

THE birds in place, by factions press'd,
To Jupiter their pray'rs address'd
By specious lies the state was vex'd,
Their counsels libellers perplex'd ;
They begg'd (to stop seditious tongues)
A gracious hearing of their wrongs.
Jove grants their suit :—the Eagle sat,
Decider of the grand debate.
    The Pie to trust and pow'r preferr'd,
Demands permission to be heard :
Says he, " Prolixity of phrase
You know I hate.   This libel says—
' Some birds there are, who, prone to noise,
Are hir'd to silence Wisdom's voice ;
And, skill'd to chatter out the hour,
Rise by their emptiness to pow'r.'
That this is aim'd direct at me,
No doubt you'll readily agree ;
Yet well this sage assembly knows—

By parts to government I rose ;
My prudent counsels prop the State ;
Magpies were never known to prate."
   The Kite rose up ; his honest heart
In virtue's sufferings bore a part :
" That there were birds of prey he knew,
So far the libeller said true ;
Voracious, bold, to rapine prone,
Who knew no interest but their own ;
Who, hovering o'er the farmer's yard,
Nor pigeon, chick, nor duckling spar'd :
This might be true, but if applied
To him, in troth the slanderer lied :
Since ignorance then might be misled,
Such things he thought were best unsaid."
   The Crow was vex'd : " As yester-morn
He flew across the new-sown corn;
A screaming boy was set for pay,
He knew, to drive the crows away ;
Scandal had found out him in turn,
And buzz'd abroad that crows love corn."
   The Owl arose with solemn face,
And thus harangu'd upon the case :
" That Magpies prate, it may be true,
A Kite may be voracious too ;
Crows sometimes deal in new-sown pease ;
He libels not that strikes at these :
The slander's here—' But there are birds
Whose wisdom lies in looks, not words,
Blunderers who level in the dark,
And always shoot beside the mark ' ·

He names not me, but these are hints
Which manifest at whom he squints ;
I were indeed that blundering fowl,
To question if he meant an owl ? ''
    " Ye wretches, hence ! " the Eagle cries,
'Tis Conscience, Conscience that applies ;
The virtuous mind takes no alarm,
Secur'd by innocence from harm ;
While Guilt and his associate, Fear,
Are startled at the passing air."

                        EDWARD MOORE.

A PLACE OF PLEASAUNCE

From " The Message "

A PLACE of pleasaunce, all o'errun
With whisperous shade, and blossoming
Of divers trees, wherein do sing
The little birds, and all together,
All day long in happy weather.
And well I ween that since the birth
Of Adam's firstborn, not on earth
Hath ever been such sweet singing
Of bird on bough, as here doth bring
Into a large and leafy ease
His sense that strayeth among the trees,
Where mingled is full many a note
Of golden-finch and speckle-throat.
Even the hoarse-chested starling
Here, where creepeth never a snarling
Gust to vex his heart, all day
Learneth a more melodious lay

Than that whereby this bird is known,
Which, otherwhere, with chiding tone,
What time the fretful Spring doth heave
The frozen North, to winds, that grieve
Round about the grave of March,
He chaunteth from the cloudy larch ·
The linnet loud, and throstle eke,
And the blackbird of golden beak,
With perpetual madrigals
Do melodise the warm green walls
Of those blossom-crownèd groves,
In whose cool hearts the cooing doves
Make murmurings innumerable,
Of sound as sweet as when a well
With noise of bubbled water leapeth
At a green couch where Silence sleepeth
Nor less, the long-voiced nightingale
Doth, deep down in bloomy vale
Delicious, pour at full noonlight
The song he hath rehearsed o'er-night ;
And many other birds be there
Of most sweet voice, and plumage rare,
And names that I not know.

    Earl of Lytton (" Owen Meredith ").

TO A BIRD

That haunted the Waters of Laken, in the Winter

O MELANCHOLY bird !—a winter's day
Thou standest by the margin of the pool,
And, taught by God, dost thy whole being school
To patience, which all evil can allay ;
God has appointed thee the fish thy prey ;
And given thyself a lesson to the fool
Unthrifty, to submit to moral rule,
And his unthinking course by thee to weigh.
There need not schools, nor the professor's chair,
Though these be good, true wisdom to impart ;
He who has not enough for these to spare
Of time or gold, may yet amend his heart,
And teach his soul by brooks and rivers fair ·
Nature is always wise in every part.

LORD THURLOW.

BIRDS ON MOUNT TARAWERA

THE wild-ducks' black and tiny fleet
Shot in and out their shy retreat ;
The cormorant left his crowded tree
And stretched his tinselled neck for sea ;
All Nature's feathered favourites poured
To their adored undoubted Lord
Of light and heat, accordance sweet
Of pure impassioned revelry ;
And honey-bird and mocking bird

And he of clearest melody,
The blossom-loving bell-bird—each
Delicious-throated devotee
In happy ignorance framed to be
Content with rapture—longing-free
For life or love they cannot reach—
Like chimes rich-tuned to heaven preferred
The praise of their mellifluous glee ;
Each lurking lyrist of the grove
With all his might sang all his love ;
Till every foliage-filled ravine
And bower of amaranthine green
Rang persevering ecstasy.

ALFRED DOMETT.

THE HABITAT OF BIRDS

BIRDS ! Birds ! ye are beautiful things,
With your earth-treading feet and your cloud
cleaving wings !
Where shall man wander, and where shall he
dwell,
Beautiful birds, that ye come not as well ?
Ye have nests on the mountain all rugged and
stark,
Ye have nests in the forest, all tangled and dark ;
Ye build and ye brood 'neath the cottagers' eaves,
And ye sleep on the sod 'mid the bonnie green
leaves ;
Ye hide in the heather, ye lurk in the brake,
Ye dive in the sweet flags that shadow the lake ·

Ye skim where the stream parts the orchard-
deck'd land,
Ye dance where the foam sweeps the desolate
strand ;
Beautiful Birds ! ye come thickly around,
When the bud's on the branch, and the snow's
on the ground ;
Ye come when the richest of roses flush out,
And ye come when the yellow leaf eddies about !

ELIZA COOK.

THE HOME OF THE WATER-OUZEL

SHUT between mighty cliffs, yon desperate pass
    Still ever upward urges its blind way
Through treeless solitudes of mountain grass,
    Uncheered by mortal sound the livelong day,
Save burrowing under rocks now smooth as glass,
    Or now unfettered sparkling into play,
Wild sunlit waters, though 'tis Michaelmas,
    Lull silence into trance with dreamlike lay.

This is the water-ouzel's shy retreat,
    There in the torrent-bed from stone to stone
She noiseless flits ; then poised on steadfast feet,
    Dipping her dusk head, she trills forth alone
Love's sunniest, airiest gossip by her nest,
One milk-white foam-flake bound across her breast.

CHARLES A. FOX.

THE LARK BY LAKE BEWA, JAPAN

THE motive of this little story,
Told in the land of the rising sun,
Is a tribute from me, and a feeling
Of thanks for a sentiment won
Back from the scenes of my childhood,
A reflection of earliest days,
A rush over time and of distance
Through the cranks of life's rough ways.
A vision of home and 'my mother
Flashes out like a light in the dark,
As I hear on this sweet May morning,
In Japan, the voice of the lark !

The breeze brings song of the boatmen,
Which ebbs with the rustle of reeds ;
The water is laughing and flashing
To the mill through its bamboo leads,
While the hills across the water
Are changing from gold to dun
As the fitful shadows wander
O'er the land of the rising sun.
   But beyond the bright blue water,
And beyond the changing hills,
To my English home and birthplace
I am borne by those wild trills.
And the road and the wide green rice-fields
And the grey-roofed cottages there,
Melt into an English meadow
And an English homestead fair :

I lie again 'mid the daisies,
Which bend in the soft-toned breeze,
That wafts the scent of the rich ripe flowers
Through the branches of blooming trees.

That's my dream while the lark was singing,
But his song was, alas, soon done :
Yet the dream was fair and pleasant
In the land of the rising sun.

ALFRED EAST.

PARTRIDGES' HAUNTS AND HABITS

STILLNESS, heart-soothing, reigns,
Save, now and then, the Partridge's late call ;
Featly athwart the ridge she runs, now seen,
Now in the furrow hid ; then screaming springs,
Joined by her mate, into the grass-field flies ;
There, 'neath the blade, rudely she forms
Her shallow nest, humble as is the lark's,
But thrice more numerous her freckled store.
Careful she turns them to her breast, and soft
With lightest pressure sits, scarce to be moved.
Yes, she will sit regardless of the scythe,
That nearer, and still nearer, sweep by sweep,
Levels the swath ; bold with a mother's fears,
She, faithful to the last, maintains her post,
And with her blood sprinkles a deeper red
Upon the falling blossoms of the field ;
While others of her kind, content to haunt
The upland ferny braes, remote from man,

Behold a plenteous brood burst from the shell,
And run ; but soon poor helpless things, return
And crowd beneath the fond inviting breast
And wings outstretching, quivering with delight.
They grow apace, but still not far they range
Till on their pinions plumes begin to shoot ;
Then by the wary parents led, they dare
To skirt the earing crofts ; at last, full-fledged,
They try their timorous wings, bending their flight
Home to their natal spot and pant amid the ferns.
Oft by the side of sheepfold, on the ground
Bared by the frequent hoof, they love to lie
And bask.   Oh, I could never tire to look
On such a scene of peacefulness as this !

JAMES GRAHAME.

ROOKS' HABITS

From " Sons of the Soil "

THE solemn caw of venerable Rook,
Flapping his wings from out the sheltered nook,
Where silent sit a conclave of his kind,
Unlike to wiser conclaves, of one mind.
Unlike themselves, when, portioned out in pairs,
The bustling stir of spring's new life was theirs,
And ceaseless din of nestlings' greedy cry,
And fluttering wings that scarce found time to fly,
Though on the blissful embassy of love,
Through the wide realm of nature free to rove.
How different seems their very nature now,
Single their cry, their movements grave and slow,

The curse of idleness has reft away
Each bustling joy that crowned their happier day ;
And far away through distant skies they roam,
Seeking the silent forest for their home.
Who has not heard their autumn voice, and found
The melody of nature in that sound ?
Harsh in itself—discordant, were it near ;
But oh ! What music to the tuneful ear.
Hath it not language for the heart as well,
Of more than man's familiar tongue can tell ?
Of blighted flowers, and scattered leaves and sighs,
And clouds that overcast the sunny skies ?
Of withered wreaths o'er faded brows that stray,
Of time, and death, and sorrow and decay ?
In one sad voice, disconsolate and drear,
Hymning a dirge for the departing year.

MRS SARAH ELLIS.

THE WOODMAN AND THE NIGHTINGALE

A WOODMAN, whose rough heart was out of tune
    (I think such hearts yet never came to good),
Hated to hear, under the stars or moon,

    One nightingale in an interfluous wood
Satiate the hungry dark with melody.
    And as a vale is watered by a flood,

Or as the moonlight fills the open sky
    Struggling with darkness—as a tuberose
Peoples some Indian dell with scents which lie

Like clouds above the flower from which they rose—
The singing of that happy nightingale
In this sweet forest, from the golden close

Of evening till the star of dawn may fail,
Was interfused upon the silentness.
The folded roses and the violets pale

Heard her within their slumbers ; the abyss
Of heaven with all its planets ; the dull ear
Of the night-cradled Earth ; the loneliness

Of the circumfluous waters. Every sphere,
And every flower and beam and cloud and wave,
And every wind of the mute atmosphere,

And every beast stretched in its rugged cave,
And every bird lulled on its mossy bough,
And every silver moth fresh from the grave

Which is its cradle (ever from below
Aspiring, like one who loves too fair, too far,
To be consumed within the purest glow

Of one serene and unapproachèd star,
As if it were a lamp of earthly light,
Unconscious, as some human lovers are,

Itself how low, how high beyond all height
The heaven where it would perish), and every form
That worshipped in the temple of the night

Was awed into delight, and by the charm
Girt as with an interminable zone ;
Whilst that sweet bird, whose music was a storm

Of sound, shook forth the dull oblivion
Out of their dreams.   Harmony became love
In every soul but one.

And so this man returned with axe and saw
    At evening close from killing the tall treen,
The soul of whom, by Nature's gentle law,

    Was each a Wood-nymph, and kept ever green
The pavement and the roof of the wild copse,
    Chequering the sunlight of the blue serene

With jagged leaves, and from the forest tops
    Singing the winds to sleep, or weeping oft
Fast showers of aèrial water-drops

    Into her mother's bosom sweet and soft,—
Nature's pure tears which have no bitterness.
    Around the cradles of the birds aloft

They spread themselves into the loveliness
    Of fan-like leaves ; and over pallid flowers
Hang like moist clouds ; or, where high branches
        kiss,

    Make a green space among the silent bowers
Like a vast fane in a metropolis,
    Surrounded by the columns and the towers

All overwrought with branch-like traceries,
  In which there is religion, and the mute
Persuasion of unkindled melodies,

  Odours, and gleams, and murmurs, which the lute
Of the blind Pilot-Spirit of the blast
  Stirs as it sails, now grave and now acute,

Wakening the leaves and waves, ere it has passed,
  To such brief unison as on the brain
One tone which never can recur has cast,

  One accent never to return again.

The world is full of Woodmen who expel
  Love's gentle Dryads from the haunts of life,
And vex the nightingales in every dell.
                    PERCY BYSSHE SHELLEY.

TO A SEA-BIRD

SAUNTERING hither on listless wings,
  Careless vagabond of the sea,
Little thou heedest the surf that sings,
The bar that thunders, the shale that rings,—
  Give me to keep thy company.

Little thou hast, old friend, that's new ;
  Storms and wrecks are old things to thee ;
Sick am I of these changes too ;
Little to care for, little to rue.—
  I on the shore, and thou on the sea.

All of thy wanderings, far and near,
  Bring thee at last to shore and me ;
All of my journeyings end them here,
This our tether must be our cheer,—
  I on the shore, and thou on the sea.

Lazily rocking on ocean's breast,
  Something in common, old friend, have we
Thou on the shingle seek'st thy nest,
I to the waters look for rest,—
  I on the shore, and thou on the sea.
                                        BRET HARTE.

CLIFF BIRDS

From " Faire-Virtue "

HERE you might through the water see the land
Appear, strowed o'er with white or yellow sand ;
Yon deeper was it, and the wind by whiffs
Would make it rise and wash the little cliffs
On which, oft pluming, sat unfrighted than
The gagling wild-goose and the snow-white swan,
With all those flocks of fowls which to this day,
Upon those quiet waters breed and play.
                                     GEORGE WITHER.

THE BELFRY PIGEON

ON the cross-beam under the Old South bell
The nest of a pigeon is builded well.
In summer and winter that bird is there,
Out and in with the morning air :

I love to see him track the street,
With his wary eye and active feet ;
And I often watch him as he springs,
Circling the steeple with easy wings,
Till across the dial his shade has pass'd,
And the belfry edge is gain'd at last.
'Tis a bird I love, with its brooding note,
And the trembling throb in its mottled throat ;
There's a human look in its swelling breast,
And the gentle curve of its lowly crest ;
And I often stop with the fear I feel—
He runs so close to the rapid wheel.

Whatever is rung on that noisy bell—
Chime of the hour or funeral knell—
The dove in the belfry must hear it well.
When the tongue swings out to the midnight moon
When the sexton cheerily rings for noon—
When the clock strikes clear at morning light—
When the child is waked with " nine at night "—
When the chimes play soft in the Sabbath air,
Filling the spirit with tones of prayer—
Whatever tale in the bell is heard,
He broods on his folded feet unstirr'd,
Or, rising half in his rounded nest,
He takes the time to smooth his breast,
Then drops again with filmèd eyes,
And sleeps as the last vibration dies.

Sweet bird ! I would that I could be
A hermit in the crowd like thee !

With wings to fly to wood and glen,
Thy lot, like mine, is cast with men ;
And daily, with unwilling feet,
I tread, like thee, the crowded street ;
But, unlike me, when day is o'er,
Thou canst dismiss the world and soar,
Or, at a half-felt wish for rest,
Canst smooth the feathers on thy breast,
And drop, forgetful, to thy nest.
                    NATHANIEL PARKER WILLIS.

TO A CITY PIGEON

STOOP to my window, thou beautiful dove !
Thy daily visits have touch'd my love.
I watch thy coming, and list the note
That stirs so low in thy mellow throat.
      ' And my joy is high
To catch the glance of thy gentle eye.

Why dost thou sit on the heated eaves,
And forsake the wood with its freshen'd leaves ?
Why dost thou haunt the sultry street,
When the paths of the forest are cool and sweet ?
      How canst thou bear
This noise of people—this sultry air ?

Thou alone of the feather'd race
Dost look unscared on the human face,
Thou alone, with a wing, to flee,
Dost love with man in his haunts to be,
      And the " gentle dove "
Has become a name for trust and love.

A holy gift is thine, sweet bird !
Thou'rt named with childhood's earliest word
Thou'rt link'd with all that is fresh and wild
In the prison'd thoughts of the city child ;
    And thy glossy wings
Are its brightest image of moving things.

It is no light chance. Thou art set apart,
Wisely by Him who has tamed thy heart,
To stir the love for the bright and fair
That else were seal'd in this crowded air ;
    I sometimes dream
Angelic rays from thy pinions stream.

Come then, ever, when daylight leaves
The page I read, to my humble eaves,
And wash thy breast in the hollow spout,
And murmur thy low sweet music out !
    I hear and see
Lessons of heaven, sweet bird, in thee !
            NATHANIEL PARKER WILLIS.

THE SNIPE AND HEATHCOCK

A Translation from the Icelandic

O 'TIS the touch of fairy hand
That wakes the spring of northern land !
It warms not there by slow degrees,
With changeful pulse, the uncertain breeze ;
But sudden on the wondering sight
Bursts forth the beam of living light,

And instant verdure springs around,
And magic flowers bedeck the ground.
Returned from regions far away,
The red-winged throstle pours his lay ;
The soaring snipe salutes the spring,
While the breeze whistles through his wing ;
And, as he hails the melting snows,
The heathcock claps his wings and crows.

WILLIAM HERBERT.

THE CUCKOO AND THE STARLING

ONE day a Cuckoo, in his flight up and down,
Fell in with a Starling escaped from the town :
" Pray what is the talk ? " he began with an air,
" Pray how do they speak of songs in the city ?
Pray what do they think of the Nightingale there ? "
' The whole of the town is in love with her ditty ! '
" And pray what remark do they make on the Lark? "
' She is high in renown with the half of the town.'
"Indeed! Well, and as to the Blackbird?"—'He, too,
Is eulogised much, here and there by a few.'
" Well, now, I've to add that I'd feel very glad
If you'd tell me the various opinions that go forth
Respecting myself and my merits and so forth."
' Why, that,' said the Starling, ' I hardly can do
For scarcely a soul ever talks about you.'
"Base ingrates! Well, then, as they grant me no praise,
I'll trumpet myself to the end of my days."
So saying, away to the forest he flew,
And ever since then has been crying, Cuckoo !

CHRISTIAN F. GELLERT.

THREE SIMILES

I.—ÆSCHYLUS : EAGLE'S FEATHER

So, in the Libyan fable it is told
That once an Eagle, stricken with a dart,
Said when he saw the fashion of the shaft,
" With our own feathers, not by others' hands,
Are we now smitten."

EDWARD H. PLUMPTRE.

II.—EAGLE'S FEATHER

To a Lady singing a Song of his Composing

CHLORIS ! yourself you so excel,
When you vouchsafe to breathe my thought,
That, like a spirit, with this spell
Of my own teaching, I am caught.

That Eagle's fate and mine are one,
Which, on the shaft that made him die,
Espied a feather of his own,
Wherewith he wont to soar so high.

Had Echo, with so sweet a grace,
Narcissus' loud complaint return'd,
Not for reflection of his face,
But of his voice, the boy had burn'd.

EDMUND WALLER.

III.—H. KIRKE WHITE : EAGLE'S FEATHER

UNHAPPY White ! while life was in its Spring,
And thy young muse just waved her joyous wing,
The spoiler came ! and all thy promise fair
Has sought the grave, to sleep for ever there.
Oh ! what a noble heart was here undone,
When Science' self destroy'd her favourite son !
Yes, she too much indulged thy fond pursuit ;
She sow'd the seeds, but Death has reap'd the fruit.
'Twas thine own genius gave the final blow,
And help'd to plant the wound that laid thee low.
So the struck Eagle, stretch'd upon the plain,
No more through rolling clouds to soar again,
View'd his own feather on the fatal dart,
And wing'd the shaft that quiver'd in his heart ·
Keen were his pangs, but keener far to feel,
He nursed the pinion which impell'd the steel ;
While the same plumage that had warm'd his nest
Drank the last life-drop of his bleeding breast.

LORD BYRON.

IX

THE FLIGHT AND FEEDING
OF BIRDS

" A flight of fowl
Scattered by winds and high tempestuous gusts."
Shakespeare.

THE BIRDS OF PASSAGE

BIRDS, joyous birds of the wandering wing !
Whence is it ye come with the flowers of spring ?—
" We come from the shores of the green old Nile,
From the land where the roses of Sharon smile,
From the palms that wave through the Indian sky,
From the myrrh-trees of glowing Araby.

" We have swept o'er cities in song renowned—
Silent they lie with the deserts round !
We have crossed proud rivers whose tide hath roll'd
All dark with the warrior-blood of old ;
And each worn wing hath regained its home,
Under peasant's roof-tree or monarch's dome."

And what have ye found in the monarch's dome,
Since last ye traversed the blue sea's foam ?—
" We have found a change, we have found a pall,
And a gloom o'ershadowing the banquet's hall,
And a mark on the floor as of life-drops spilt—
Nought looks the same, save the nest we built ! "

O joyous birds ! it hath still been so ;
Through the halls of kings doth the tempest go !
But the huts of the hamlet lie still and deep,
And the hills o'er their quiet a vigil keep :
Say what have ye found in the peasant's cot,
Since last ye parted from that sweet spot ?—

"A change we have found there—and many a change!
Faces and footsteps, and all things strange !
Gone are the heads of the silvery hair,
And the young, that were, have a brow of care,
And the place is hushed where the children played—
Nought looks the sáme, save the nest we made ! "

Sad is your tale of the beautiful earth,
Birds that o'ersweep it in power and mirth !
Yet through the wastes of the trackless air
Ye have a guide, and shall *we* despair ?
Ye over desert and deep have passed—
So may *we* reach our bright home at last !

Mrs Felicia Hemans.

THE FLIGHT OF BIRDS

From " Amyntor and Theodora "

The birds of passage transmigrating come,
Unnumber'd colonies of foreign wing,
At Nature's summons their aërial state
Annual to found, and in bold voyage steer
O'er this wide ocean ; through yon pathless sky,
One certain flight to one appointed shore,
By Heaven's directive spirit here to raise
Their temporary realm, and form secure,
Where food awaits them copious from the wave,
And shelter from the rock their nuptial leagues ;
Each tribe apart, and all on tasks of love,
To hatch the pregnant egg, to rear and guard
Their helpless infants, piously intent.

At twilight hour, remote and hollow heard
Through wintry pines high waving o'er the steep
Of sky-crown'd Apennine ; the sea-pie ceas'd
At once to warble ; screaming from his nest
The fulmar soar'd, and shot a westward flight
From shore to sea.

DAVID MALLET.

A THRONG OF BIRDS
From " The Story of Rimini "

ANON the sweet birds, like a sudden throng
Of happy children, ring their tangled song
From out the greener trees ; and then a cloud
Of cawing rooks breaks o'er them, gathering loud
Like savages at ships ; and then again
Nothing is heard but their own stately train,
Or ring-dove that repeats his pensive plea,
Or startled gull up-screaming toward the sea.

LEIGH HUNT.

FLIGHT OF THE CRANES
From " The Battle of the Pigmies and Cranes "

FROM far the mingling clamours rise,
Loud and more loud rebounding through the skies.
From skirt to skirt of heaven, with stormy sway,
A cloud rolls on, and darkens all the day.
Near and more near descends the dreadful shade ;
And now in battalious array display'd,
On bounding wings, and screaming in their ire,
The cranes rush onward, and the fight require.

JAMES BEATTIE.

MIGRATION OF THE CRANES AND SWALLOWS·

WHERE the tall Crane or winding Swallow goes,
Fearful of gathering winds and falling snows ;
If into rocks or hollow trees they creep,
In temporary death confin'd to sleep,
Or conscious of the coming evil, fly
To milder regions and a southern sky ?

                              MATTHEW PRIOR.

THE FLIGHT OF THE WILD GEESE

RAMBLING along the marshes,
On the bank of the Assabett,
Sounding myself as to how it went,
Praying that I might not forget,
And all uncertain
Whether I was in the right,
Toiling to lift Time's curtain,
And if I burnt the strongest light,—
Suddenly,
High in the air,
I heard the travell'd geese
Their overture prepare.

Stirred above the patcht ball,
The wild geese flew,
Nor near so wild as that doth me befall,
Or, swollen Wisdom ! you.

In the front there fetch'd a leader,
Him behind the line spread out,
And waved about,
As it was near night,
When these air-pilots stop their flight.

Cruising off the shoal dominion
Where we sit ;
Depending not on their opinion,
Nor hiving sops of wit ;

Geographical in tact,
Naming not a pond or river ;
Pull'd with twilight down, in fact,
In the reeds to quack and quiver ;—
There they go,
Spectators at the play below,
Southward in a row.

Cannot laud and map the stars
The indifferent geese ;
Nor taste the sweetmeats in odd jars ;
Nor speculate and freeze ;
Rancid weasands need be well,
Feathers glossy, quills in order ;
Starts this train, yet rings no bell,—
Steam is raised without recorder.

" Up, my feather'd fowl ! all ! "
Saith the goose commander ;
" Brighten your bills, and flirt your pinions,
My toes are nipp'd—let us render

Ourselves in soft Guatemala,
Or suck puddles in Campeachy ,
Spitzbergen-cake cuts very frosty,
And the tipple is not leechy !

" Let's brush loose for any creek,
There lurk fish and fly,
Condiments to fat the weak,
Inundate the pie.
Flutter not about a place,
Ye concomitants of space ! "

Mute the listening nations stand
On that dark receding land ;
How faint their villages and towns,
Scatter'd on the misty downs !
A meeting-house
Appears no bigger than a mouse !
How long ?—
Never is a question ask'd,
While a throat can lift the song,
Or a flapping wing be task'd.

All the grandmothers about
Hear the orators of heaven ;
Then put on their woollens stout,
And cower o'er the hearth at even,
And the children stare at the sky,
And laugh to see the long black line so high

Thence once more I heard them say,—
" 'Tis a smooth, delightful road ;
Difficult to lose the way,
And a trifle for a load."

'Twas our forte to pass, for this
Proper sack of sense to borrow
Wings and legs, and bills that clatter,
And the horizon of To-morrow.
WILLIAM ELLERY CHANNING.

ON THE DEPARTURE OF THE NIGHTINGALE

SWEET poet of the woods, a long adieu !
  Farewell, soft minstrel of the early year !
Ah ! 'twill be long ere thou shalt sing anew,
  And pour thy music on the night's dull ear.
Whether on spring thy wandering flights await,
  Or whether silent in our groves you dwell,
The pensive muse shall own thee for her mate,
  And still protect the song she loves so well.
With cautious step the love-lorn youth shall glide
  Through the lone brake that shades thy mossy nest;
And shepherd girls from eyes profane shall hide
  The gentle bird who sings of pity best :
For still thy voice shall soft affections move,
And still be dear to sorrow and to love !
MRS CHARLOTTE SMITH.

ITYLUS

SWALLOW, my sister, oh, sister swallow,
  How can thine heart be full of the spring ?
    A thousand summers are over and dead.
What hast thou found in the spring to follow ?
  What hast thou found in thine heart to sing ?
    What wilt thou do when the summer is shed ?

Oh, swallow, sister, oh, fair swift swallow,
  Why wilt thou fly after spring to the south,
  The soft south whither thine heart is set ?
Shall not the grief of the old time follow ?
  Shall not the song thereof cleave to thy mouth ?
  Hast thou forgotten ere I forget ?

Sister, my sister, oh, fleet sweet swallow,
  Thy way is long to the sun and the south ;
  But I, fulfilled of my heart's desire,
Shedding my song upon height, upon hollow,
  From tawny body and sweet small mouth
  Feed the heart of the night with fire.

I, the nightingale, all spring through,
  Oh, swallow, sister, oh, changing swallow,
  All spring through till the spring be done,
Clothed with the light of the night on the dew,—
  Sing, while the hours and the wild birds follow,
  Take flight and follow and find the sun.

Sister, my sister, oh, soft light swallow,   [chamber,
  Though all things feast in the spring's guest-
  How hast thou heart to be glad thereof yet ?
For where thou fliest I shall not follow,
  Till life forget and death remember,
  Till thou remember and I forget.

Swallow, my sister, oh, singing swallow,
  I know not how thou hast heart to sing.
  Hast thou the heart ? is it all past over ?
Thy lord the summer is good to follow,
  And fair the feet of thy lover the spring :
  But what wilt thou say to the spring, thy lover ?

Oh, swallow, sister, oh, fleeting swallow,
　My heart in me is a molten ember,
　　And over my head the waves have met.
But thou wouldst tarry or I would follow,
　Could I forget or thou remember,
　　Couldst thou remember and I forget.

Oh, sweet stray sister, oh, shifting swallow,
　The heart's division divideth us.
　　Thy heart is light as a leaf of a tree ;
But mine goes forth among sea-gulfs hollow,
　To the place of the slaying of Itylus,
　　The feast of Daulis, the Thracian Sea.

Oh, swallow, sister, oh, rapid swallow,
　I pray thee sing not a little space.
　　Are not the roofs and the lintels wet ?
The woven web that was plain to follow,
　The small slain body, the flowerlike face,
　　Can I remember if thou forget ?

Oh, sister, sister, thy first-begotten !
　The hands that cling and the feet that follow,
　　The voice of the child's blood crying yet,
Who hath remembered me ? who hath forgotten ?
　Thou hast forgotten, oh, summer swallow,
　　But the world shall end when I forget.
　　　　　　　ALGERNON CHARLES SWINBURNE.

THE FIRST SWALLOW

I HEARD the wheat-ear singing in the dale,
I saw the ouzel curtsey to the sun,
And cried, " The days of winter sure are done,
The spring upon the mountains doth prevail,
Soon shall the cuckoo come to tell her tale."
E'en as I spake where Calder's ripples run
To seek the shining Solway, there came one
Songless but sweeter than the nightingale.

From silent wastes and those dumb Memphian hills
    Where dead men slumber in Sakkarah's dunes,
        He came, he could not speak our English tongue,
But as he flashed above the daffodils
    On bluest April air he wrote in runes
        That Love was near, and Life again was young.
                              H. D. RAWNSLEY.

THE FIRST SWALLOW OF SPRING

THE gorse is yellow on the heath,
    The banks with speedwell flowers are gay,
The oaks are budding ; and beneath,
The hawthorn soon will bear the wreath,
    The silver wreath of May.

The welcome guest of settled Spring,
    The swallow, too, is come at last ;
Just at sunset, when thrushes sing,
I saw her dash with rapid wing,
    And hail'd her as she pass'd.

Come, Summer visitant, attach
  To my reed-roof your nest of clay ;
And let my ear your music catch,
Low twittering underneath the thatch,
  At the grey dawn of day.
                    MRS CHARLOTTE SMITH.

THE SWALLOW'S RETURN

WELCOME, welcome, feathered stranger,
  Now the sun bids nature smile ;
Safe arrived, and free from danger,
  Welcome to our blooming isle !
Still twitter on my lowly roof,
  And hail me at the dawn of day,
Each morn the recollected proof
  Of time that ever fleets away.

Fond of sunshine, fond of shade,
  Fond of skies serene and clear,
Ev'n transient storms thy joy invade
  In fairest seasons of the year ·
What makes thee seek a milder clime,
  What bids thee shun the wintry gale,
How know'st thou thy departing time ?
  Hail ! wondrous bird ! hail, Swallow, hail

Sure something more to thee is given
  Than myriads of the feathered race,
Some gift divine, some spark from Heaven,
  That guides thy flight from place to place

Still freely come, still freely go,
  And blessings crown thy vigorous wing,
May thy rude flight meet no rude foe,
  Delightful messenger of Spring !
                    ROBERT FRANKLIN.

A WELCOME TO THE FIRST SWALLOW OF SPRING

WELCOME, dear Swallow, to thy well known nest
  Preserved for thy return with anxious care !
Well pleased I saw thee cleave the yielding air,
  And haste to be again my cheerful guest !

Oh, could my verse ungrateful man persuade
  To pay the tribute which thy labours claim !
No ruthless hand thy dwelling should invade,
  Nor at thy life the murderous tube should aim

Thou on the busy wing at early morn
  Shalt dart, like lightning, thro' the wide expanse,
Where noxious insects float in mazy dance,
  And shed their poison on the withering corn.

From such by thee relieved, our fields rejoice ;
  The flowers unfold their variegated hues !
And shall we greet thee with unfriendly voice,
  Or the warm covert of the roof refuse.

Shall the rude African the stork adore,
  That frees him from the reptiles of the Nile ?
And shall we drive thee from a thankless shore,
  Regardless of thy free, unpurchased toil ?

Welcome, dear Swallow, to thy well known nest ;
   Here sit secure, and pour thy artless song ;
In safety here thy weary pinions rest,
   And soothe with lullabies thy callow young.

ANON.

THE LAST SWALLOW

ONE latest, solitary swallow flies
   Across the sea, rough autumn-tempest tost,
   Poor bird, shall it be lost ?
Dropped down into this uncongenial sea,
      With no kind eyes
      To watch it while it dies,
Unguessed, uncared for, free ·
      Set free at last,
      The short pang past,
In sleep, in death, in dreamless sleep locked fast.

CHRISTINA G. ROSSETTI.

THE FLIGHT OF THE SWALLOWS

From " A Doubting Heart "

WHERE are the swallows fled ?
   Frozen and dead,
Perchance upon some bleak and stormy shore.
   O doubting heart !
   Far over purple seas,
   They wait, in sunny ease,
   The balmy southern breeze,
To bring them to their northern homes once more.

ADELAIDE ANNE PROCTER.

THE SEVEN WHITE SWANS

From " The Land East of the Sun "

HE started up, for through the trees
A mighty rushing sound he heard,
As of the wings of many a bird ;
And, stark away, with beating heart,
He put the hawthorn twigs apart,
And yet saw no more wondrous thing
Than seven white swans, who on wide wing
Went circling round, till one by one
They dropped the dewy grass upon.
He smiled thereat, and thought to shout
And scare them off ; but yet a doubt
Clung .to him, as he gazed on those,
And in the brake he held him close,
And watched them bridle there, and preen
Their snowy feathers well beseen ;
So near they were, that he a stone
Might have cast o'er the furthest one
With his left hand, as there he lay.

WILLIAM MORRIS.

THE MOTHER BIRD

From " Paradiso," canto xxiii.

E'EN as the bird, who 'mid the leafy bower
Has, in her nest, sat darkling through the night
With her sweet brood ; impatient to descry
Their wished looks, and to bring home their food,
In the fond quest, unconscious of her toil ;

She, of the time prevenient, on the spray
That overhangs their couch, with wakeful gaze
Expects the sun, nor ever, till the dawn,
Removeth from the east her eager ken,
So stood the dame erect.

DANTE.

BIRDS FEEDING

From " The Fair Penitent "

BIRDS, great Nature's happy commoners,
That haunt the woods, the meads and flowery
gardens,
Rifle the sweets and take the choicest fruits,
Yet scorn to ask the lordly owner's leave.

NICHOLAS ROWE.

ROOKS FEEDING AND PLAYING

WINNOWING the high pure ether go the Rooks
Down to the sea in intermittent trains,
Far from their inland roost, on the flat mead,
To tear up tufts of grass for grubs below,
And stalking forage on the shelly shore.
Sagacious birds ! what time the sun goes down
With streaks and spots on his distempered face,
High in the airy firmament, a troop
Of maddest revellers, see them whirling round ;
And oft with sidelong flight, slant down the sky
They go ; and oft with clanging wings, the one
Depending as if broke, swooping they fall
Near to the ground, then upward shoot again ;

They scream, they mix, they thwart, they eddy
  round
And round tumultuous, till all heaven is filled
With a wild storm of birds !   By this they show
Presence of windy blasts ; but when, as now,
They take the morn afar, expect the day
To close in beauty as it has begun.

THOMAS AIRD.

BEES THE FOOD OF BIRDS

The poet Addison in his translation of Vergil's *Georgics*, iv. 14, has, by
  a misunderstanding of the Latin "merops," a bee-eater, attributed
  to the woodpeckers a practice followed by the bee-eater.

NOR must the lizard's painted brood appear,
Nor woodpecks, nor the swallow harbour near ;
They waste the swarms, and as they fly along,
Convey the tender morsels to their young.

JOSEPH ADDISON.

X
CLASSICAL AND FABULOUS BIRDS

" Nay, Jupiter now that usurps the command,
Appears with an eagle, appointed to stand
As his emblem of empire ; a striking example
Of authority once so extended and ample :
And each of the gods had his separate fowl,
Apollo a Hawk, and Minerva an Owl."

ARISTOPHANES.

THE CROW AND THE PITCHER

THE bird of Phœbus, parched with thirst's dire pain,
A housewife's pitcher spied, for catching rain :
He perched, loud croaking, on the brim, but no—
Too short his beak, the water much too low !
Thy power then, Phœbus, in the bird inspired
An artifice to gain what he desired
With gathered pebbles, quickly to the brink
He raised the water's level, and could drink.

BIANOR.

IBYCUS AND THE CRANES

Incident used for one of Schiller's Poems

IBYCUS, bent the desert to explore,
There robbers slew thee on the lonely shore ;
Thy cries brought down a passing flock of cranes,
Who came and witnessed thy last dying pains ;—
And not in vain. A Fury, ire-inflamed,
Avenged thy death, which those good birds pro-
  claimed,
On Corinth's ground. By greed of lucre driven,
Ye robbers, fear ye not the wrath of Heaven ?
Ægysthus, when he doomed a Bard to die,
Did not escape the black-robed Fury's eye.

" Greek Anthology."

A KITE'S CONTEST WITH AN EAGLE

Translated from the Latin of Melchior de Polignac

AMONG the Kites, one, bold beyond compare,
Had erst in harrying doves employed his care ;
At length, he—urged by fate or love of fame—
Disdained such fleeing birds and booty tame.
The Eagle, king of birds, he now provokes
To deadly strife ; with beak and wing-sent strokes,
Two or three times he dares the passing foe.
Insulted thus, no angry feelings glow
Within the Eagle's lordly heart—his flight
Sweeps calmly onward through the clouds and light.
The Kite waxed bold, waylays the homeward
    track ;
A feather plucked—trophy of quick attack—
His bill adorns.   Enough an Eagle's breast
Has borne with patience and hot rage suppressed !
Gripped is the rival, barely spared his life,
And on a rock is left—so ends the strife—
The plumeless hero, longing to be dead
To save the shame of that crestfallen head.
Undaunted still in heart, weak, shivering, bare,
On worms he feeds ; wrath, vengeance nursing
    there,
Till, with new garb and full-recovered might,
The day expected dawns,—off sails the Kite
Intent by guile (force can no hope bestow)
To match himself with his great-minded foe.

A bridge there was, by fret of stream and years
Worn out ; 'mid rotting planks a gap appears ;
The avenger destines this, a sure deceit,
If fortune favour for the foe's defeat.
He first creeps in, next passing tries its size
With cautious wings, then headlong from the skies
Shoots through.   Well-proved in all, he rises where
His conqueror ranges in the spacious air.
Straightway, as if to assault, he darts below
The indignant Eagle to invite the blow.
The royal bird prepares, and speeds his way
To rend the rebel and with death repay ;
But the false Kite darts to the ambush-cleft,
And passes safe ; headlong, of heed bereft,
Blind fury urging and the hope of spoil
Soon to reward him for the warlike toil,—
Right in the yawning hole, impetuous springs
The luckless Eagle, struggling by the wings,
Though half his body clears the narrow space.
Back flies the Kite from a near lurking-place ;
Then to avenge his wrongs, he tears the plumes
From the struck captive, and his way resumes.

C. L. Brain.

THREE EPITAPHS FROM CATULLUS III

1.—Lesbia's Bird

Ye Cupids, droop each little head,
Nor let your wings with joy be spread,
My Lesbia's favourite bird is dead,
   Whom dearer than her eyes she loved ·

For he was gentle, and so true,
Obedient to her call he flew,
No fear, no wild alarm he knew,
    But lightly o'er her bosom moved ·

And softly fluttering here and there,
He never sought to cleave the air,
But chirrup'd oft, and, free from care,
    Tuned to her ear his grateful strain.
Now having pass'd the gloomy bourne
From whence he never can return,
His death and Lesbia's grief I mourn,
    Who sighs, alas ! but sighs in vain.

Oh ! curst be thou, devouring grave !
Whose jaws eternal victims crave,
From whom no earthly power can save,
    For thou hast ta'en the bird away !
From thee, my Lesbia's eyes overflow,
Her swollen cheeks with weeping glow ;
Thou art the cause of all her woe, ·
    Receptacle of life's decay.
                                        LORD BYRON.

II.—LESBIA'S SPARROW

TELL me not of joy ! there's none,
Now my little sparrow's gone ;
    He, just as you, would sigh and woe.
He would chirp and flatter me ;
    He would hang the wing awhile,
    Till at length he saw me smile,
Lord ! how sullen he would be !

He would catch a crumb, and then
Sporting let it go again,
  He from my lip would moisture sip,
He would from my trencher feed ;
    Then would hop and then would run,
    And cry *fillip* ! when he'd done ;
Oh ! whose heart can choose but bleed ?

Oh ! how eager would he fight,
And ne'er hurt though he did bite ·
  No morn did pass, but on my glass
He would sit, and mark, and do
    What I did ; now ruffle all
    His feathers o'er, now let them fall,
And then straightway sleek them too.

Whence will Cupid get his darts
Feathered now, to pierce our hearts ?
  A wound he may, not love, convey,
Now this faithful bird is gone
    Oh ! let mournful turtles join
    With loving redbreasts, and combine
To sing dirges o'er his stone.
WILLIAM CARTWRIGHT.

III.—ON THE DEATH OF A PET SPARROW

*This the Editor believes is the first Scots Translation
of Catullus III*

COME, lads an' lasses, lovers a',
Come mourn wi' me, ye callants bra',
The bird my dearie cherishèd
Mair than her ain twa een is dead.

The sweet wee birdie ken'd her weel
    As ony bairn her mither kens,
    An' hoppin' roun'
    And up an' down,
Ne'er wander't aff to ither frien's,
But nestlin' til his mistress' breast,
For her alane wad pipe his best.
But noo 'tis gaun yon dusky track
Whaur ne'er a traveller turns back.
Foul fa' ye, fient, auld greedy carl,
That rives the bonnie frae the warl' ;
    Wee winsome birdie, stol'n frae me
    Ill was the deed,
    Aye maun ye dree't !
My lassie's bonnie een for thee
Are red wi' greetin' wearilie.
                    H. F. MORLAND SIMPSON.

ON THE RETURN OF THE SWALLOW

*A Translation of a very ancient Greek Carol preserved
by Athenæus*

THE Swallow ! the Swallow she does with her bring
Soft seasons, and all the delights of the spring ·
The Swallow ! the Swallow ! we're sure we are
    right,
For her back is all black, and her breast is all white.
From your stores, ye good housewives, produce, if
    you please,
Lumps of figs, jugs of wine, and some wheat and
    some cheese,

With some hen eggs the Swallow will well be
content,
Must we go then, or shall we have anything sent ?
We will not allow you to do as you choose,
To give or give not, to comply or refuse ;
But will certainly take from its hinges the door,
Or bear off the good dame as she sits on the floor ;
She is little and light, and we can manage her
sure.
Open, open the door to the Swallow—for we
Are playful young children, not men—you may see.

THE NEST SO HARD TO BUILD, NOW ROBBED

This poem is translated from the "Shi King" of Confucius, the old
poetry-classic of the Chinese, which represents every phase of
society in China three thousand years ago as portrayed by them-
selves. This Ode is said, by the learned translator, to have been
written by the Duke of Chow to vindicate his fidelity at a time
when he was accused of treachery towards the young King Ch'ing.

O HAWK ! O robber-hawk !
My young ones from me thou hast torn ;
My nest I pray thee spare.
With toil and tender care
I reared these young ones now I mourn.

Ere rain-clouds hid the sky
The mulberry bark I brought to bind
My lattice and my door.
You folks below me more
Would dare molest me, I opined.

With claws I pulled and tore ;—
With tugging at each stalk I met,
    With getting in my store,
    My beak grew very sore ;
Said I, " No house have I as yet."

My wings are worn and frayed ;
All torn and tattered is my tail ;
    My nest is hard to gain,
    Rocked, thrashed by wind and rain :
Nought can I do but shriek and wail.
                    WILLIAM JENNINGS.

CHAUNT TO THE SACRED IBIS OF EGYPT

O SACRED Bird !
Thou didst wander through the ancient courts of
    Egypt !
Treasured of the Pharaohs ;
Loved by all the Land !
None hadst thou to fear—
None ! not even the Hawk of Horus !
For didst thou not announce the rising of the Nile
To the worshippers of Isis, of Osiris ?
But where are those resplendent courts now,
The Temples and the Tombs ?
Aye, some still are left,
But their ancient people have departed.
Yet how great they are,
These memorials of the gods of Egypt ;
How far beyond realisation, shrouded in mystery

And thou, Bird that of old wert sacred,
Thou still at times art seen,
But thy glory, too, has vanish'd
Though the glamour of thy name remains,
O Sacred Ibis of the Nile !
With the greatness of the Pharaohs didst thy glory
    fade ·
            But why ?
Fame, where art thou gone ?
And the Pyramids,
And the Tombs of Egypt's Great Ones, echoing from
    the Past
Reply ·
            " Where art thou gone ?
            Where art thou gone ? "

                        R. M. INGERSLEY.

THE PHŒNIX AND THE TURTLE

LET the bird of loudest lay,
On the sole Arabian tree,
Herald sad and trumpet be,
To whose sound chaste wings obey.

But thou shrieking harbinger,
Foul precurrer of the fiend,
Augur of the fever's end,
To this troop come thou not near !

From this session interdict
Every fowl of tyrant wing,
Save the eagle, feather'd king ·
Keep the obsequy so strict

Let the priest in surplice white,
That defunctive music can,
Be the death-divining swan,
Lest the requiem lack his right. .

And thou treble-dated crow,
That thy sable gender makest
With the breath thou givest and takest,
'Mongst our mourners shalt thou go.

Here the anthem doth commence ·
Love and constancy is dead ;
Phœnix and the turtle fled
In a mutual flame from hence.

So they loved, as love in twain
Had the essence but in one ;
Two distincts, division none :
Number there in love was slain.

Hearts remote, yet not asunder ;
Distance, and no space was seen
'Twixt the Turtle and his queen
But in them it were a wonder.

So between them love did shine,
That the turtle saw his right
Flaming in the phœnix' sight ;
Either was the other's mine.

Property was thus appall'd,
That the self was not the same ;
Single nature's double name
Neither two nor one was call'd.

Reason, in itself confounded,
Saw division grow together,
To themselves yet either neither,
Simple were so well compounded.

That it cried, How true a twain
Seemeth this concordant one !
Love hath reason, reason none,
If what parts can so remain.

Whereupon it made this threne
To the phœnix and the dove,
Co-supremes and stars of love,
As chorus to their tragic scene.

THRENOS

Beauty, truth, and rarity,
Grace in all simplicity,
Here enclosed in cinders lie.

Death is now the phœnix' nest ;
And the turtle's loyal breast
To eternity doth rest,

Leaving no posterity :
'Twas not their infirmity,
It was married chastity.

Truth may seem, but cannot be ,
Beauty brag, but 'tis not she ;
Truth and beauty buried be.

To this urn let those repair
That are either true or fair ;
For these dead birds sigh a prayer.

WILLIAM SHAKESPEARE.

THE NEW-BORN PHŒNIX

WHEN the new-born Phœnix first is seen
Her feathered subjects all adore their queen.
And while she makes her progress through the East,
From every grove her numerous train's increased ;
Each poet of the air her glory sings,
And round him the pleased audience clap their wings.
JOHN DRYDEN.

THE EAGLE, OWL AND PHŒNIX

SOME fowls there be that have so perfect sight,
  Against the sun their eyes for to defend ;
  And some, because the light does them offend,
Never appear but in the dark or night ;
Others rejoice to see the fire so bright,
  And ween to play in it, as they pretend,
  But find contrary of it that they intend.
SIR THOMAS WYATT.

THE PARROT

PYTHAGORAS, an ancient Sage, opin'd
That form, and shape were indexes of mind ;
And minds of men, when they departed hence,
Would all be form'd according to this sense :
Some animal, or human shape again,
Would shew the minds of all the former men.

.   .   .   .

Plain in four-footed animals, let's try
Instance, that first occurs, in such as fly ·

The Parrot shews, by its unmeaning prate,
Full many a talker's metamorphos'd fate,
Whose tongue outstrips the clapper of a mill,
And still keeps saying the same nothing still:
As full the city, and as full the court,
As India's woods, with creatures of this sort,
If rightly the gay feather'd bird foretells
The future shape of eloquenter Belles,
Or Beaux, transmigrated, the human dolls
Will talk, and shine caress'd in pretty polls.

JOHN BYROM.

THE CARRIER PIGEON

I AM now Anacreon's slave,
And to me intrusted have
All the o'erflowings of his heart
To Bathyllus to impart :
Each soft line, with nimble wing,
To the lovely boy I bring.

ANACREON.

THE QUELÉTZÛ

" Now the first bird that sang on earth was the Quelétzû."—*Mexican Mythology.*

UP in the air,
Like a spirit in prayer,
With the wings of a dove, and the heart of a rose,
And a bosom as white as the Zàraby snows,
When the hurricane blows !

In the light of the day,
Like a soul on its way
To the gardens of God, it was loosed from the earth ;
And the song that it sang was a pæan of mirth
For the raptures of birth.

The song that it sang
Like an echo out-rang
From the cloud to the copse, and the copse to the
    cloud ;
And the hills and the valleys responded aloud,—
And the rivers were proud.

If you think of the rush
Of the wind, and the flush
Of a morning in May when the sun is in view,
You will know what is meant by the flight from the
    dew
Of the first Quelétzû.

If you think of these things
You will dote on the wings
Of the wonderful bird in its upward career ;
And the legends thereof will be sweeter to hear
Than the song of a seer.

You will know what is meant
By the pinioned ascent
Of an angel of grace when its mission is done,
And the knowledge of this will be second to none
Which the ages have spun.

For the lark in its nest
Is a minstrel at best,
And the music it makes is the mirth of a kiss
That is flung to the skies in a frenzy of bliss
On the morning's abyss.

And the nightingale's note
Is a sob from its throat,
And the gurgle thereof is a rapture of pain ;
For the roses are sad,—and the lilies complain,—
When the silence is slain.

All the larks in the world
With their feathers unfurled,
And the nightingales, too, in their tender despair,—
All the birds that we know have a sorrow to share
With the natives of air.

But the first Quelétzû,
When it sprang to the blue,
Had the heart of a rose, and the wings of a dove ;
And the song that it sang to the angels above
Was the music of love.

ERIC MACKAY.

THE ROC-BIRD IN THE ORIENT TALE

From the Poem entitled " Milton "

THE lovers met in twilight and in stealth.
Like to the Roc-bird in the Orient Tale,
That builds its nest in pathless pinnacles,
And there collects and there conceals the wealth,
Which paves the surface of the Diamond Vale,
Love hoards aloof the glories that it stealeth ;
And gems, but found in life's enchanted dells,
On airy heights that kiss the heaven concealeth.

LORD BULWER LYTTON.

THE JACKDAW OF RHEIMS

THE Jackdaw sat on the Cardinal's chair !
Bishop and abbot, and prior were there ;
  Many a monk, and many a friar,
  Many a knight, and many a squire,
With a great many more of lesser degree,—
In sooth a goodly company ;
And they served the Lord Primate on bended knee.
  Never, I ween, was a prouder seen,
Read of in books, or dreamt of in dreams,
Than the Cardinal Lord Archbishop of Rheims !

  In and out through the motley rout,
That little Jackdaw kept hopping about ;
  Here and there like a dog in a fair,
  Over comfits and cakes, and dishes and plates,
Cowl and cope, and rochet and pall,
Mitre and crosier ! he hopp'd upon all !

With saucy air, he perch'd on the chair
Where, in state, the great Lord Cardinal sat
In the great Lord Cardinal's great red hat ;
   And he peer'd in the face of his Lordship's Grace,
With a satisfied look, as if he would say,
" We two are the greatest folks here to-day'! "
   And the priests, with awe, as such freaks they saw,
Said, "The Devil must be in that little Jackdaw!"

The feast was over, the board was clear'd,
The flawns and the custards had all disappear'd,
And six little Singing-boys,—dear little souls !
In nice clean faces, and nice white stoles,
   Came, in order due, two by two,
Marching that grand refectory through !
A nice little boy held a golden ewer,
Emboss'd and fill'd with water, as pure
As any that flows between Rheims and Namur,
Which a nice little boy stood ready to catch
In a fine golden hand-basin made to match.
Two nice little boys, rather more grown,
Carried lavender-water, and eau-de-Cologne ;
And a nice little boy had a nice cake of soap,
Worthy of washing the hands of the Pope.
   One little boy more a napkin bore,
Of the best white diaper, fringed with pink,
And a Cardinal's Hat mark'd in " permanent ink."

The great Lord Cardinal turns at the sight
Of these nice little boys dress'd all in white :
   From his finger he draws his costly turquoise ;
And, not thinking at all about little Jackdaws,

Deposits it straight by the side of his plate,
While the nice little boys on his Eminence wait ;
Till, when nobody's dreaming of any such thing,
That little Jackdaw hops off with the ring !

There's a cry and a shout, and a deuce of a rout,
And nobody seems to know what they're about,
But the monks have their pockets all turn'd inside out ;
  The friars are kneeling, and hunting, and feeling
The carpet, the floor, and the walls, and the ceiling.
  The Cardinal drew off each plum-colour'd shoe,
And left his red stockings exposed to the view ;
  He peeps, and he feels in the toes and the heels ;
They turn up the dishes,—they turn up the plates—
They take up the poker and poke out the grates,
  —They turn up the rugs, they examine the mugs :—
But, no!—no such thing ;—they can't find the ring !
And the Abbot declared that, " when nobody
    twigg'd it,
Some rascal or other had popp'd in, and prigg'd it ! "

The Cardinal rose with a dignified look,
He call'd for his candle, his bell, and his book !
  In holy anger, and pious grief,
  He solemnly cursed that rascally thief !
He cursed him at board, he cursed him in bed ;
Form the sole of his foot to the crown of his head ;
He cursed him in sleeping, that every night
He should dream of the devil, and wake in a fright ;
He cursed him in eating, he cursed him in drinking,
He cursed him in coughing, in sneezing, in winking ;

He cursed him in sitting, in standing, in lying ;
He cursed him in walking, in riding, in flying,
He cursed him in living, he cursed him dying !—
Never was heard such a terrible curse !
But what gave rise to no little surprise,
Nobody seem'd one penny the worse !

The day was gone, the night came on,
The Monks and the Friars they search'd till dawn ;
When the Sacristan saw, on crumpled claw,
Come limping a poor little lame Jackdaw !
No longer gay, as on yesterday ;
His feathers all seem'd to be turn'd the wrong way ;—
His pinions droop'd—he could hardly stand,—
His head was as bald as the palm of your hand ;
His eye so dim, so wasted each limb,
That, heedless of grammar, they all cried, " THAT'S
    HIM !—
That's the scamp that has done this scandalous thing !
That's the thief that has got my Lord Cardinal's Ring !"

The poor little Jackdaw, when the monks he saw
Feebly gave vent to the ghost of a caw ;
And turn'd his bald head, as much as to say ;
" Pray, be so good as to walk this way ! "
Slower and slower he limp'd on before,
Till they came to the back of the belfry door,
Where the first thing they saw, 'midst the sticks
    and the straw
Was the ring in the nest of that little Jackdaw !
Then the great Lord Cardinal call'd for his book,
And off that terrible curse he took ;

The mute expression served in lieu of confession,
And, being thus coupled with full restitution,
The Jackdaw got plenary absolution !
—When those words were heard, that poor little
   bird
Was so changed in a moment, 'twas really absurd,
   He grew sleek, and fat ; in addition to that,
A fresh crop of feathers came thick as a mat !

His tail waggled more even than before ;
But no longer it wagged with an impudent air,
No longer he perch'd on the Cardinal's chair.
   He hopp'd now about with a gait devout ;
At Matins, at Vespers, he never was out ;
And, so far from any more pilfering deeds,
He always seem'd telling the Confessor's beads.
If any one lied,—or if any one swore,—
Or slumber'd in prayer-time and happen'd to snore,
   That good Jackdaw, would give a great " Caw "
As much as to say, " Don't do so any more ! "
While many remark'd, as his manners they saw,
That they "never had known such a pious Jackdaw!"
   He long lived the pride of that country side,
And at last in the odour of sanctity died ;
   When, as words were too faint, his merits to paint,
The Conclave determined to make him a Saint ;
And on newly-made Saints and Popes, as you know,
It's the custom, at Rome, new names to bestow,
So they canonised him by the name of Jim Crow !

                        RICHARD HARRIS BARHAM
                        (" Thomas Ingoldsby ").

XI
BIBLICAL BIRDS, LEGENDS, AND BIRD LESSONS

" Perchance the bald old eagle
　　On grey Beth-peor's height,
Out of his rocky eyrie,
　　Looked on the wondrous sight ;
Perchance the lion stalking
　　Still shuns that hallowed spot,
For beast and bird have seen and heard
　　That which man knoweth not."
MRS ALEXANDER.

A FAREWELL TO ADAM AND EVE

From " The Drama of Exile "

BIRD SPIRIT

I AM the nearest nightingale
That singeth in Eden after you ;
And I am singing loud and true,
And sweet,—I do not fail.
I sit upon a cypress bough,
Close to the gate ; and I fling my song
Over the gate and through the mail
Of the warden angels marshalled strong,—
    Over the gate and after you !
And the warden angels let it pass,
Because the poor brown bird, alas !
    Sings in the garden, sweet and true.

And I build my song of high pure notes,
    Note over note, height over height,
    Till I strike the arch of the Infinite
And I bridge abysmal agonies
With strong, clear calms of harmonies,—
And something abides, and something floats,
In the song which I sing after you :
    Fare ye well, farewell !

The creature-sounds, no longer audible,
    Expire at Eden's door !
    Each footstep of your treading
Treads out some cadence which ye heard before.
    Farewell ! the birds of Eden,
    Ye shall hear nevermore.

               ELIZABETH BARRETT BROWNING.

THE DOVE FROM THE ARK

RIDE on :—the ark, majestic and alone
On the wide waste of the careering deep,
Its hull scarce peering through the night of clouds,
Is seen.   But lo ! the mighty deep has shrunk !
The ark from its terrific voyage rests
On Ararat ! The raven is sent forth,
Send out the dove, and as her wings far off
Shine in the light, that streaks the severing clouds,
Bid her speed on, and greet her with a song :—

　　" Go, beautiful and gentle dove,—
　　　But whither wilt thou go ?
　　For though the clouds ride high above,
　　　How sad and waste is all below ! "
The wife of Shem, a moment to her breast
Held the poor bird, and kiss'd it.   Many a night
When she was listening to the hollow wind
She press'd it to her bosom, with a tear ;
And when it murmur'd in her hand, forgot
The long, loud tumult of the storm without.
She kisses it, and, at her father's word,
Bids it go forth.

　　　The dove flies on !   In lonely flight
　　　　She flies from dawn to dark ;
　　　And now amid the gloom of night,
　　　　Comes weary to the ark.

　　" Oh ! let me in "—she seems to say,
　　" For long and lone has been my way ;
　　Oh ! once more, gentle mistress, let me rest,
　　And dry my dripping plumage on thy breast."

So the bird flew to her who cherish'd it.
She sent it forth again out of the ark ;
Again it came at evening fall, and lo,
An olive-leaf pluck'd off, and in its bill.
And Shem's wife took the green leaf from its bill,
And kiss'd its wings again, and smilingly
Dropp'd on its neck one silent tear of joy.
She sent it forth once more and watch'd its flight,
Till it was lost amid the clouds of heaven :
Then, gazing on the clouds where it was lost,
Its mournful mistress sung this last farewell :—

" Go, beautiful and gentle dove,
    And greet the morning ray ;
For lo ! the sun shines bright above,
    And night and 'storm are pass'd away
No longer drooping, here confin'd,
    In this cold prison dwell ,
Go, free to sunshine and to wind,
    Sweet bird, go forth, and fare-thee-well.

" Oh ! beautiful and gentle dove,
    Thy welcome sad will be,
When thou shalt hear no voice of love
    In murmurs from the leafy tree ·
Yet freedom, freedom thou shalt find,
    From this cold prison cell ;
Go, then, to sunshine and to wind,
    Sweet bird, go forth, and fare-thee-well."
                    WILLIAM LISLE BOWLES.

THE WINGS OF THE DOVE

Oh ! for thy wings, thou dove !
Now sailing by with sunshine on thy breast ;
  That, borne like thee above,
I, too, might flee away, and be at rest !

  Where wilt thou fold those plumes,
Bird of the forest-shadows, holiest bird ?
  In what rich leafy glooms,
By the sweet voice of hidden waters stirred ?

  Over what blessed home,
What roof with dark, deep summer foliage crowned,
  O fair as ocean's foam !
Shall thy bright bosom shed a gleam around ?

  Or seek'st thou some old shrine
Of nymph or saint, no more by votary wooed,
  Though still, as if divine,
Breathing a spirit o'er the solitude ?

  Yet wherefore ask thy way ?
Blest, ever blest, whate'er its aim, thou art !
  Unto the greenwood spray,
Bearing no dark remembrance at thy heart

  No echoes that will blend
A sadness with the whispers of the grove ;
  No memory of a friend
Far off, or dead, or changed to thee, thou dove

Oh ! to some cool recess
Take, take me with thee on the summer wind,
　Leaving the weariness
And all the fever of this life behind ·

　The aching and the void
Within the heart whereunto none reply,
　The young bright hopes destroyed—
Bird ! bear me with thee through the sunny sky !

　Wild wish, and longing vain,
And brief upspringing to be glad and free !
　Go to thy woodland reign ;
My soul is bound and held—I may not flee.

　For even by all the fears
And thoughts that haunt my dreams—untold, un
　known,
　And burning woman's tears,
Poured from mine eyes in silence and alone ;

　Had I thy wings, thou dove !
High 'midst the gorgeous Isles of Cloud to soar,
　Soon the strong cords of love
Would draw me earthwards—homewards—yet once
　more.

Mrs Felicia Hemans.

BIRDS FORBIDDEN AS FOOD BY THE LEVITICAL LAW

See Leviticus xi. 13–19 and Deuteronomy xiv. 12–19

OF feath'red foules that fanne the bucksom aire,
Not all alike weare made for foode to men,
For, these thou shalt not eat doth God declare,
Twice tenne their nombre, and their flesh unclene ;
Fyrst the great Eagle, byrde of feignèd Jove,
Which Thebanes worshippe and diviners love.

Next Ossifrage and Ospray (both one kinde,)
Of luxurie and rapine, emblems mete,
That haunte the shores, the choicest preye to finde,
And brast the bones, and scoope the marrow swete
The Vulture, void of delicace and feare,
Who spareth not the pale dede man to teare :

The tall-built Swann, faire type of pride confest ;
The Pelicane, whose sons are nurst with bloode.
Forbidd to man ! she stabbeth deep her breast,
Self-murtheresse through fondnesse to her broode ;
They too that range the thirstie wilds emong,
The Ostryches, unthoughtful of their yonge.

The Raven, ominous (as Gentiles holde,)
What time she croaketh hoarsely *à la morte* ;
The Hawke, aerial hunter, swifte and bolde,
In feats of mischief trayned for disporte :
The vocal Cuckowe, of the faulcon race,
Obscene intruder in her neighbor's place ·

The Owle demure who loveth not the lighte
(Ill semblance she of wisdome to the Greeke,)
The smallest foul's dradd foe, the coward Kite,
And the stille Herne, arresting fishes meeke ;
The glutton Cormorante, of sullen moode,
Regarding no distinction in his foode :

The Storke which dwelleth on the fir-tree toppe,
And trusteth that no power shall hir dismaye,
As kings, on their high stations place' thir hope,
Nor wist that there be higher farre than theye ;
The gay Gier-Eagle, beautifull to viewe,
Bearyng within a savage herte untrewe.

The Ibis, whome in Egypte Israel found,
Fell byrde ! that living serpents can digest ;
The crested Lapwynge, wailing shrill arounde,
Solicitous, with no contentment blest ;
Last the foul Batt of byrde and beaste fyrst
    bredde,
Flitting with littel leathren sailes dispredde.
                  "Bibliotheca Biblica," 1725.

QUAILS AND MANNA

How quick rose their murmuring, their murmuring,
    their murmuring,
(Deep is the plaint that hungry hearts supply) :—
  " When the flesh-pots were our stay,
  Then our labours ceased with day,
  Then at night we restful lay,
                  Now we die."
'Gainst Aaron and Moses thus greediwise they cry.

The birds heard the murmuring, the murmuring, the
    murmuring ;
Swift from the sea the evening camp toward,
    Up flew the eager quail
    With wing-beats loud as hail,
    And, to still the human wail,
                On the sward
They fell, and gladly die at the biddance of their
    Lord..

A truce to their murmuring, their murmuring, their
    murmuring,
The feasters sleep at ease ; but the Angels work in-
    stead :
    Round the camp their myriads flew—
    Where they touched the starlit dew,
    There a seed-like treasure grew,
                Heavenly Bread
WHAT IS THIS ? they wakening cried, and reaped
    it ere it fled.

                                    D.

THE OSTRICH

A Paraphrase upon Job xxxix.

THE peacock, not at thy command, assumes
His glorious train ; nor ostrich her rare plumes.
She drops her eggs upon the naked land,
And wraps them in a bed of hatching sand,
Exposèd to the wand'ring traveller,
And feet of beasts, which those wild deserts rear.

She as a step-mother betrays her own,
Left without care, and presently unknown ;
By God depriv'd of that intelligence
Which Nature gives ; of all most void of sense.
Her feet the nimble rider leave behind,
And, when she spreads her sails, outstrip the wind.

GEORGE SANDYS.

ELIJAH AND THE RAVENS

SORE was the famine throughout all the bounds
Of Israel, when Elijah, by command
Of God, journeyed to Cherith's failing brook ;
No rain-drops fell, no dew-fraught cloud, at morn,
Or closing eve, creeps slowly up the vale ;
The withering herbage dies ; among the palms,
The shrivelled leaves send to the summer gale
An autumn rustle ; no sweet songster's lay
Is warbled from the branches ; scarce is heard
The rill's faint brawl. The prophet looks around,
And trusts in God, and lays his silvered head
Upon the flowerless bank ; serene he sleeps,
Nor wakes till dawning ; then with hands enclasped,
And heavenward face, and eyelids closed, he prays
To Him who manna on the desert showered,
To Him who from the rock made fountains gush :
Entranced the man of God remains ; till roused
By sound of wheeling wings, with grateful heart,
He sees the ravens fearless by his side
Alight, and leave the heaven-provided food.

JAMES GRAHAME.

ELIJAH FED BY RAVENS

ELIJAH's example declares,
  Whatever distress may betide,
The saints may commit all their cares
  To Him who will surely provide ;
When rain long withheld from the earth
  Occasioned a famine of bread,
The prophet, secured from the dearth,
  By ravens was constantly fed.

More likely to rob than to feed
  Were ravens who lived upon prey ;
But when the Lord's people have need,
  His goodness will find out a way
This instance to those may seem strange
  Who know not how faith can prevail ;
But sooner all nature shall change
  Than one of God's promises fail.

Nor is it a singular case ·
  The wonder is often renewed ;
And many can say, to His praise,
  He sends them by ravens their food ·
Thus worldlings, though ravens indeed,
  Though greedy and selfish their mind,
If God has a servant to feed,
  Against their own wills can be kind.

Thus Satan, that raven unclean,
  Who croaks in the ears of the saints,
Compelled by a power unseen
  Administers oft to their wants ;

God teaches them how to find food,
From all the temptations they feel ;
This raven who thirsts for my blood
Has helped me to many a meal.

How safe and how happy are they
Who on the Good Shepherd rely !
He gives them out strength for their day,
Their wants He will surely supply ;
He, ravens and lions can tame,
All creatures obey His command ;
Then let me rejoice in His name,
And leave all my cares in His hand.

JOHN NEWTON.

GOD'S CARE OF BIRDS

OUR bark is on the waters ! wide around
The wandering wave ; above, the lonely sky
Hush ! a young sea-bird floats, and that quick cry
Shrieks to the levelled weapon's echoing sound :
Grasp its lank wing, and on, with reckless bound
Yet, creature of the surf, a sheltering breast
To-night shall haunt in vain thy far-off nest,
A call unanswered search the rocky ground.
Lord of leviathan ! when Ocean heard
Thy gathering voice, and sought his native breeze ;
When whales first plunged with life, and the
proud deep
Felt unborn tempests heave in troubled sleep,
Thou didst provide, even for this nameless bird,
Home and a natural love amid the surging seas.

ROBERT STEPHEN HAWKER.

GOD'S BIRD

NAY, not Thine eagle, Lord ;
  No golden eagle I,
That creep half-fainting on the sward
  And have not wings to fly.

Nor yet Thy swallow dear,
  That, faring home to Thee,
Looks on the storm and hath no fear
  And broods above the sea.

Nor yet Thy tender dove,
  Meek as Thyself, Thou Lamb !
I would I were the dove, Thy love,
  And not the thing I am !

But take me in Thy hand,
  To be Thy sparrow, then ;
Were two sparrows in Holy Land,
  One farthing bought the twain.

Make me Thy sparrow, then,
  That trembles in Thy hold ;
And who shall pluck me out again
  And cast me in the cold ?

But if I fall at last,
  A thing of little price,
If Thou one thought on me hast cast,
  Lo, then my paradise !
        MRS KATHARINE TYNAN HINKSON.

TWO NIGHTINGALES

Translated from " Procopii Mariale Festivale,"
Seventeenth Century

Two nightingales we often hear
Down in some valley singing :
'Tis wonder-sweet when far and near
They set the place a-ringing :
Their carols charm the passer-by
As vie they one with other,
Yet either would far liefer die
Than give way to his brother.

Two nightingales, I hear them yet ·
An Angel sent from glory,
Yet not by chance, to Nazaret,
Into one upper-storey.
How sweetly sung that Virgin bright,
The blissful Maid, Maria ;
No mortal tongue can sing aright
Her dulcet harmonïa.

'Twas no mere echo of thin air—
Her voice with his united ;
Would God I had been standing there—
My heart had been ignited.
No sweeter song in heavenly hall
Than this is sung ; no, never ;
When Hallows chant in chorus all
" Thy will be done " for ever.

GEORGE RATCLIFFE WOODWARD.

THE NOËL OF THE BIRDS

THE SUMMONS OF THE ANGELS TO THE BIRDS ON
THE EVE OF THE NATIVITY

CAME a voice from the sky
In a mid-winter night,
" I will show you ' The Light,'
All ye birds who can fly—
From afar ! From afar !
To the East ! To the East !
Ye must follow the Star."

THE ANSWER OF THE BIRDS

'' With the Angels we'll fly,
And our tribute we'll bring
To present to ' the King,' ''
Said the birds in reply—
" From afar ! From afar !
To the East ! To the East
We will follow the Star."

THE STAR GUIDES THE BIRDS TO BETHLEHEM

And the Star led them on—
By its light they were led
To the rude cattle-shed
Where the " Saviour " was born.
From their homes ! From afar
To the Birth-place of Christ
They had followed the Star.

The Songs of the Birds
Then the birds stood around
And sang each a sweet air
To the Infant so fair—
Who applauded the sound.
" From our homes ! From afar ! "
Said the birds to the Child,
" We have come with the Star."

The Song of the Swallow
" Oh ! the housetop is cold,"
Sang the sweet Hirondelle—
" I will build a new cell—
I'm a bricklayer bold—
From my home ! From afar !
I came with the Angels,
I came with the Star."

The Song of the Skylark
" I'm the Herald of Day,"
Sang the Lark from the sky,
" Higher ! Higher ! I fly
As I pour forth my lay—
From on high ! From afar !
Sweetest music I'll sing
By the side of the Star."

The Song of the Dove
" I bring peace," said the Dove—
" From the ' Father ' I bring,
And for ever I'll sing
Words of infinite love—

From the sky !   From afar !
I bring peace unto all
From the land of the Star ! "

THE SONG OF THE GOLDEN-CRESTED WREN

" I am small," sang the Wren,
" My gold feathers I bring
As tribute to the King,
The Redeemer of Men,
And I've flown from afar,
Little bird that I am—
By the help of the Star."

THE SONG OF THE NIGHTINGALE

" I'm the Minstrel of Night,"
Sang the sweet Nightingale.
" When all other songs fail
Mine alone shall delight
The Sweet Child from afar !
Whose Advent to the World
Is proclaim'd by the Star."

THE SONG OF ALL THE BIRDS

From each bird there arose
Songs of Peace and Good-will,
That the wide world should fill,
As the Angels foretold.
The Angels from afar !—
Sent as heralds of Peace,
They had followed the Star.

THE SONG OF THE LITTLE CHILDREN

" Let us join with the birds
In their praise of the ' King,'
With their songs as they sing,
Let us mingle our words,
And praise Him—from afar !
Who came here for us all,
And was shown by the Star."

BY A NUN.

AN EASTER LEGEND OF THE SKYLARK

THERE is a legend somewhere told
Of how the skylark came of old
   To the dying Saviour's cross,
And, encircling round that form of pain,
Poured forth a wild lamenting strain
   As if for human loss.

Pierced by those accents of despair,
Upon the little mourner there
   Turning His fading eyes,
The Saviour said, " Dost thou so mourn,
And is thy fragile heart so torn,
   That Man, thy Brother, dies ?

" O'er all the world uplifted high,
We are alone here, thou and I ;
   And near to heaven and thee,
I bless thy pity-guided wings,
I bless thy voice, the last that sings
   Love's requiem to Me !

" Sorrow shall cease to fill thy song ;
Those frail and fluttering wings grow strong,
   Thou shalt no longer fly,
Earth's captive—nay, but boldly dare
The azure vault, and upward bear
   Thy raptures to the sky ! "

So passed the Saviour, but the lark,
   Could not his grief abate ;
And, nigh the watchers of the tomb,
Still mourning through days of grief and gloom,
   With note disconsolate.

But when to those sad mourners came,
In rose and amethyst of flame,
   The Dawn Miraculous,
Song in which sorrow had no part.
Burst from the lark's triumphant heart—
   Sweet and tumultuous !

An instant, as with rapture blind,
He faltered ; then, his Lord to find,
   Straight to the ether flew,—
Rising where falls no human tear,
Singing where still his song we hear
   Piercing the upper blue.

                              FLORENCE COATES.

THE LEGEND OF THE CROSSBILL

From the German of Julius Mosen

ON the cross the dying Saviour
Heavenward lifts his eyelids calm,
Feels, but scarcely feels, a trembling
In his pierced and bleeding palm.

And by all the world forsaken,
Sees He how with zealous care
At the ruthless nail of iron
A little bird is striving there.

Stained with blood and never tiring,
With its beak it doth not cease,
From the cross 'twould free the Saviour,
Its Creator's Son release.

And the Saviour speaks in mildness
" Blest be thou of all the good !
Bear, as token of this moment,
Marks of blood and holy rood ! "

And that bird is called the Crossbill ;
Covered all with blood so clear,
In the groves of pine it singeth
Songs, like legends, strange to hear.
                    HENRY W. LONGFELLOW.

A LEGEND OF THE ROBIN REDBREAST

(Why the Robin's Breast is Red)

THE Saviour, bowed beneath His cross, climbed up
the dreary hill,
And from the agonising wreath ran many a crimson
rill ;
The cruel Roman thrust Him on with unrelenting
hand,
Till, staggering slowly 'mid the crowd He fell upon
the sand.

A little bird that warbled near, that memorable day,
Flitted around and strove to wrench one single thorn
away.
The cruel spike impaled his breast, and thus, 'tis
sweetly said,
The robin has his silver vest incarnadined with red.

Ah, Jesu ! Jesu ! Son of Man ! My dolour and my
sighs
Reveal the lesson taught by this winged Ishmael of
the skies.
I, in the palace of delight or cavern of despair,
Have plucked no thorns from Thy dear brow, but
planted thousands there !

JAMES RYDER RANDALL.

THE COMPASSIONATE BULBUL

WHILE our Lord lay in the tomb,
Cold and still in earth's dark womb,
A bulbul from the olive shade,
All through the night its homage paid.

Saddest music ever heard,
Was the plaint of that small bird,
Flooding with its melody
That new rock-cave by Calvary.

When the sun's first shining ray
Tipped the clouds on Easter-day,
His mate's eggs were changed in hue,
Sparkling gold, red, crimson, blue.

Mindful of that singer lone
O'er the sepulchre's sealed stone,
Easter eggs unto this day,
Are often decked with colours gay.

ADA LOVEGROVE.

THE ROBIN

MY old Welsh neighbour over the way
    Crept slowly out in the sun of spring,
Pushed from her ears the locks of gray,·
    And listened to hear the robin sing.

Her grandson, playing at marbles, stopped,
    And, cruel in sport as boys will be,
Tossed a stone at the bird, who hopped
    From bough to bough in the apple-tree.

" Nay!" said the grandmother, "have you not
   heard,
   My poor, bad boy ! of the fiery pit,
And how, drop by drop, this merciful bird
   Carries the water that quenches it ?

" He brings cool dew in his little bill,
   And lets it fall on the souls of sin ·
You can see the mark on his red breast still
   Of fires that scorch as he drops it in.

" My poor Bron rhuddyn ! my breast-burned bird,
   Singing so sweetly from limb to limb,
Very dear to the heart of our Lord
   Is he who pities the lost like Him ! "

" Amen ! " I said to the beautiful myth ;
   " Sing, bird of God, in my heart as well
Each good thought is a drop wherewith
   To cool and lessen the fires of hell.

" Prayers of love like rain-drops fall,
   Tears of pity are cooling dew,
And dear to the heart of our Lord are all
   Who suffer like Him in the good they do   "
                    JOHN GREENLEAF WHITTIER.

EIDER DUCKS

A Saxon Legend of St Cuthbert

OTHERS came
And thus demanded : " Rumour fills the world,
Father, that birds miraculous crowned thine isle,
And awe-struck let thee lift them in thy hand,
Though scared by all beside." Smiling once more,
The Saint made answer, " True, and yet not true !
Sea-birds elsewhere beheld not through that isle ;
A breed so loving and so firm in trust
That, yet unharmed by man, they flee not man ;
Wondering they gaze ; who wills may close upon
 them !
I signed a league betwixt that race and man,
Pledging the mariners who sought my cell
To reverence still that trust."

AUBREY DE VERE.

THE SERMON OF ST FRANCIS TO THE BIRDS

Up soared the lark into the air,
A shaft of song, a wingèd prayer,
As if a soul, released from pain,
Were flying back to heaven again.

St Francis heard ;. it was to him
An emblem of the Seraphim ;
The upward motion of the fire,
The light, the heat, the heart's desire.

Around Assisi's convent gate
The birds, God's poor who cannot wait,
From moor and mere and darksome wood
Came flocking for their dole of food.

" O brother birds ! " St Francis said,
" Ye come to me and ask for bread,
But not with bread alone to-day
Shall ye be fed and sent away.

" Ye shall be fed, ye happy birds,
With manna of celestial words ;
Not mine, though mine they seem to be,
Not mine, though they be spoke through me.

" O doubly are ye bound to praise
The great Creator in your lays ;
He giveth you your plumes of down,
Your crimson hoods, your cloaks of brown.

" He giveth you your wings to fly
And breathe a purer air on high,
And careth for you everywhere,
Who for yourselves so little care ! "

With flutter of swift wings and songs
Together rose the feathered throngs,
And singing scattered far apart ;
Deep peace was in St Francis' heart.

He knew not if the brotherhood
His homily had understood ;
He only knew that to one ear
The meaning of his words was clear.

HENRY W. LONGFELLOW.

A LEGEND WITHIN A LEGEND

St Francis fain would preach to the birds.
He sat him down in a quiet nook,
With finger uplifted and open book,
And they all came circling to hear his words.

They flew from north, south, east and west ·
The giant eagle, the dove, the wren,
The swallow, the robin held dear by men
For his trustfulness and his crimson vest ;

The linnet, the peacock, the swan, the crow ;
The lark and the sorrowful nightingale ;
The sea-mew borne on the sobs of the gale,
And brown little sparrows ranged close in a row.

St Francis prayed, and his voice rang sweet.
He preached God's truths in a tone inspired ;
With loving fervour his heart was fired
For the feathered creatures about his feet.

He stretched his hands, and he blessed them all.
He blessed them once and be blessed them twice ;
His tears came fast as he blessed them thrice,
God's beautiful songsters both great and small.

For joy they sang 'as away they flew,
Passed swift as a rainbow that fades from sight ;
The woods dusk'd sudden of colour and light,
But sweet echoes clung to the trees like dew.

The shadows of evening crept o'er the wold ;
St Francis pillowed his head and dreamed ;
And, as he slumbered, to him it seemed
That the lesson he'd taught was strangely retold.

Again the sky glittered with beat of wings.
The birds crowded back and dropt to ground.
They perched on the bushes, they fluttered around ;
The grass space was filled, with the lovely things.

" O   man ! "   so   they   twittered—" O   man,   you
    would preach
To us, who rise upward while you sit and wait ;
You count grains of dust, we float to heav'n's gate ;
You   dread   the   sun's   glare,   though   its   glory   you
    teach

" Then hearken our rede.   The Lord's bidding we do.
We are messengers, types, what you will, whom He
    sends
With the flowers to beautify earth ; thus He lends
Some   threads   from   His   robe   your   poor   world   to
    endue."

To the saint, in procession, each bird flits anear,
And tells of its mission.   " From even until morn
I sing," quoth the nightingale, " pierced by a thorn,
Till dark depths of pain I no longer fear."

" I am weakest of all the birds that be,"
Chirped the wren, " yet fire I brought of yore,
A power and blessing unknown before."
Said the kingfisher :   " Storms lull to calm for me.

"Those halcyon days are mine, when the breath
Of Eden but parts the west wind's lips."
"And I," piped the redwing, "guard fisher-ships,
And give good luck to the nets beneath."

"I listened," the lark said, "but yester-morn
To an angel that carolled at heav'n's own door,
And the jewel-strung notes for evermore
I'll trill from my nest in the yellow corn."

"Alas!" quoth the peacock, "some term me vain,
Yet a picture of life's immortality,
From ancient time hath each sage held me,
For eternity's emblems my plumage stain."

"Nay," sang the robin, "I chose to bear
Unto souls in pain cool water to drink ;
What though I singed my breast at the brink
Of the fiery gulf that was raging there ? "

"I," cried the woodpecker, "brought spring-root
To unlock the treasures of elves and gnomes."
"But I bring joy to the poorest homes,"
The sweet thrush warbled. "Ah me! I am mute,"

The swan sighed low. "Yet, when death shall numb
These pinions, and stay their beauteous flight,
My soul will burst with song's delight,
And make earth's music wax poor and dumb."

" 'Tis given to me the form to wear
Of God's own Spirit and tenderest love ;
A message of purity," crooned the dove,
" To sinful mortals I gladly bear."

" But the Saviour hung on the shameful rood,"
The cross-bill spake ; " I sought to draw
A cruel nail for His ease ; He saw,
And bless'd my wings with His glorious blood."

Now came a rushing sound that fill'd
The tremulous air, and an eagle sped,
As lightning shaft hurled from overhead,
To bear his witness in cry that thrill'd.

" Lo ! I have seen far beyond man's ken,
I, bid to climb to the Lord's high throne,
Of all His creatures preferred alone
To guide an apostle's inspired pen."

The eagle ceased, and from out the crowd
Throbbed forth a pæan of love and praise
" *Te Deum Laudamus*, all Thy ways
Are wondrous and good ! " Thus the birds sang
    loud.

And their *Gloria in excelsis* broke
From the fringe of the woods to the distant mere,
With a rapture of voices strong and clear—
St Francis turned in his sleep, and woke.

New dawn in the east showed faint and dim—
A saffron girdle across the grey.
The daisies opened to greet the day.
The sparrows were chirping their morning hymn.

LADY LINDSAY.

WALTER VON DER VOGELWEID

VOGELWEID the Minnesinger,
  When he left this world of ours,
Laid his body in the cloister,
  Under Würtzberg's minster towers.

And he gave the monks his treasures,
  Gave them all with this behest ·
They should feed the birds at noontide
  Daily on his place of·rest ;

Saying " From these wandering minstrels
  I have learned the art of song ;
Let me now repay the lessons
  They have taught so well and long."

Thus the bard of love departed ;
  And fulfilling his desire,
On his tomb the birds were feasted
  By the children of the choir.

Day by day, o'er tower and turret,
  In foul weather and in fair,
Day by day in vaster numbers,
  Flocked the poets of the air.

On the tree whose heavy branches
  Overshadowed all the place,
On the pavement, on the tombstone,
  On the poet's sculptured face.

On the cross-bars of each window,
  On the lintel of each door,
They renewed the War of Wartburg,
  Which the bard had fought before.

There they sang their merry carols,
  Sang their lauds on every side ;
And the name their voices uttered
  Was the name of Vogelweid.

Till at length the portly abbot
  Murmured, " Why this waste of food ?
Be it changed to loaves henceforward
  For our fasting brotherhood."

Then in vain o'er tower and turret,
  From the walls and woodland nests,
When the minster bells rang noontide,
  Gathered the unwelcome guests.

Then in vain, with cries discordant,
  Clamorous round the Gothic spire,
Screamed the feathered Minnesingers
  For the children of the choir.

Time has long effaced the inscriptions
On the cloister's funeral stones,
And tradition only tells us
Where repose the poet's bones.

But around the vast cathedral,
By sweet echoes multiplied,
Still the birds repeat the legend,
And the name of Vogelweid.
HENRY W. LONGFELLOW.

THE BIRD

From " Silex Scintillans "

HITHER thou com'st : the busy wind all night
Blew through thy lodging, where thy own warm
wing
Thy pillow was.   Many a sullen storm,
For which coarse man seems much the fitter born,
Rain'd on thy bed
And harmless head.

And now as fresh and cheerful as the light
Thy little heart in early hymns doth sing
Unto that Providence, whose unseen arm
Curb'd them, and cloth'd thee well and warm.
All things that be praise Him ; and had
Their lesson taught them when first made.
HENRY VAUGHAN.

THE MERLE AND NIGHTINGALE

This poem is one of the best of Dunbar's moral ones. In it he represents a contest between a merle and a nightingale as to the merits of earthly and heavenly love. The stanzas of the merle end with a recommendation of a "life in Love's service." The nightingale declared that "All love is lost but upon God alone." The nightingale won over the merle, who at last confessed her error, and sang too, "All love is lost but upon God alone."

THEN sang they both with voices loud and clear,
The Merle sang, "Man, love God that has thee wrought."
The Nightingale sang, "Man, love the Lord most dear,
That thee and all this world made of nought."
The Merle said, "Love Him that thy love has sought
Fro' heaven to earth, and here took flesh and bone."
The Nightingale sang, "And with His death thee bought ;
All love is lost but upon Him alone."

WILLIAM DUNBAR.

BIRDS AS TEACHERS OF HUMILITY

THE bird that soars on highest wing,
    Builds on the ground her lowly nest ;
And she that doth most sweetly sing,
    Sings in the shade when all things rest ·
In lark and nightingale we see
What honour hath *humility*.

The saint that wears heaven's brightest crown,
  In deepest adoration bends ;
The weight of glory bows him down,
  Then most, when most his soul ascends ·
Nearest the throne itself must be
The footstool of *humility*.

JAMES MONTGOMERY.

THE STORK

THE stork's an emblem of true piety ;
Because, when age has seized and made his dam
Unfit for flight, the grateful young one takes
His mother on his back, provides her food,
Repaying thus her tender care of him
Ere he was fit to fly.

FRANCIS BEAUMONT.

DESPONDENCY IN SPRING

BEAUTIFUL robin ! with thy feathers red
  Contrasting, flower-like, with the soft green tree,
Making thy little flights, as thou art led
  By things that tempt a simple one like thee.
I would that thou couldst warble me to tears
As lightly as the birds of other years !
  Idly to lie beneath an April sun,
Pressing the perfume from the tender grass ;
  To watch a joyous rivulet leap on

With the clear tinkle of a music glass,
And, as I saw the early robin pass,
  To hear him through his little compass run—
Only with joys like these to overflow
Is happiness my heart will no more know.
NATHANIEL PARKER WILLIS.

MAN'S MORTALITY

LIKE to the damask rose you see,
Or like a blossom on a tree,
Or like a dainty flower of May,
Or like the morning to the day,
Or like the sun, or like the shade,
Or like the gourd which Jonas had,
E'en such is man ;—whose thread is spun,
Drawn out, and cut, and so is done.—
The rose withers, the blossom blasteth,
The flower fades, the morning hasteth,
The sun sets, the shadow flies,
The gourd consumes ;—the man he dies.
Like to the grass that's newly sprung,
Or like a tale that's new begun,
Or like the bird that's here to-day,
Or like the pearly dew of May,
Or like an hour, or like a span,
Or like the singing of a swan,
E'en such is man ;—who lives by breath,
Now here, now there, in life and death.—

The grass withers, the tale is ended,
The bird is flown, the dew's ascended,
The hour is short, the span not long,
The swan's near death—man's life is done.
SIMON WASTELL.

STABILITY OF SCIENCE

THE feeble sea-birds, blinded in the storms,
On some tall light-house dash their little forms,
And the rude granite scatters for their pains
Those small deposits that were meant for brains.
Yet the proud fabric in the morning's sun
Stands all unconscious of the mischief done ;
Still the red beacon pours its evening rays
For the lost pilot with as full a blaze,
Nay, shines, all radiance, o'er the scattered fleet
Of gulls and boobies brainless at its feet.
I tell their fate, though courtesy disclaims
To call our kind by such ungentle names ;
Yet, if your rashness bid you vainly dare,
Think of their doom, ye simple, and beware !
OLIVER WENDELL HOLMES.

THE NIGHTINGALE

SOLE singer in the world of dreams,
  Whose voice, outringing clear and far
Into the empty darkness, seems
  An echo from a distant star,

Thou comest, as God's angels will,
    When day and all its noisier mirth,
Gone past us like a wind, are still :
    The stars in heaven and thou on earth.

Thou singest yet in all the years,
    In all the years the stars arise,
When sleep has dulled our heedless ears
    And weighs like death upon our eyes.

And ah ! outworn with sordid cares,
    We drowse in other glooms supine,
Blind even to greater light than theirs,
    And deaf to loftier songs than thine.

But still they shine though none should see ;
    And singest thou, unheard, forgot,
Save in lone night-times, it may be,
    When they and thou shall know it not,

Their shining makes some pathway bright ;
    One hears thee as he toils along,
And passes onward through the night,
    Glad in their splendour, and thy song.

                         A. St John Adcock.

THE CUCKOO'S CALL

The Celtic superstition is that a long journey lies before you in the direction you are looking when you hear the cuckoo first in spring.

THERE'S a long good-bye for you and me,
And a long good-bye for all ;
For I stood yestreen above the sea,
And I heard the cuckoo's call !

And the shadows crept across the deep,
The waves were hushed and still ·
And we looked where the loved ones lie asleep
In the graveyard on the hill.

Oh, my heart grew like a house of dreams
Where mournful echoes dwell,
And a thought lay o'er the hills and streams
That words can never tell.

Oh, the long road's waiting you and me—
The long road waits us all ;
For we stood yestreen above the sea,
And heard the cuckoo's call !

LAUCHLAN MACLEAN WATT.

THE WINGED WORSHIPPERS

To Two Swallows in a Church

GAY, guiltless pair !
What seek ye from the fields of heaven ?
Ye have no need of prayer,
Ye have no sins to be forgiven.

Why perch ye here,
Where mortals to their Maker bend ?
Can your pure spirits fear
The God ye never could offend ?

Ye never knew
The crimes for which we come to weep :
Penance is not for you,
Bless'd wanderers of the upper deep !

To you 'tis given
To wake sweet nature's untaught lays ;
Beneath the arch of heaven
To chirp away a life of praise.

Then spread each wing,
Far, far above, o'er lakes and lands,
And join the choirs that sing
In yon blue dome not rear'd with hands

Or, if ye stay,
To note the consecrated hour,
Teach me the airy way,
And let me try your envied power !

Above the crowd
On upward wings could I but fly,
I'd bathe in yon bright cloud,
And seek the stars that gem the sky.

'Twere heaven indeed,
Through fields of trackless light to soar,
On nature's charms to feed,
And nature's own great God adore.

CHARLES SPRAGUE.

THE VAIN TOUCAN, THE HORNBILL AND THE LITTLE GREEN TODY

(A BIRD LESSON)

IN a certain great forest, of which I've heard,
All things were at peace, both with beast and with
    bird.
Ill-will and dissension, all vanity, guile,
Tabooed by the birds as excessively vile !
At last rose a Toucan, a raucous old bird,
Who averred that his beak was quite the last word
In size and in structure, utility, length,
In ornamentation, capacity, strength.
He issued a challenge to all the birds there
To find such another with it to compare !
His listeners, vexed by this very vain speech,
To keep the peace fled from his garrulous screech ;
Save one little Tody, in brilliant green,
With delicate hues of a glossy soft sheen,
Who answered the Toucan in accents demure :—
" Your beak is a wonder ! but don't be too sure,
It cannot be equalled or even excelled
By birds, my good sir, whom you never beheld ! "
The Toucan shrieked long when he heard the bird
    small
In dainty green habit, and loud did he call
That his challenge held good for aye and a day !
Then raised up his bill and flew off on his way.
But the little Green Tody was satisfied quite,
Though before him there lay a most hazardous flight

If he wished to accomplish his object with skill !
'Twas to visit the haunt of an ancient Hornbill !
At once he set out for the Old World, and flew
Through skies that were stormy and skies that were
    blue.
Many wonderful sights did he see on his way,
But he stayed not his flight nor made any delay
Save to eat and to rest ; and at last he drew nigh
To the land that he came to seek, far through the sky ;
And now it was twilight ! He entered the shade
Of an old, vast forest, and there in a glade,
Through the aisles of the trees, with the light growing
    dim,
He espied a weird figure ; 'twas equally grim
As any mad Toucan he ever had seen.
" That must be the Hornbill I look for, I ween ! "
Quoth the little Green Tody ; and next did alight
On a neighbouring tree, and with words very trite
Addressed the old Hornbill, explaining his case
And ending his speech with admirable grace,
Saying, " Now you know this vain-glorious bird,
This Toucan, of whom you have possibly heard,
Imagines he owns the most marvellous beak,
Perhaps, just to teach him opinions more meek,
By my side you'll return to the land far away
Where the beak of the Toucan at present holds sway
His colours may rival all birds of the wood ;
His bill equal yours ! but 'tis lacking a *hood* !
If any may humble the pride of the Toucan
There is not a doubt, ancient bird, but that you
   can ! "

The Hornbill, on hearing the Green Tody's tale
Agreed to go with him o'er mountain and vale !
So back o'er the forests, o'er lake, sea, and hill
Flew the small green bird and the ancient Hornbill.
Very little indeed now remains to be told ;
The Toucan once more, looking wonderfully bold,
Was haranguing the birds on the same old romance
Of his glorious beak ; when on chancing to glance
Through trees in the distance, he saw with a thrill
The Tody, but—who owns that terrible bill ?
When, seeing its beak with the horn on its head,
Not waiting to argue, he instantly fled !
The little Green Tody, his object obtained,
Flew calmly away, but his lesson remained
In the mind of the Toucan, who, never again,
In spite of his beak, was accused of being vain !

R. M. INGERSLEY.

THE THRUSH AND THE PIE

(A TALE)

CONCEAL'D within an hawthorn bush,
We're told that an experienced Thrush
Instructed, in the prime of spring,
Many a neighb'ring bird to sing :
She caroll'd, and her various song
Gave lessons to the list'ning throng ·
But (th'entangling boughs between)
'Twas her delight to teach unseen.

At length the little wond'ring race
Would see their fav'rite face to face :
They thought it hard to be deny'd,
And begg'd that she'd no longer hide,
O'er-modest, worth's peculiar fault.
Another shade the tut'ress sought,
And, loth to be too much admir'd,
In secret from the bush retir'd.

An impudent, presuming Pie,
Malicious, ignorant, and sly,
Stole to the matron's vacant seat,
And in her arrogance elate,
Rush'd forward—with—" My friends, you see
The mistress of the choir in me ;
Here be your due devotion paid ;
I am the songstress of the shade."

A linnet, that sat list'ning nigh,
Made the impostor this reply :
" I fancy, Friend ! that vulgar throats
Were never form'd for warbling notes ;
But if these lessons came from you,
Repeat them in the public view
That your assertions may be clear,
Let us behold as well as hear."

The length'ning song, the soft'ning strain,
Our chatt'ring Pie attempts in vain ;
For, to the fool's eternal shame,
All she could compass was a scream

The birds, enrag'd, around her fly,
Nor shelter nor defence is nigh :
The caitiff wretch, distress'd—forlorn,
On ev'ry side is peck'd and torn,
Till, for her vile atrocious lies,
Under their angry beaks she dies.
Such be his fate whose scoundrel claim
Obtrudes upon a neighbour's fame.
                                JOHN CUNNINGHAM.

THE RAVEN

ONCE upon a midnight dreary, while I pondered,
    weak and weary,
Over many a quaint and curious volume of forgotten
    lore—
While I nodded, nearly napping, suddenly there
    came a tapping,
As of some one gently rapping, rapping at my
    chamber door ;
" 'Tis some visitor," I muttered, " tapping at my
    chamber door—
        Only this, and nothing more."

Open here I flung the shutter, when, with many a
    flirt and flutter,
In there stepped a stately Raven of the saintly days
    of yore ;
Not the least obeisance made he, not a minute
. stopped or stayed he ;

But with mien of lord or lady, perched above my
  chamber door
Perched upon a bust of Pallas, just above my
  chamber door—
    Perched, and sat, and nothing more.

Then this ebon bird beguiling my sad fancy into
  smiling,
By the stern and grave decorum of the countenance
  it wore,
" Though thy crest be shorn and shaven, thou," said
  I, " art sure no craven,
Ghastly, grim, and ancient Raven, wandering from
  the nightly shore
Tell me what thy lordly name is on the night's
  Plutonian shore ! "
    Quoth the Raven · " Never more."

But the Raven still beguiling all my sadness into
  smiling,
Straight I wheeled a cushioned seat in front of bird
  and bust and door ;
Then upon the velvet sinking, I betook myself to
· linking
Fancy unto fancy, thinking what this ominous bird
  of yore—
What this grim, ungainly, ghastly, gaunt and omin-
  ous bird of yore
    Meant in croaking " Never more."

And the Raven, never flitting, still is sitting, still is
sitting,
On the pallid bust of Pallas, just above my chamber
door ;
And his eyes have all the seeming of a demon's that
is dreaming,
And the lamplight, o'er him streaming, throws his
shadow on the floor ;
And my soul from out that shadow that lies floating
on the floor,
    Shall be lifted—never more !

EDGAR ALLAN POE.

THE MARINER AND THE ALBATROSS

From " The Rime of the Ancient Mariner "

AT length did cross an Albatross ·
Thorough the fog it came ;
As if it had been a Christian soul,
We hailed it in God's name.

.   .   .   .   .

In mist or cloud, on mast or shroud,
It perched for vespers nine ;
Whiles all the night, through fog-smoke white,
Glimmered the white moon-shine.

*The ancient Mariner inhospitably killeth the pious
bird of good omen.*

And I had done a hellish thing,
And it would work 'em woe ;
For all averred, I had killed the bird
That made the breeze to blow.
"Ah, wretch ! " said they, "the bird to slay,
That made the breeze to blow ! "

Ah ! well-a-day ! what evils looks
Had I from old and young !
Instead of the cross, the Albatross
About my neck was hung.

Beyond the shadow of the ship,
I watched the water-snakes ·
They moved in tracks of shining white,
And when they reared, the elfish light
Fell off in hoary flakes.

O happy living things ! no tongue
Their beauty might declare ·
A spring of love gushed from my heart,
And I blessed them unaware !
Sure my kind saint took pity on me,
And I blessed them unaware.

The selfsame moment I could pray ;
And from my neck so free
The Albatross fell off, and sank
Like lead into the sea.
                    SAMUEL TAYLOR COLERIDGE.

MY WINGS

YE are my wings, dear suffering birds,
That tell us daily how to fly,
And teach me, if in broken words,
New charity.
Ye do uplift me and the globe,
Which but for sorrows could not rise,
That are the jewels in the robe
Of Paradise.

F. W. ORDE WARD.

HEAVEN FLIES DOWN ON LITTLE WINGS

From " Clear Waters "

ANGELS to me no message bring ·
I cannot hear their harps accord ·
But often from a sparrow's wing
There falls the glory of the Lord.

FREDERICK LANGBRIDGE.

GOLDEN WINGS

LISTEN, sweet dove, unto my song,
And spread thy golden wings on me;
Hatching my tender heart so long,
Till it get wing, and fly away with thee.

GEORGE HERBERT.

DAWN AND THE KING'S FUNERAL

20th May 1910

"Weep not"

With what an importunity of praise,
 What splendid carelessness of cheerful song
 These birds begin their rapturous matin song
While still the stars go down their silver ways ;
For us to-day the funeral trumpets raise
 Imperious wail, the rolling drums prolong
 Our lamentation, tyrannous and strong
Death calls for tears and every heart obeys.

But as I listen to the birds at dawn
 New hope has birth, " Weep not," they seem to cry,
 " There are whole worlds that know not any pain.
The King you loved is momently withdrawn,
 He has but gone to win full empery
 And comes to claim Love's spirit throne and
 reign."

H. D. Rawnsley.

XII

BIRDS AFTER THEIR KIND

" Ye Birds that fly through the fields of air,
What lessons of wisdom and truth ye bear ;

Beautiful Birds of lightsome wing,
Bright creatures that come with the voice of Spring;

Swift Birds, that skim o'er the stormy deep,
Who steadily onward your journey keep ;

Sweet Birds, that breathe the spirit of song,
And surround Heaven's gate in melodious throng."

C. W. THOMPSON.

BEAUTIFUL THROSTLE

From " Unstrung Links "

BEAUTIFUL throstle, that warbled so sweetly,
Dull is the winter unblest by thy song,
And my heart, saddened, is mourning and waiting,
Waiting to hear thee with yearnings so strong ;
Bird of the silver song, come with the summer,
Come when the daisies bespangle the lea,
And when the woodlands with song are redolent,
Beautiful throstle, come whistle to me !
Beautiful bird !
Beautiful bird !
Come into the willow and sing to me.

There's a sweet grot not far down in the garden,
Roses down there in the summer will grow,
And a tall willow bends over the arbour,
Though now its branches are covered with snow ;
Come in the summer, and there in the arbour
I'll listen enraptured, my soul roaming free ;
I'll tune my sad lyre to the song thou art singing,
Beautiful throstle, come whistle to me !
Beautiful bird !
Beautiful bird !
Come into the willow and sing to me.
                                    JOHN ROWELL WALLER.

THRUSH

Sᴡᴇᴇᴛ Thrush ! whose wild untutor'd strain
  Salutes the opening year,
Renew tho'se melting notes again
  And soothe my ravish'd ear.

Though in no gaudy plumage dress'd,
  With glowing colours bright,
Nor gold, nor scarlet on thy breast
  Attracts our wondering sight;

Yet not the pheasant or the jay,
  Thy brothers of the grove,
Can boast superior worth to thee,
  Or sooner claim our love.

How could we transient beauty prize
  Above melodious art !
Their plumage may seduce our eyes,
  Thy song affects our heart.

While evening spreads her shadowy veil,
  With pensive steps I'll stray,
And soft on tiptoe gently steal
  Beneath thy favourite spray.

Thy charming strain shall doubly please,
  And more my bosom move,
Since Innocence attends these lays
  Inspired by Joy and Love.

ANON.

FIELDFARES

How blue above our head the sky !
How brown below the path we tread,
By silent carpet overspread
From sombre larches standing by !
The berries in the hedge are red,
On which the birds should sure have fed,
Alas ! they long ago have fled
Who feel the frost and die.

But hark ! a foreign note I hear,
Along the fell, behind the wall,
A language I must needs recall,
Old talk made new with every year !
O'er northern seas, thro' sleet and squall,
These birds have come for festival,
And on the coral berries fall
To keep their Christmas cheer.

With " tsik-tsak " high and " tsik-tsak " low—
While perched far off their pickets stand—
These wandering birds possess the land
Our Norseman fathers used to know.
In voice, half quarrel, half command,
They wrangle on, the robber band—
Swift-wingèd Vikings from the strand
Of ice and winter snow.

I clap my hands, away they speed !
What matters where they rest to-night,
Beyond this vale are berries bright
And food where'er they wish to feed !

They know no law of tenant-right,
They only know they love the light ;
One law alone can guide their flight--
The law of Nature's need.

Ye red-backed rangers over sea,
    Ye grey-winged rovers of the field,
    Who, from what English roses yield,
Find life from lea to lea !
    Those hearts must sure be hard and steeled
    Who have no founts of faith unsealed
    By your wild carelessness revealed,
This winter morn to me.

                    H. D. RAWNSLEY.

THE FIELDFARE

WHEN wildly wave the poplar tops,
And scattered leaves the greensward mottle,
A worn invader seeks the copse.
    She lights beneath the stunted bush,
    And seems, to hasty eyes, a thrush,
But lacks the music of his throttle.

From freezing fiords has lain her way,
Where pines adorn some rock Norwegian :
There stands her home where skies are gray.
    But now she seeks the English fields,
    Where short November herbage yields
A refuge from that stormy region.

From year to year, when Winter's breath
Enshrouds the hills in misty sadness,
She flees as from the stroke of death ;
   Yet evermore, from year to year,
   As soon as earliest buds appear,
She seeks her motherland with gladness.

Nor egg nor nursling will she leave
Within these hateful, strange dominions,
But hastes her homestead to retrieve.
   Would Heaven that every human breast
   With such unfailing truth were blest
As gilds the fieldfare's faithful pinions !

E. W. LUMMIS.

THE BLACKBIRD

O BLACKBIRD ! sing me something well ·
   While all the neighbours shoot thee round,
   I keep smooth plats of fruitful ground,
Where thou may'st warble, eat and dwell.

The espaliers and the standards all
   Are thine ; the range of lawn and park
   .The unnetted black-hearts ripen dark,
All thine, against the garden wall.

Yet, tho' I spared thee all the spring,
   Thy sole delight is, sitting still,
   With that gold dagger of thy bill
To fret the summer jenneting.

A golden bill ! the silver tongue,
   Cold February loved, is dry :
   Plenty corrupts the melody
That made thee famous once, when young :

And in the sultry garden-squares,
   Now thy flute-notes are changed to coarse,
   I hear thee not at all, or hoarse
As when a hawker hawks his wares.

Take warning ! he that will not sing
   While yon sun prospers in the blue,
   Shall sing for want, ere leaves are new,
Caught in the frozen palms of Spring.
                    ALFRED, LORD TENNYSON.

BLACKBIRDS

CHRIST'S LITTLE CHRYSOSTOMS

YE merles with golden bills and throbbing throats,
   O tiny Chrysostoms of Christ's dear birds
Shaking the dewdrops from your shining coats,
   God's wingèd words ;
Loud rings your waking music every morn
   Like messages which high the church bells raise,
Forth from your shrine of shadowed thistle and thorn
   Calling to praise.

Singing in secret, yet your cry is clear,
   Priests of earth's matins, ye who not do swerve
Daily from offerings due, that men may hear
   And likewise serve ;

That warning shout of Advent-tide and Lent
    Has sounded through the centuries, as it bare
Summons for sinners early to repent,
    Purgèd through prayer.

The burden of the ages through it peals
    And gathers substance in that homely song,
Whereto the world (it rocks and rests and heals)
    Yet rolls along ;
Great congregations under the dim skies
    Stir at the mystic passion of your strain,
The Holy Baby on Mary's Breast still lies
    Blessèd through pain.

Perpetual hold ye Christmas (through the years)
    Now mixed and one with Easter's radiant Dawn,
With all sweet smiles and all sweet happier tears
    Together drawn ;
Your chant a challenge is and makes us feel
    .How more than near the Love that seemeth loss
Shelters and shrives us, as we humbly kneel
    Under the Cross.

O as ye bid us to the Altar's rite
    And awful act our glory and our shame,
I see great doors that open infinite
    In Jesu's Name ;
Ten thousand times ten thousand choirs are there
    And many a priest with many a reverend robe,
Girding in one grand worship everywhere
    The suppliant globe.

Ring on like matin bells and ring away
  Sloth and indifference from the Church's track,
Ring down the barriers of unfaith's delay
  Keeping Christ back ;
And let Love bridge indeed the land and sky
  Each morn with Christmas—Easter's endless birth,
That God may enter in His sanctuary—
  Redeemèd earth.

                              F. W. ORDE WARD.

THE WHEATEAR

FROM that deep shelter'd solitude,
Where in some quarry wild and rude
Your feather'd mother rear'd her brood,
    Why, pilgrim, did you brave
The upland winds so bleak and keen,
To seek these hills—whose slopes between
Wide stretch'd in grey expanse is seen
    The ocean's toiling wave ?

Did instinct bid you linger here,
That broad and restless ocean near,
And wait, till with the waning year,
    These northern gales arise ?
Which, from the tall cliff's rugged side,
Shall give your soft light plumes to glide
Across the channel's refluent tide
    To seek more favouring skies ?

Alas ! and has not instinct said,
That luxury's toils for you are laid,
And that by groundless fears betrayed,
    You ne'er perhaps may know
Those regions where the embowering vine
Loves round the luscious fig to twine,
And mild the suns of Winter shine,
    And flowers perennial blow ?

To take you, shepherd-boys prepare
The hollow turf, the wiry snare,
Of those weak terrors well aware,
    That bid you vainly dread
The shadows floating o'er the downs,
Or murmuring gale, that round the stones
Of some old beacon, as it moans,
    Scarce moves the thistle's head.

And if a cloud obscure the sun,
With faint and fluttering heart you run,
And to the pitfall you should shun,
    Resort in trembling haste ;
While on that dewy cloud so high,
The lark, sweet minstrel of the sky,
Sings in the morning's beamy eye,
    And bathes his spotted breast.

Ah ! simple bird, resembling you
Are those, that with distorted view,
Through life some selfish end pursue
    With low inglorious aim ;

They sink in blank oblivious night,
While minds superior dare the light,
And high on honour's glorious height
    Aspire to endless fame.
                    MRS CHARLOTTE SMITH.

SONG OF THE WHINCHAT

WE left a land where all look'd sad,
    With tokens known too well ;
Where the leaves in Autumn's livery clad,
    Look'd brightly ere they fell :
A land of dying beauty, where
All show'd decay and change were there.

We came again.   The earth had thrown
    Her faded mantle by,
And bright the bursting foliage shone
    Beneath the sunny sky ;
While from its deep mysterious source
The stream of life ran forth its course.
                    W. E. EVANS.

THE STONECHAT

WHY art thou ever flitting to and fro ?
—Plunge through these whins, their thorns will let
    thee know.
There are five secrets brooding here in night,
Which my good mate will duly bring to light ;
Meanwhile she sees the ants around her throng,
And hears the grasshopper chirp all day long.
                    JAMES MONTGOMERY.

SONG OF THE REDSTART

—HE who'd hear the redstart's note,
And catch my lonely strain,
Must follow me to spots remote,
Far from the haunts of men ;
Where the loud din of busy life
Ne'er falls upon the ear,
And all is still, save the soft strife
Of waters flowing near.

Now pause awhile ! in this calm scene
You'll hear the redstart sing,
For on that stone of mossy green
I rest my weary wing.
And deep into the solitude
Flows forth my short wild song ;
You'll hear it here, but ne'er renew'd
In the world's busy throng.

W. E. EVANS.

THE PRISONER TO A ROBIN THAT CAME TO HIS WINDOW

WELCOME ! welcome ! little stranger,
Welcome to my lone retreat,
Here, secure from every danger,
Hop about, and chirp, and eat.
Robin ! how I·envy thee,
Happy child of liberty !

Hunger never shall distress thee,
  While my meals one crumb afford,
Colds and cramps shall ne'er oppress thee,
  Come and share my humble board ·
Robin, come and live with me,
Live,—yet still at liberty.

Soon shall Spring, with smiles and blushes,
  Steal upon the blooming year ;
Then, amid the verdant bushes,
  Thy sweet song shall warble clear ;
Then shall I too, joined with thee,
Taste the sweets of liberty.

Should some rough, unfeeling Dobbin,
  In this iron-hearted age,
Seize thee on thy nest, my Robin,
  And confine thee in a cage ;
Then, poor Robin, think of me,
Think—and sigh for liberty.

Liberty ! thou brightest treasure
  In the crown of earthly joys,
Source of gladness, soul of pleasure,
  All delights besides are toys :
None but prisoners like me
Know the worth of liberty.

                              JAMES MONTGOMERY.

TO A REDBREAST

LITTLE bird, with bosom red,
Welcome to my humble shed !
Courtly domes of high degree
Have no room for thee and me.
Pride and pleasure's fickle throng
Nothing mind an idle song.

Daily near my table steal,
While I pick my scanty meal.
Doubt not, little though there be,
But I'll cast a crumb to thee ;
Well rewarded, if I spy
Pleasure in thy glancing eye,
See thee, when thou'st ate thy fill,
Plume thy breast and wipe thy bill.

Come, my feathered friend, again,
Well thou know'st the broken pane.
Ask of me thy daily store ;
Go not near Avaro's door :
Once within his iron hall,
Woeful end shall thee befall.
Savage !—he would soon divest
Of its rosy plumes thy breast ;
Then, with solitary joy,
Eat thee, bones and all, my boy !
JOHN LANGHORNE.

THE MERRIEST BIRD ON BUSH OR TREE

THE merriest bird on bush or tree
　Was Robin of the grove,
When, in the jocund springtime, he
　Sang to his nestling love.
Unknowing he the art to frame
　Methodic numbers vain,
But as each varied feeling came
　He wove it in his strain.
　　With freedom gay
　　He poured his lay,
While heaved his little breast of fire,
To rival all the woodland choir.

GERALD GRIFFIN.

TO THE ROBIN

I WISH I could welcome the spring, bonnie bird,
　With a carol as joyous as thine ;
Would my heart were as light as thy wing, bonnie bird,
　And thine eloquent spirit-song mine !

The bloom of the earth and the glow of the sky
　Win the loud-trilling lark from his nest ;
But though gushingly rich are his pæans on high,
　Yet, sweet Robin, I like thee the best.

I've been marking the plumes of thy scarlet-faced
　suit,
　And the light in thy pretty black eye ;
Till my harpstring of gladness is mournfully mute,
　And I echo thy note with a sigh.

For you perch on the bud-cover'd spray, bonnie bird,
  O'er the bench where I chance to recline ;
And you chatter and warble away, bonnie bird,
  Calling up all the tales of " Lang Syne."

They sang to my childhood the ballad that told
  Of " the snow coming down very fast " ;
And the plaint of the Robin, all starving and cold ;
  Flung a spell that will live to the last.

How my tiny heart struggled with sorrowful heaves,
  That kept choking my eyes and my breath ;
When I heard of thee spreading the shroud of green
    leaves
  O'er the little ones lonely in death.

I stood with delight by the frost-chequer'd pane,
  And whisper'd, " See, see, Bobby comes ! "
While I fondly enticed him again and again
  With the handful of savoury crumbs.

There were traps—there were nets, in each thicket
    and glen,
  That took captures by night and by day ;
There were cages for chaffinch, for thrush, and for
    wren,
  For linnet, for sparrow, and jay.

But if ever thou chanced to be caught, bonnie bird,
  With what eager concern thou wert freed ,
Keep a Robin enslaved ! why, 'twas thought, bonnie
    bird,
  That " bad luck " would have followed the deed.

They wonder'd what led the young dreamer to rove
In the face of a chill winter wind ;
But the daisy below, and the Robin above,
Were bright things that I ever could find.

Thou wert nigh when the mountain streams gladden'd
the sight,
When the autumn's blast smote the proud tree ;
In the corn-field of plenty, or desert of blight,
I was sure, bonnie bird, to see thee.

I sang to thee then as thou sing'st to me now,
And my strain was as fresh and as wild ;
Oh, what is the laurel Fame twines for the brow,
To the wood-flowers pluck'd by the child !

Oh, would that, like thee, I could meet with all
change,
And ne'er murmur at aught that is sent !
Oh, would I could bear with the dark and the fair ;
And still hail it with voice of content !

How I wish I could welcome the spring, bonnie bird,
With a carol as joyous as thine ;
Would my heart were as light as thy wing, bonnie
bird,
And thy beautiful spirit-song mine !

ELIZA COOK.

TO THE REDBREAST

UNHEARD in summer's flaring ray,
  Pour forth thy notes, sweet singer,
Wooing the stillness of the autumn day
  Bid it a moment linger,
    Nor fly
Too soon from winter's scowling eye.

The blackbird's song at eventide,
  And hers, who gay ascends,
Filling the heavens far and wide,
  Are sweet. But none so blends,
    As thine,
With calm decay, and peace divine.
GEORGE CORNISH.

THE ROBIN

RAINCLOUDS go ! and let me gaze once more
Upon the purple sun-kissed hills.
(But still the robin gaily trills
Singing of all the tempest holds in store.)

Grey mists depart ! and let me see again
Elidre's tops and Dafydd's hoary head.
(Yet still the robin sings up overhead
Singing of sheets of cheerless driving rain.)

Oh, darkness fly and show once more to me
Llewellyn's peak and Tryfan's triple crest.
(But still the robin sings with scarlet breast
Singing of stormclouds gathered o'er the sea.)
E. V. PALGRAVE SIMPSON.

TO A ROBIN

Aw like to yer a throstle sing ·
    It seawnds so sweet an' clear ;
Aw like to yer a blackbird too,
    When spring is drawin' near.
O' t'other brids are just as sweet,
    When nature is in·prime ;
But give to me that little brid
    That sings i' th' winter time.

He comes when frost and snow lie deep,
    He'll come in sleet an' rain,
Then for eawr scanty crumbs he'll sing,
    An' tap at th' window pane.
He never wings his flight fro' whoam
    To seek a foreign clime,
But stops to cheer eawr lonesome hearts,
    An' sings i' th' winter time.

When summer days are past an' gone,
    An' t'other brids are mute,
Ther' comes a seawnd o' melody
    Like some enchanted flute.
It brings to mind a tinklin' brook,
    Or bells that sweetly chime,
So perfect is the harmony
    He sings i' th' winter time.

Neaw o' yo' great musicianers,
    That dwell on flats an' sharps,
Fotch o' yo're modern instruments,
    Yo're ancient lutes an' harps,

An' if yo' fancy yo' con sing,
　An' think yo're voice sublime,
Just come an' yer yon little brid
　That sings i' th' winter time.

Sing on, sweet little minstrel,
　Till thy brief gamut's done,
An' while theaw'rt sweetly singin' may
　Theaw never yer a gun.
Aw'd like to wring that rascal's neck,
　An' think it were no crime,
That tries to shoot a brid 'at sings
　So sweet i' th' winter time.
JOSEPH CRONSHAW.

THE BLUEBIRD

THE HERALD OF SPRING

WHEN Winter's cold tempests and snows are no more,
　Green meadows and brown furrow'd fields re-
　appearing,
The fishermen hauling their shad to the shore,
　And cloud-cleaving geese to the lakes are a-
　steering ;
When first the lone butterfly flits on the wing,
　When red glow the maples, so fresh and so pleasing,
O then comes the Bluebird, the herald of Spring !
　And hails with his warblings the charms of the
　season.

Then loud-piping frogs make the marshes to ring ;
  Then warm glows the sunshine, and fine is the
    weather ;
The blue woodland flowers just beginning to spring,
  And spicewood and sassafras budding together · ´
O then to your gardens, ye housewives, repair,
  Your walks border up, sow and plant at your
    leisure
The Bluebird will chant from his box such an air,
  That all your hard toils will seem truly a pleasure !

He flits through the orchard, he visits each tree,
  The red-flowering peach, and the apple's sweet
    blossoms ;
He snaps up destroyers wherever they be,
  And seizes the caitiffs that lurk in their bosoms ;
He drags the vile grub from the corn it devours,
  The worms from the webs, where they riot and
    welter ;
His song and his services freely are ours,
  And all that he asks is—in Summer a shelter.

The ploughman is pleas'd when he gleans in his train,
  Now searching the furrows—now mounting to
    cheer him ;
The gardener delights in his sweet, simple strain ;
  And leans on his spade to survey and to hear him ;
The slow lingering schoolboys forget they'll be chid,
  While gazing intent as he warbles before them
In mantle of sky-blue, and bosom so red,
  That each little loiterer seems to adore him.

When all the gay scenes of the Summer are o'er,
And Autumn slow enters so silent and sallow,
And millions of warblers, that charm'd us before,
Have fled in the train of the sun-seeking Swallow;
The Bluebird, forsaken, yet true to his home,
Still lingers and looks for a milder to-morrow,
Till forc'd by the horrors of Winter to roam,
He sings his adieu in a lone note of sorrow

While Spring's lovely season, serene, dewy, warm,
The green face of earth, and the pure blue of
heaven,
Or love's native music have influence to charm
Or sympathy's glow to our feelings are given,
Still dear to each bosom the Bluebird shall be;
His voice, like the thrillings of hope, is a treasure;
For, through bleakest storms, if a calm he but see,
He comes to remind us of sunshine and pleasure.

ALEXANDER WILSON.

THE MOCKING-BIRD

From " Evangeline "

THEN from a neighbouring thicket the Mocking-bird,
wildest of singers,
Swinging aloft on a willow spray that hung o'er the
water,
Shook from his little throat such floods of delirious
music,
That the whole air and the woods and the waves
seemed silent to listen.

x

Plaintive at first were the tones and sad ; then soar-
ing to madness
Seemed they to follow or guide the revel of frenzied
Bacchantes.
Single notes were then heard, in sorrowful, low
lamentation ;
Till, having gathered them all, he flung them abroad
in derision,
As when, after a storm, a gust of wind through the
tree-tops
Shakes down the rattling rain in a crystal shower on
the branches.

HENRY W. LONGFELLOW.

TO THE OREGON ROBIN IN ALASKA

O VARIED THRUSH ! O Robin strange !
Behold my mute surprise.
Thy form and flight I long have known,
But not this new disguise,

I do not know thy slaty coat,
Nor vest with darker zone ;
I'm puzzled by thy recluse ways
And song in monotone.

I left thee 'mid my orchard's bloom,
When May had crowned the year ;
Thy nest was on the apple bough,
Where rose thy carol clear.

Thou lurest now through fragrant shades,
  Where hoary spruces grow ;
Where floor of moss enfolds the foot,
  Like depths of fallen snow.

Loquacious ravens clack and croak
  Nor hold me in my quest ;
The purple grosbeaks perch and sing
  Upon the cedar's crest.

But thou art doomed to shun the day,
  A captive of the shade ;
I only catch thy stealthy flight
  Athwart the forest glade.

Thy voice is like a hermit's reed
  That solitude beguiles ;
Again 'tis like a silver bell
  Adrift in forest aisles.

Throw off, throw off this masquerade
  And don thy ruddy vest,
And let me find thee, as of old,
  Beside thy orchard nest.
                          JOHN BURROUGHS.

THE NIGHTINGALE

So thick the boughis and the leavis green
Beshaded all the alleys that there were,
And midst of every arbour might be seen
The sharpe greene sweete juniper,

Growing so fair with branches here and there,
That, as it seemed to a lyf without,
The boughis spread the arbour all about.

And on the small greene twistis sat
The little sweete nightingale, and sung
So loud and clear, the hymnis consecrat
Of Iovis use, now soft, now loud among,
That all the gardens and the wallis rung
Right of their song.
                        KING JAMES I. OF SCOTLAND.

THE NIGHTINGALE

THE Nightingale, as soon as April bringeth
Unto her rested sense a perfect waking,
While late-bare earth, proud of new clothing,
    springeth,
Sings out her woes, a thorn her song-book making,
    And mournfully bewailing ;
    Her throat in tunes expresseth
    What grief her breast oppresseth
For Tereus' force on her chaste will prevailing.

O Philomela fair, O take some gladness,
That here is juster cause of plaintful sadness ·
    Thine earth now springs, mine fadeth ;
Thy thorn without, my thorn my heart invadeth.

Alas ! she hath no other cause of anguish
But Tereus' love, on her by strong hand wroken,
Wherein she suffering, all her spirits languish,
Full womanlike complains her will was broken.

But I, who, daily craving,
Cannot have to content me,
Have more cause to lament me,
Since wanting is more woe than too much having.

O Philomela fair, O take some gladness
That here is juster cause of plaintful sadness ·
Thine earth now springs, mine fadeth ;
Thy thorn without, my thorn my heart invadeth.

SIR PHILIP SIDNEY.

MOURNFUL PHILOMEL

OUR mournful Philomel,
    That rarest tuner,
Henceforth in April
    Shall wake the sooner,
And to her shall complain
    From the thick cover,
Redoubling every strain
    Over and over :
For when my love too long
    Her chamber keepeth ;
As though it suffered wrong,
    The morning weepeth.
        On thy bank
        In a rank
        Let thy swans sing her,
    And with their music
        Along let them bring her.

MICHAEL DRAYTON.

NO BIRD LIKE THE NIGHTINGALE

A graceful Compliment to Elizabeth of Bohemia

You meaner beauties of the night,
    That poorly satisfy our eyes,
More by your number than your light,
    You common people of the skies,
    What are you, when the Moon shall rise ?

You curious chanters of the wood
    That warble forth dame Nature's lays,
Thinking your passions understood
    By your weak accents ; what's your praise
    When Philomel her voice doth raise ?

                           SIR HENRY WOTTON.

TO THE NIGHTINGALE

SWEET bird ! that sing'st away the early hours
Of winters past, or coming void of care,
Well pleasèd with delights which present are,
Fair seasons, budding sprays, sweet-smelling flowers ;
To rocks, to springs, to rills, from leafy bowers,
Thou thy Creator's goodness dost declare,
And what dear gifts on thee He did not spare,
A stain to human sense in sin that lowers.
    What soul can be so sick which by thy songs
    (Attired in sweetness) sweetly is not driven
    Quite to forget earth's turmoils, spite, and wrongs,
    And lift a reverend eye and thought to heaven ?
    Sweet, artless songster ! thou my mind dost raise
    To airs of spheres—yes, and to angels' lays.
        WILLIAM DRUMMOND OF HAWTHORNDEN.

THE NIGHTINGALE

HARK ! how through many a winding note,
  She now prolongs her lays ;
How sweetly down the void they float
The breeze their magic path attends,
The stars shine out ; the forest bends,
  The wakeful heifers gaze.

Whoe'er thou art, whom chance may bring
  To this sequester'd spot,
If then the plaintive Syren sing,
Oh ! softly tread beneath her bower,
And think of Heaven's disposing power,
  Of man's uncertain lot.

Oh ! think o'er all this mortal stage,
  What mournful scenes arise ;
What ruin waits on kingly rage ;
How often virtue dwells with woe ,
How many griefs from knowledge flow ;
  How swiftly pleasure flies.

Oh ! sacred bird, let me at eve
  Thus wandering all alone,
Thy tender counsel oft receive,
Bear witness to thy pensive airs,
And pity Nature's common cares,
  Till I forget my own.

  MARK AKENSIDE.

THE NIGHTINGALE

From " Minstrelsy of the Woods "

BEAUTIFUL nightingale ! who shall portray
All the varying turns of thy flowing lay ?
And where is the lyre, whose chords shall reply
To the notes of thy changeful melody ?
We may linger indeed, and listen to thee,
But the linkèd chain of thy harmony
It is not for mortal hands to unbind,
Nor the clue of thy mazy music to find.
Thy home is the wood on the echoing hill,
Or the verdant banks of the forest rill ;
And soft as the south wind the branches among,
Thy plaintive lament goes floating along.

SIR WALTER SCOTT.

THE NIGHTINGALES

—ALL is still,
A balmy night ! and though the stars be dim,
Yet let us think upon the vernal showers
That gladden the green earth, and we shall find
A pleasure in the dimness of the stars.
And hark ! the Nightingale begins its song,
" Most musical, most melancholy " bird !
A melancholy bird ?   Oh ! idle thought !
In nature there is nothing melancholy.
But some night-wandering man, whose heart was
     pierced
With the remembrance of a grievous wrong,

Or slow distemper, or neglected love,
(And so, poor wretch ! filled all things with himself,
And made all gentle sounds tell back the tale
Of his own sorrow) he, and such as he,
First named these notes a melancholy strain,
And many a poet echoes the conceit ;

     —We may not thus profane
Nature's sweet voices, always full of love
And joyance ! 'Tis the merry Nightingale
That crowds and hurries, and precipitates
With fast thick warble his delicious notes,
As he were fearful that an April night
Would be too short for him to utter forth
His love chant, and disburden his full soul
Of all its music.
     And I know a grove
Of large extent, hard by a castle huge,
Which the great lord inhabits not ; and so
This grove is wild with tangling underwood,
And the trim walks are broken up, and grass,
Thin grass and kingcups, grow within the paths.
But never elsewhere in one place I knew
So many nightingales ; and far and near,
In wood and thicket, over the wide grove,
They answer and provoke each other's songs,
With skirmish and capricious passagings,
And murmurs musical and swift jug-jug,
And one low piping sound more sweet than all—
Stirring the air with such a harmony,
That should you close your eyes, you might almost

Forget it was not day ! On moonlit bushes,
Whose dewy leaflets are but half disclosed,
You may perchance behold them on the twigs,
Their bright, bright eyes, their eyes both bright and
  full,
Glistening, while many a glow-worm in the shade
Lights up her love-torch

           And oft, a moment's space,
What time the moon was lost behind a cloud,
Hath heard a pause of silence, till the moon
Emerging, hath awakened earth and sky
With one sensation, and those wakeful birds
Have all burst forth in choral minstrelsy,
As if some sudden gale had swept at once
A hundred airy harps !
               SAMUEL TAYLOR COLERIDGE.

ODE TO A NIGHTINGALE

MY heart aches, and a drowsy numbness pains
  'My senses, as though of hemlock I had drunk,
Or emptied some dull opiate to the drains
  One minute past, and Lethe-wards had sunk ·
'Tis not through envy of thy happy lot,
  But being too happy in thine happiness—
    That thou, light-wingèd Dryad of the trees,
      In some melodious plot
Of beechen green, and shadows numberless,
  Singest of summer in full-throated ease.

O, for a draught of vintage ! that hath been
  Cool'd a long age in the deep-delvèd earth,
Tasting of Flora and the country green,
  Dance, and Provençal song, and sunburnt mirth
O for a beaker full of the warm South,
  Full of the true, the blushful Hippocrene,
    With beaded bubbles winking at the brim,
      And purple-stainèd mouth ;
  That I might drink, and leave the world unseen,
    And with thee fade away into the forest dim.

Fade far away, dissolve, and quite forget
  What thou among the leaves hast never known,
The weariness, the fever, and the fret
  Here, where men sit and hear each other groan ;
Where palsy shakes a few, sad, last grey hairs,
  Where youth grows pale, and spectre-thin, and
      dies ;
  Where but to think is to be full of sorrow
      And leaden-eyed despairs,
  Where Beauty cannot keep her lustrous eyes,
    Or new Love pine at them beyond to-morrow.

Away ! away ! for I will fly to thee,
  Not charioted by Bacchus and his pards,
But on the viewless wings of Poesy,
  Though the dull brain perplexes and retards ·
Already with thee ! tender is the night,
  And haply the Queen-Moon is on her throne,

Cluster'd around by all her starry fays ;
    But here there is no light,
Save what from heaven is with the breezes blown
    Through verdurous glooms and winding mossy
        ways.

I cannot see what flowers are at my feet,
    Nor what soft incense hangs upon the boughs,
But, in embalmed darkness, guess each sweet
    Wherewith the seasonable month endows
The grass, the thicket, and the fruit-tree wild ;
    White hawthorn, and the pastoral eglantine ;
        Fast-fading violets cover'd up in leaves ;
            And mid-May's eldest child,
The coming musk-rose, full of dewy wine,
    The murmurous haunt of flies on summer eves.

Darkling I listen ; and for many a time
    I have been half in love with easeful Death,
Call'd him soft names in many a musèd rhyme,
    To take into the air my quiet breath ;
Now more than ever seems it rich to die,
    To cease upon the midnight with no pain,
        While thou art pouring forth thy soul abroad
            In such an ecstasy !
Still would'st thou sing, and I have ears in vain—
    To thy high requiem become a sod.

Thou wast not born for death, immortal Bird !
    No hungry generations tread thee down ;
The voice I hear this passing night was heard
    In ancient days by emperor and clown :

Perhaps the self-same song that found a path
Through the sad heart of Ruth, when, sick for home,
She stood in tears amid the alien corn ;
The same that oft-times hath
Charm'd magic casements, opening on the foam
Of perilous seas, in faery lands forlorn.

Forlorn ! the very word is like a bell
To toll me back from thee to my sole self !
Adieu ! the fancy cannot cheat so well
As she is fam'd to do, deceiving elf.
Adieu ! adieu ! thy plaintive anthem fades
Past the near meadows, over the still stream,
· Up the hillside ; and now 'tis buried deep
In the next valley-glades :
Was it a vision, or a waking dream ?
Fled is that music—do I wake or sleep ?

JOHN KEATS.

PHILOMELA

HARK ! ah, the Nightingale !
The tawny-throated !
Hark ! from that moonlit cedar what a burst
What triumph ! hark—what pain !

O Wanderer from a Grecian shore,
Still, after many years, in distant lands,
Still nourishing in thy bewilder'd brain
That wild, unquench'd, deep-sunken, old-world pain—
Say, will it never heal ?

And can this fragrant lawn
With its cool trees, and night,
And the sweet tranquil Thames,
And moonshine, and the dew,
To thy rack'd heart and brain
  Afford no balm ?

Dost thou to-night behold
Here, through the moonlight on this English grass,
The unfriendly palace in the Thracian wild ?
  Dost thou again peruse
With hot cheeks and sear'd eyes
The too clear web, and thy dumb Sister's shame ?
  Dost thou once more assay
Thy flight, and feel come over thee,
Poor Fugitive, the feathery change
Once more, and once more seem to make resound
With love and hate, triumph and agony,
Lone Daulis, and the high Cephissian vale ?
  Listen, Eugenia—
How thick the bursts come crowding through the
    leaves !
  Again—thou hearest !
Eternal passion !
Eternal pain !
                                MATTHEW ARNOLD.

LE ROSSIGNOL

Translated by Ashmore Wingate

LIKE flocks of noisy birds that madly fare,
All my past memories round me beat the air ·
Beat 'gainst the foliage of my heart so bleached,
My heart which its bent alder trunk hath reached
E'en where Regret's cold violet stream doth show,
That melancholy close at hand doth flow.
They beat, their evil clamour, by degrees,
Which a moist vapour, mounting, doth appease,
Now penetrates so far to the tree's core
That in an instant I can hear nought more—
Nought, save a voice that a lost name doth sing,
Nought, save this voice, a voice so languishing !
Of my dear first bird-love so far away,
Singing as erst upon that primal day.
While in the moon's sad splendour which doth rise
So solemn and so pale, this night which lies
Full pensively, and heavy with the Spring,
And silence, and obscure imagining,
On the blue glass, wind-ruffled, rocks to sleep
The tree which throbs, the bird which now doth weep.

PAUL VERLAINE.

THE WHITETHROAT

COME, come ye, to the green, green woods !
Loudly the blackbird is singing ;
The squirrel is feasting on blossoms and buds,
And the curlèd fern is springing.

Here ye may sleep in the wood so deep
  While the moon is so warm and so weary,
And sweetly awake, when the sun through the brake,
  Bids the Fauvet [1] and Whitethroat sing cheery.
                                    RICHARD HOWITT.

SONG OF THE BLACKCAP

FOR many a mile by day and night,
Our little wings with pinions light,
  Their weary task have plied.
And now we come, all peril past,
Back to the hazel copse at last,
  The well-known stream beside.

The land we left had dainty food
To feed our young, and tangled wood
  To screen our simple nest ;
Full softly breathed the spicy air,
And all around look'd bright and fair ;
  But that was not our rest.

O'er the dark bosom of the deep
Our journey lay, no rest or sleep
  Our weary pinions knew ;
But through the blue unclouded sky
With lusty wing we soar'd on high,
  And strong in hope we flew.

_____

[1] The lesser Whitethroat.

But on we went ; for land and life
Before us lay ; beneath, the strife
Of ocean's raging tide.
And now we come, all peril past,
Back to our hazel copse at last,
The well-known stream beside.

W. E. EVANS.

GARDEN WARBLERS

WHILE April skies to grove and field
Alternate shade and sunshine yield,
I hear thy sweet and mellow strain,
And give thee welcome once again.
Come, build within my hawthorn bower,
And shade thy nurslings with its flower ;
Or where my wreathèd woodbines twine,
Make thee a home for thee and thine.

H. G. A.

THE SONG OF THE GOLDEN CRESTED WREN

OUR nest hangs high on yon tall tree
    With tiny cords suspended,
And few its narrow door can see,
    By clustering leaves defended.
With roots and moss we wove it round,
    With ivy tendrils twined it,
While all around we lichens bound,
    With down and feathers lined it.

So sly upon the hanging bough
  With artful care we tied it,
No restless jay or thieving crow
  With peering look hath spied it.
The cat may look with wistful eye,
  Along the branches running,
But though she try, we're far too high,
  And laugh at all her cunning.

When the storm blows, the pliant spray
  Bends gently to its power,
The hanging leaves all fresh and gay
  Keep off the pelting shower :
The brood within, in merry plight,
  Care not for wind or weather ;
Through the dark night and cheerful light
  They all are warm together.

And soon all strong abroad they'll go,
  Their waving cradle leaving,
Their airy course from bough to bough
  On tiny pinion cleaving.
And though they lie so callow here,
  In the soft nest reclining,
They'll soon appear in brighter gear,
  With crowns of bright gold shining.

                                W. E. EVANS.

THE CHIFF-CHAFF

LITHE of body, dusk of hue,
Little courier of the sun,
We have waited long for you.
Flower-time, shower-time has begun.
Larch is greening everywhere,
Birch-tree fragrance fills the air.

Poet, welcome to the west,
Ranging from your Asian grove
To the " Islands of the blest,"
To the land of food and love,
Tell us, prithee, how you found
Your remembered mating ground.

By the ilex and the pine
Did you see our budding thorn ?
Thro' the olives and the vine
Were our verdurous pastures borne ?
Did pale lakes and mountains grey
Haunt you hither all the way ?

Or where palms and cactus crest
All sweet privacy forbid,
Had you vision of a nest
In some English dingle hid ?
Tell us wanderer over seas
Was your lodestar one of these ?

Nay, but singing, ringing clear
  Speed the message down the wind
That the guerdon of last year
  Led you, joy of soul to find
That one sweetheart, tried and true,
Thro' a whole world followed you.

Sing and ring, thro' trackless air
  She, you love, is following now,
Soon your ecstasy will share,
  Soon will warble from the bough,
And to listening ears shall prove
How adventuresome is Love.
                    H. D. RAWNSLEY.

WILLOW-WARBLER

FAREWELL, sweet bird ! thou still hast been
Companion of our Summer scene,
Lov'd inmate of our meadows green
        And rural home :
The music of thy cheerful song
We've loved to hear ; and all day long
See thee on pinion, fleet and strong,
        About us roam.

And dost thou no wise lore impart ?
Yes, still thou bidd'st us act our part
With body prompt and willing heart,
        While Summer lasts :

Prepar'd the course to take, that He
For us appoints, who summons thee
To climes of grateful warmth to flee
 From wintry blasts.

Oh, may that warning voice be heard
Howe'er revealed ! To thee, sweet bird,
The tongue that speaks the instructive word
 Within thee dwells :
To us where'er around we look,
Each passing wing, the field, the brook,
But most His own unerring Book
 God's wisdom tells.

That Book directs our mental sight
To mark the migratory flight,
With powers surpassing human might
 On thee impress'd :—
And trains by thy observant kind
Man's wilful and reluctant mind,
Its refuge in God's laws to find
 And there to rest.

ANON.

SONG OF THE WOOD WARBLER

'TIS hard our little nest to make,
 And rear our tender brood,
And then a weary flight to take
 Far from the beechen wood ;

Far from the Summer-haunted dell,
From each dear spot we loved so well,
To some far-distant land, all new and strange,
Where still the flowers will fade, and still the seasons
    change.

For, oh ! as soon as yon green corn
    Shall wave its yellow hair,
And the branches of that scented thorn
    Its crimson berries bear ;
When on the hill the fern grows brown,
And swollen streams are rushing down,
We must away, and leave them all behind,
Borne off like falling leaves strewn by the Autumn
    wind.

                                    W. E. Evans.

SONG OF THE REED BIRD

In the calm night when all is still,
    And not a voice is heard around,
Save the wild stream that from the hill
    Falls down with dashing sound ;
        When o'er the heath,
        The cold damp breath
Bends the tall rush with passing wing,
Upon its waving head alone I sing.

How sweet to me this quiet hour,
    When day hath hush'd his voices loud ;
And all earth owns night's silent power,
    Wrapt in her stilly shroud !

My lowly song,
That 'mid the throng
Of day's gay songsters was not heard,
Hath now at length the lonely echoes stirr'd.

When day shone bright, loud, joyous notes
From thousand voices hail'd his smile,
As when the pealing organ floats
Along the shafted aisle.
But I sing best,
When all's at rest,
As when escaped from crowd and glare,
Some faithful heart sends forth its lonely prayer.

W. E. EVANS.

SONG OF THE SEDGE WARBLER

By yon fair willow'd stream,
When June, array'd in flowers,
Shines with her sunny gleam,
I spend my lonely hours.
Wary and shy,
From man's keen eye
I softly hide, and sing my song unseen,
Close in the willow bush beneath the tresses green.

The stream's soft voice I love
Flowing beneath the bough,
When the waving branches move
To the water rippling through.

Sweet to my ear
That murmur clear ;
And when the sun rides high, the busy hum
Of myriad insect wings that love the glowing sun.

Where the calm stream is seen
  Beneath the bough to glide,
And the brakes of hawthorn green
⁻ Its gentle ripples hide ;
    'Twas there I first
    The egg-shell burst,
And from my nest looked out with wondering eye ;
'Twas there my weak wings made their first essay to
    fly.
                              W. E. EVANS.

SONG OF THE HEDGE SPARROW

MANY a sweeter voice than mine
  Sounds in the summer bower ;
And birds in gayer plumage shine,
  Or sing with deeper power :
But do not turn your eye away
  Because I'm brown and plain ;
Nor scorn the simple songster's lay,
  Though sung in lowly strain.
                              W. E. EVANS.

THE CANADIAN SONG-SPARROW

FROM the leafy maple ridges,
From the thickets of the cedar,
From the alders by the river,
From the bending willow branches,
From the hollows and the hill sides,
Through the lone Canadian forest,
Comes the melancholy music,
Oft repeated—never changing—
    " All—is—vanity—vanity—vanity."

Where the farmer ploughs his furrow,
Sowing seed with hope of harvest,
In the orchard white with blossom,
In the early field of clover,
Comes the little brown-clad singer,
Flitting in and out of bushes,
Hiding well behind the fences,
Piping forth his song of sadness—
    " Poor—hu—manity—manity—manity."
                                    J. D. EDGAR.

THE DIPPER OR WATER-OUZEL

THE Bird
Is here—the solitary bird that makes
The rock his sole companion. Leafy vale,
Green bower, and hedge-row fair, and garden rich
With buds and bloom, delight him not ;—he bends
No spray, nor roams the wilderness of boughs,

Where love and song detain a million wings,
Through all the Summer morn—the Summer eve ;—
He has no fellowship with waving woods,—
He joins not in their merry minstrelsy,—
But flits from ledge to ledge, and through the day
Sings to the highland waterfall—that speaks
To him in strains he loves and lists
For ever.

NOEL T. CARRINGTON.

THE DIPPER

AT the waterfall's edge where the rainbow springs
    From its mystic valley of spray,
The white-breasted ouzel sits and sings,
    Perched on a stone of grey.

He joins his song with the words of the brook,
    With a note so sweet and rare,
That the elves of the forest come out to look,
    Thinking that Pan is there.

His mate's in her hidden nest of moss,
    Away from all prying eyes,
Where 'tis cloaked by the falling water's floss,
    And the sprays that upwards rise.
Whilst he and the rivulet join their song
In melodious choir the whole day long.

E. V. PALGRAVE SIMPSON.

OXEYE OR GREAT TIT

Loud chatters from his ivied hold
The blackcapped Oxeye, fierce and bold.
And see, alarmed, before me flit
Of smaller size, his brother Tit ;
Vest yellowish green, and bonnet blue,
Now up and down, and through and through,
O'er trunk and branch, with prying beak
And restless eye, he climbs, to seek,
Close lodged within the creviced wood
Or moss-clad bark, his insect food.
His haunt the larvas' known resort ;
Nor less the homestead's stable court
Attracts him ; thence with pilfered grain
He hies him to his bush again,
And first the precious morsel draws
With sounding bill and grasping claws.

BISHOP MANT.

THE TITMOUSE

You shall not be overbold
When you deal with Arctic cold,
As late I found my lukewarm blood
Chilled wading in the snow-choked wood.
How should I fight ? my foeman fine
Has million arms to one of mine :
East, west, for aid I looked in vain,
East, west, north, south, are his domain.

Miles off, three dangerous miles, is home ;
Must borrow his winds who there would come.
Up and away for life ! be fleet !—
The frost-king ties my fumbling feet,
Sings in my ears, my hands are stones,
Curdles the blood to the marble bones,
Tugs at the heart-strings, numbs the sense,
And hems in life with narrowing fence.
Well in this broad bed he and sleep,—
The punctual stars will vigil keep,—
Embalmed by purifying cold ;
The winds shall sing their dead-march old,
The snow is no ignoble shroud,
The moon thy mourner, and the cloud.

Softly,—but this way fate was pointing,
'Twas coming fast to such anointing,
When piped a tiny voice hard by,
Gay and polite, a cheerful cry,
Chic-chicadeedee! saucy note
Out of sound heart and merry throat,
As if it said, " Good-day, good sir !
Fine afternoon, old passenger !
Happy to meet you in these places,
Where January brings few faces."

This poet, though he lived apart,
Moved by his hospitable heart,
Sped, when I passed his sylvan fort,
To do the honours of his court,

As fits a feathered lord of land ;
Flew near, with soft wings grazed my hand,
Hopped on the bough then, darting low,
Prints his small impress on the snow,
Shows feats of his gymnastic play,
Head downward, clinging to the spray.

Here was this atom in full breath,
Hurling defiance at vast death ;
This scrap of valour just for play
Fronts the north wind in waistcoat grey,
As if to shame my weak behaviour ;
I greeted loud my little saviour,
You pet ! what dost here ? and what for ?
In these woods, thy small Labrador,
At this pinch wee San Salvador !
What fire burns in that little chest
So frolic, stout, and self possest ?

Henceforth I wear no stripe but thine ;
Ashes and jet all hues outshine.
Why are not diamonds black and grey,
To ape thy dare-devil array ?
And I affirm, the spacious North
Exists to draw thy virtue forth.
I think no virtue goes with size ;
The reason of all cowardice
Is, that men are overgrown,
And, to be valiant, must come down
To the Titmouse dimension.

'Tis goodwill makes intelligence,
And I began to catch the sense
Of my bird's song : " Live out of doors
In the great woods, on prairie floors.
I dine in the sun ; when he sinks in the sea,
I too have a hole in a hollow tree ;
And I like less when Summer beats
With stifling beams on these retreats,
Than noontide twilights which snow makes
With tempest of the blinding flakes.
For well the soul, if stout within,
Can arm impregnably the skin ;
And polar frost my frame defied,
Made of the air that blows outside."

With glad remembrance of my debt,
I homeward turn ; farewell, my pet !
When here again thy pilgrim comes,
He shall bring store of seeds and crumbs.
Doubt not, so long as earth has bread,
Thou first and foremost shalt be fed ;
The Providence that is most large
Takes hearts like thine in special charge,
Helps who for their own need are strong,
And the sky doats on cheerful song.
Henceforth I prize thy wiry chant
O'er all that mass and minster vaunt ;
For men mis-hear thy call in Spring,
As 'twould accost some frivolous wing,
Crying out of the hazel copse, *Phe-be !*
And, in winter, *Chic-a-dee-dee !*

I think old Cæsar must have heard
In northern Gaul my dauntless bird,
And, echoed in some frosty wold,
Borrowed thy battle-numbers bold.
And I will write our annals new,
And thank thee for a better clew,
I, who dreamed not when I came here,
To find the antidote of fear,
Now hear thee say in Roman key,
Pæan! Veni, vidi, vici.
RALPH WALDO EMERSON.

THE BLUE-TIT

A FLUTTER of wings and a flash of blue,
And there my brave little friend are you !
Perched on the cocoanut, prying around,
Now at the window, now at the ground,
With your small head cocked in a knowing way,
And bright little, fierce little eyes, that say
" What of the fellow who stands and stares ?
Is he friend or foe
That he marks me so ?
He forgets his manners—but then, who cares ?

" Here is a prize it were sin to lose ;
And when times are bad can we hope to choose
Exactly whom we would care to meet ?
The main thing is to have food to eat ;
When it freezes and blows, and sleets and snows,
One can't be particular—so here goes !

And, though it's rather a tactless whim,
He may stand and look
If it suits his book ;
I don't intend to be scared by him."

Little tit, blue-tit, am I so rude,
Seeing that I provide the food,
And never have grudged a taste of the best,
In winter-time, to a feathered guest ?
Only, I like to watch you there,
You tiny thing with the jaunty air ;
And, manners or no, I intend to stay
And gaze at will
As you take your fill
Of the soft white nut on the ivy spray.

For it warms my heart, when it's glum and sad,
And the world seems doomed to be always bad,
And the great hope dwarfed by the little mind,
And the great light scorned by the inly blind,
To see you busy, and keen, and bold,
And undismayed by the parching cold ;
For you don't despair, and you don't complain ;
And where I should mope
You are full of hope
And sure that Spring will return again.

G. F. BRADBY.

BLUE TITMOUSE

WHERE is he, that giddy sprite,
Blue-cap with his colours bright ;
Who was blest as bird could be,
Feeding on the apple-tree ;
Made such wanton sport and rout
Turning blossoms inside out ?
Hung with head toward the ground,
Bound himself and then unbound ;
Lithest, quickest harlequin,
Prettiest tumbler ever seen,
Light of heart and light of limb,
What has now become of him ?

WILLIAM WORDSWORTH.

COAL-TIT

THE little Tomtit ! the little Tomtit !
    What a joyous bird is he !
And he loveth about in the sun to flit,
    And to perch on the orchard tree.
When the shining buds begin to peep,
With his sharp *twit-twit*, and his shrill *cheep-cheep*,
From morn till night 'tis his to keep
    As busy, as busy can be.

The little Tomtit has a little black cap,
    And, oh ! such a twinkling eye,
And his tiny wings they go flip-flap,
    As he utters his shrill sharp cry :

And he looks as proud as an eagle can,
That sits on a rock the sun to scan ;
And he says to the gardener, " Come, my man,
We ought to be friends—you and I."
But the gardener loves not the little Tomtit,
For he sees the ground beneath
With buds bestrewn ; and he vows, at noon,
Ere night to be his death.
But surely this is a cruel speech,
For a worm hath eaten the heart of each ;
If the fatal shot should the poor bird reach,
The innocent suffereth.

                                        H. G. A.

THE NUTHATCH

From " The Ornithologist"

A slightly wounded Nuthatch was put in a wooden cage, which it
    tapped, giving occasion for the observation that it was nailing its
    own coffin, for it died in two days.

UNCEASING the toil of that captive one,
From the dawn of the day to the set of sun ;
When the shadows of night around him fell.
There was silence and peace in his lowly cell ;
For the prisoner's weary toil was o'er,
And the requiem-strain was heard no more.

Dost weep for the captive ?   Weep freely, then ;
But knowest thou not there are captive men ?
Oh ! canst thou not hear how their plaintive wail
Is borne from afar on the ocean gale ?
Weep, weep, for the captive on land and sea,
And pray for that hour when the slave shall be free.

THE WREN

From " Minstrelsy of the Woods "

SMALL as thou art, thou gem-like bird,
   Yet thou hast made thy nest on high ;
And there thy warbling voice is heard,
   Singing thy children's lullaby.
Lovely bird ! with thy golden crown,
   A kind and tender nurse art thou,
Making thy nest of moss and down
   And hanging it on the bending bough.
There, rocked by the wave of the zephyrs' wings,
Amid the green branches it lightly swings,
And a few clustering leaves of the forest-tree,
Will serve to shelter thy cradle and thee ;
Concealing thee safely from every eye,
Until danger and fear have pass'd thee by.

SIR WALTER SCOTT.

THE PLEA OF THE LYRE-BIRD

MONARCH in Austral's wild domain,
   King of its birds am I,
Of those that fleetly scour the plain,
   Or wing the cloudless sky.
Long ere the white-man's hovering sail
   Was sighted off the coast,
My graceful, Grecian lyre-like tail
   Was the native's joy and boast.

I love my vast and sunny land,
  Through its bush and scrub I roam,
Where tall, umbrageous fern-trees stand
  Behold my peaceful home.
Dear to me are its forests wide
  Where no man yet hath trod,
With floral gifts on every side
  Fresh from its virgin sod.

I range the steep Blue Mountains
  Where the matchless Waratah,
With flowers like heart-shaped fountains
  Gleams blood-red from afar.
Amid the deep recesses
  Of the scented gum-trees' shade
The Wattle's feathery tresses
  Festoon the bush cascade.

But now I fear my regal sway
  Will soon be owned no more,
Too late I mourn the fatal day
  My foeman stepped ashore ;
Where his invading footsteps bend
  My royal line gives place,
His march of triumph I attend,
  I serve his home to grace.

Oh ! white-man, cease this deadly strife,
  Put up your trap and gun ;
Let me still lead a happy life,
  Leave me my forest run ;

'Tis with no wish my plumes to vaunt,
I make a faltering plea,
Within my wide ancestral haunt
Can we not both be free ?
                              ADA LOVEGROVE.

BELL-BIRDS

THE bell-birds in the magic woods,
    Oh, hearken to the witching strain ·
It flows and fills in silver floods,
    And fills and flows again.

A golden dawn, with blood-red wings,
    Flies low along the shades of night.
Oh, hearken how the carol springs,
    And trembles with delight.

The forest leaves are all afire,
    The bell-birds skim from bough to bough ;
Oh, listen to the holy choir,
    So liquid and so low.

Oh, hush ! oh, hear ! a goblin chime,
    The dew-drop trembles on the branch ;
A solo sweet, a scattered rhyme,
    A golden avalanche.

The fruits are picked, the lovely throng
    Have flown, and sung their parting strain ;
But such a witchery of song
    We shall not hear again.
                              WILLIAM SATCHELL.

TO THE MOKO-MOKO OR BELL-BIRD

I
MERRY chimer, merry chimer,
Oh, sing once more,
Again outpour,
Like some long-applauded mimer,
All thy vocal store.

II
Thy short but oft-repeated song,
At early dawn,
Awakes the morn,
Telling that joys to thee belong,
Greeting day new-born.

III
Alas ! we now but seldom hear
Thy rich, full note
Around us float,
For thou seem'st doomed to disappear,
E'en from woods remote.

IV
Some say the stranger honey-bee,
By white men brought,
This ill hath wrought ;
It steals the honey from the tree
And it leaves thee nought.

V
The songsters of our Fatherland
We hither bring,
And here they sing,
Reminding of that distant strand
Whence old mem'ries spring.

VI

But as the old, we love the new ;
Fain we'd retain
Thy chiming strain,
Thy purple throat and olive hue—
Yet we wish in vain.

VII

Thy doom is fixed by nature's law—
Why ?   none can tell.
Therefore, farewell,
We'll miss thy voice from leafy shaw—
Living silver bell.

VIII

Why should we ever know new joys,
If thus they pass ?
Leaving, alas !
Wistful regret, which much alloys
All that man now has.

ALEXANDER WILLIAM BATHGATE.

THE SUNBIRDS

EACH spangled back bright sprinkled specks adorn,
Each plume imbibes the rosy tinctured morn ;
Spread on each wing the florid season's glow,
Shaded and verged with the celestial bow ;
Where colours blend an ever-varying dye,
And wanton, in their gay exchanges vie.

ANON.

THE WAGTAIL

From the French of Dovalle

The word used in the French is *Bergeronnette*, little shepherdess, and
the translator is of opinion that the poet refers to the white wagtail,
a species (some think, merely a variety) quite common in France.
The term *Bergeronnette* for the species is perhaps chosen as more
popular and poetic than the masculine noun, *Hochequeue* (wagtail).

BIRD of the fields, poor wee rustic,
Wagtail unrestful ever,
Who bound'st along, all sprightly, quick,
Singing a ditty clever.

Fine Shepherdess ! thou lov'st to whirl
Where flocks crop their refection ;
By meadow-stream skip, skip, and twirl
To cast thine own reflection.

Now hie thee off, with changeful grace,
Peck flower-tips in rapture,
Or skirmish round kine's feet apace,
Bright coloured flies to capture.

Play on thy games, herd-loving bird !
Wee wagtail lightly flying ;
For I'll protect thee, trust my word,
If hawk overhead be spying.

How high he be, I yet can strike,
　Then, birdie, sing ; . . . to-morrow,
When I walk forth, near me I'd like
　Thy pranks to cheer my sorrow.

Thy short sweet song is my delight,
　No other friends now heed me ;
Fly, wagtail, fly—thou dear winged sprite
　Before my steps to lead me.

C. L. BRAIN.

THE SHRIKE

WITH eager eye, and half-expanded wings,
　The Butcher-bird sits watching for its prey,
　Amid the sunshine of a summer's day,
And many a wary glance around he flings.
In mid-air flit and flutter glittering things,
　Enjoying all life's pleasures while they may,
　Unconscious that the spoiler lurketh aye
Where pleasure sweetly to the charmed ear sings
There is a whirring sound—a sudden cry ;—
　The Butcher-bird hath darted from his twig ;
A form the less is in the sunny sky,
　But who shall heed its loss ? that moment, big
With fate to one, hath passed unmarked of all
So man sinks down, and dies, in life's great carnival.

PRIDEAUX J. SELBY.

THE TYRANT FLYCATCHER

BEHOLD him now, his little family flown,
Meek, unassuming, silent and alone ;
Lured by the well-known hum of favourite bees
As slow he hovers o'er the garden trees ;
Straight he alights, and from the pear-tree spies
The circling stream of humming insects rise ;
Selects his prey ; darts on the busy brood,
And shrilly twitters over his savoury food.
                                    ALEXANDER WILSON.

THE SWALLOW

No bird art thou, but a quick beauteous thought
    Sent down from Heaven to make the earth more
        bright
    And kindle in our homes a happy light,
Through the dim ages that for day have fought ;
Thy presence is an inspiration, wrought
    Of softest sound that bursts in sweetest sight,
Yet comes as angel songs, unbid, unbought,
    And lives in love when it has taken flight.

Thy palace is the air, thy roof the sky,
    Thy pillow but the cloud that cannot rest
    And drifts a rose in Space's purple breast ;
A wingèd thought thou must for ever fly
    Along thy sunbeam track, a blessing blest,
Mixed with the echoes of eternity.
                                F. W. ORDE WARD.

THE MARTLET

HARK ! the martlet twittering by
The crevice, while her twittering brood
Beneath some shadowy wall-flower lie,
In the high air of solitude !
She alone, sky-loving bird,
In that lofty clime is heard ;
But loftier far from cliff remote
Up springs the eagle, like a thought,
And pois'd in heaven's resplendent zone,
Gazes a thousand fathom down,
While his wild and fitful cry,
Blends together sea and sky.
And a thousand songs, I trow,
From the wakened world below
Are ringing through the morning glow.
Music is there on the shore,
Softening sweet the billowy roar ;
For bold and fair in every weather,
The seamews shrill now flock together,
Or wheeling off in lonely play,
Carry their pastimes far away,
To little isles and rocks of rest,
Scattered o'er the ocean's breast,
Where these glad creatures build their nest.
JOHN WILSON (" Christopher North ").

THE GREEN LINNET

BENEATH these fruit-tree boughs that shed
Their snow-white blossoms on my head,
With brightest sunshine round me spread
    Of spring's unclouded weather,
In this sequestered nook how sweet
To sit upon my orchard-seat !
And flowers and birds once more to greet
    My last year's friends together.

One have I marked, the happiest guest
In all this covert of the blest :
Hail to thee, far above the rest
    In joy of voice and pinion !
Thou, Linnet ! in thy green array,
Presiding spirit here to-day,
Dost lead the revels of the May,
    And this is thy dominion.

While birds, and butterflies, and flowers,
Make all one band of paramours,
Thou, ranging up and down the bowers,
    Art sole in thy employment ;
A life, a presence like the air,
Scattering thy gladness without care,
Too blest with any one to pair,
    Thyself thy own enjoyment.

Amid yon tuft of hazel-trees
That twinkle to the gusty breeze,
Behold him perched in ecstasies,
    Yet seeming still to hover ;

There, where the flutter of his wings
Upon his back and body flings
Shadows and sunny glimmerings,
    That cover him all over.

My sight he dazzles, half deceives,
A brother of the dancing leaves ;
Then flits, and from the cottage-eaves
    Pours forth his song in gushes ;
As if by that exulting strain,
He mocked and treated with disdain
The voiceless form he chose to feign,
    While fluttering in the bushes.
                    WILLIAM WORDSWORTH.

HAWFINCH

OH, gentle Finch ! that lovest in retirèd spots to
    dwell,
And singest, with an inward voice, thy sweet songs
    morn and eve,
Thou'rt like a cloister'd eremite, or nun within her
    cell,
That never, for the busy world, that solitude would
    leave—
Whose life is as a quiet stream, that glideth soft along,
    And murmurs to the leafy boughs, that shield it
    from the sun,
And to the lovely flowers, that bloom its verdant
    banks among,
    Of peace, and praise, and thankfulness, until its
    race be run.

The stillness of the leafy wood—the silence and the
   cahn
Pervading in the solitude, are pleasant unto thee ;
Thou cherishest no evil thought, thou dreamest not
   of harm,
   And therefore is thy bosom from all care and
   sorrow free !
The same boughs rustle over thee, the same stream
   glideth by,
   With silver voice, that to thy song responses
   uttereth,—
And where thine eyes first opened, to that patch of
   azure sky,
   That looketh like an angel face, thou closest them
   in death.
                                             H. G. A.

THE GOLDFINCH

THE mellow autumn sunshine
   Falls over land and sea,
And rosy fruit is glowing
   Upon the orchard tree,
The golden grain is garnered,
   The thistles' purple crown
Is changed to silvery masses
   Of floating, glistening down !

And round them on the hillside,
   And by the sunlit bay,
Or on the dusty roadside
   The merry finches play,
They cling to tall stems, feasting
   On ripened silver seed,

Or chase it through the sunshine
With graceful airy speed.

Their gold-barred pinions flutter
Around the thistles tall,
With joyous chirp they summon
Their comrades, one and all ;
From plant to plant they hover,
This gay-hued goldfinch band,
Their low, sweet warble ringing
Across the sunlit land !

MAUD E. SARGENT.

THE HOUSE-SPARROW

TOUCH not the little Sparrow, who doth build
His home so near us.   He doth follow us
From spot to spot amidst the turbulent town,
And ne'er deserts us.   To all other birds
The woods suffice, the rivers, the sweet fields,
And Nature in her aspect mute and fair ;
But he doth herd with men.   Blithe servant ! live,
Feed and grow cheerful !   On my window's ledge
I'll leave thee every morning some fit food,
In payment of thy service.—Doth he serve !—
Ay, serves and teaches.   His familiar voice,
His look of love, his sure fidelity,
Bid us be gentle with so small a friend ;
And much we learn from acts of gentleness.
Doth he not teach ?—Ay, and doth serve us too,
Who clears our homes from many a toilsome thing,
Insect or reptile ! and when do we mark

With what nice care he builds his nest, and guards
His offspring from all harm, and how he goes,
A persevering, bold adventurer,
'Midst hostile tribes, twenty times big as he,
Skill, perseverance, courage, parent's love,—
In all these acts we see, and may do well
In our own lives, perhaps, when need doth ask,
To imitate the little household bird.
Untiring follower ! what-doth chain thee here !
What bond's 'tween thee and man ! Thy food the same
As theirs who wing the woods,—thy voice as wild,
Thy wants, thy power, the same ; we nothing do
To serve thee, and few love thee ; yet thou bang'st
About our dwellings, like some humble friend,
Whom custom and kind thoughts do link to us,
And no neglect can banish.
                              So, long live
The household Sparrow ! may he thrive for ever !
For ever twitter forth his morning song,
A brief, but sweet domestic melody !
Long may he live ! and he who aims to kill
Our small companion, let him think how he
Would feel, if great men spurn'd him from their hearths,
Or tyrant doom'd him, who had done no wrong,
To pains or sudden death.   Then let him think,
And he will spare this little trustful bird ;
And his one act of clemency will teach
His heart a lesson that shall widen it,
For nothing makes so bright the soul, as when
Pity doth temper wisdom.
                              BARRY CORNWALL.

MY CHAFFINCH

His hours he spends upon a fragrant fir ·
  His merry " chink," his happy " Kiss me, dear,"
Each moment sounded, keeps the copse astir.
Loudly he challenges his rivals near,
Anon aslant down to the ground he springs,
Like to a sunbeam made of coloured wings.

The firm and solid azure of the ceil
  That struck by hand would give a hollow sound,
A dome turned perfect by the sun's great wheel,
  Whose edges rest upon the hills around,
Rings many a mile with blue enamelled wall ;
His fir-tree is the centre of it all.

A lichened cup he set against the side
  High up this mast, earth-stepped, that could not
    fail,
But swung a little as a ship might ride,
  Keeping an easy balance in the gale ;
Slow-heaving like a gladiator's breast,
Whose strength in combat feels an idle rest.

Whether the cuckoo or the chaffinch most
  Do triumph in the issuing of their song ?
I say not this, but many a swelling boast
  They throw each at the other all day long.
Soon as the nest had cradled eggs a-twin
The jolly squirrel climbed to look therein.

Adown the lane athwart this pleasant wood
  The broad-winged butterflies their solace sought ;
A green-necked pheasant in the sunlight stood,
  Nor could the rushes hide him as he thought.
A humble-bee through fern and thistle made
A search for lowly flowers in the shade.

A thing of many wanderings, and loss,
  Like to Ulysses on his poplar raft,
His treasure hid beneath the tunnelled moss
  Lest that a thief his labour steal with craft,
Up the round hill, sheep-dotted, was his way,
Zigzagging where some new adventure lay.

" My life and soul," as if he were a Greek,
  His heart was Grecian in his greenwood fane ;
" My life and soul," through all the sunny week
  The chaffinch sang with beating heart amain.
" The humble-bee the wide wood-world may roam ;
One feather's breadth I shall not stir from home."

No note he took of what the swallows said
  About the firing of some evil gun,
Nor if the butterflies were blue or red, ,
  For all his feelings were intent in one.
The loving soul, a-thrill in all his nerves,
A life immortal as a man's deserves.

                              RICHARD JEFFERIES.

THE LINNET

SOME humble heart is sore and sick with grief,
 And straight thou comest with thy gentle song
 To wile the sufferer from his hate or wrong,
By bringing nature's love to his relief.
 Thou churnest by the sick child's window long,
 Till racking pain itself be wooed to sleep ;
And when away have vanished flower and leaf,
 Thy lonely wailing voice for them doth weep—
 Linnet ! wild linnet !

God saw how much of woe, and grief, and care,
 Man's faults and follies on the earth would make ;
 And thee, sweet singer, for His creatures' sake,
He sent to warble wildly everywhere.
 And by our souls to love to wake.
 Oh ! blessed wandering spirit ! unto thee
Pure hearts are knit, as unto things too fair,
 And good, and beautiful of earth to be—
 Linnet ! wild linnet !

ROBERT NICOLL.

TO A SCOTCH LINNET

" HEATHER Lintie, tell me, pray,
 Why you do not fly away ? "

Heather Lintie plumed her wing,
Sang about a happy nest,
Made with one who loved her best
 In the spring.

Where beneath a boulder-stone
In the heather all together,
  Warmly nestle, all her own.
Heather Lintie will not roam
From her sweet and hidden home.
  So she sings, but not alone,
    Loving and rejoicing.
            FRANCES RIDLEY HAVERGAL

THE CANARY'

SINCE fate of sailors hourly varies,
  Lest doubts should wound my anxious breast,
This pretty bird, from the Canaries,
  Jack brought, to set my heart at rest :
" His life is charm'd, and when with sadness,"
  Cried he, " his notes he mournful gives,
      Then cherish care,
      Indulge despair ;
But sweetly, if they thrill with gladness,
Rejoice, and know your lover lives ·
      Attentive mark !
      Hark ! hark !
Rejoice, and know your lover lives."

Each hour, while my poor bosom flutters,
  Relying on my lover's word,
Anxious to hear the song he utters,
  I listen to my pretty bird :
But, thanks to Heaven ! never with sadness
Has he yet mourn'd ; even now he gives
      (To silence care,
      And chase despair,)

His sprightly notes with joy and gladness ;
And thus I know my lover lives,
Attentive mark !
Hark ! hark !
'Tis thus I know my lover lives.

But see, he's here ! my heart's contented—
Sweet warbler, truly did'st thou speak.
" Dear love ! " cried Jack, " 'twas all invented,
Lest thy poor heart my fate might break.
Love taught the cheat, to cheer thy sadness,
And cheats of love true love forgives ;
This anxious care
Heal'd thy despair ;
Birds always sing with joy and gladness ;
Thy love to thee and honour lives ·
Attentive mark !
Hark ! hark !
Thy love to thee and honour lives."

CHARLES DIBDIN.

THE YELLOW HAMMER

I

A YELLOW-HAMMER in the rain !
And that on this Carinthian plain,
So far, so far from home !
It fills me with old childish years :
And then these happy, happy tears,
Do what I will they come !

II

Behold him now : he never stops
Among the pattering raindrops
A blithe disturbance making,
Beating for ever on one key,
Pleased with his own monotony,
And his wet feathers shaking.

III

What tender memories are bound
To this familiar hedge-row sound !
The creature's homely glee
Associates me with the hours,
When, so pure childhood willed, all showers
Were sunshine showers to me.

IV

Away he goes and hammers still
Without a rule but his free will,
A little gaudy Elf !
And there he is within the rain
And beats and beats his tune again,
Quite happy in himself.

V

Within the heart of this great shower
He sits,.as in a secret bower,
With curtains drawn about him :
And part in duty, part in mirth,
He beats, as if upon the earth
Rain could not fall without him.

F. W. FABER.

THE BOB O'LINKUM

Thou vocal sprite ! thou feather'd troubadour !
  In pilgrim weeds through many a clime a ranger,
Comest thou to doff thy russet suit once more,
  And play in foppish trim the masquing stranger ?
Philosophers may teach thy whereabouts and
    nature ;
  But, wise as all of us, perforce, must think 'em,
The schoolboy best hath fix'd thy nomenclature,
  And poets too must call thee Bob o' Linkum

Say ! art thou, long 'mid forest glooms benighted,
  So glad to skim our laughing meadows over,
With our gay orchards here so much delighted,
  It makes thee musical, thou airy rover ?
Or are those buoyant notes the pilfer'd treasure
  Of fairy isles, which thou hast learn'd to ravish
Of all their sweetest minstrelsy at pleasure,
  And, Ariel-like, again on men to lavish ?

They tell sad stories of thy mad-cap freaks ;
  Wherever o'er the land thy pathway ranges,
And even in a brace of wandering weeks,
  They say, alike thy song and plumage changes :
Here both are gay ; and when the buds put forth,
  And leafy June is shading rock and river,
Thou art unmatch'd, blithe warbler of the north !
  When through the balmy air thy clear notes quiver.

Joyous, yet tender, was that gush of song
　　Caught from the brooks, where, 'mid its wildflowers
　　smiling,
The silent prairie listens all day long,
　　The only captive to such sweet beguiling ;
Or didst thou, flitting through the verdurous halls
　　And column'd aisles of western groves symphonious
Learn from the tuneful woods rare madrigals,
　　To make our flowering pastures here harmonious ?

Caught'st thou thy carol from Ottawa maid,
　　Where, through the liquid fields of wild rice plash-
　　ing,
Brushing the ears from off the burden'd blade,
　　Her birch canoe o'er some lone lake is flashing ?
Or did the reeds of some savannah south
　　Detain thee while thy northern flight pursuing,
To place those melodies in thy sweet mouth
　　The spice-fed winds had taught them in their woo-
　　ing.

Unthrifty prodigal ! is thought of ill
　　Thy ceaseless roundelay disturbing ever ?
Or doth each pulse in choiring cadence still
　　Throb on in music till at rest for ever ?
Yet, now in wilder'd maze of concord floating,
　　'Twould seem that glorious hymning to prolong,
Old Time, in hearing thee, might fall a doting,
　　And pause to listen to thy rapturous song !

TO THE LAPLAND LONGSPUR

Oh ! thou northland bobolink,
Looking over summer's brink,
Up to winter, worn and dim,
Peering down from mountain rim,
Peering out on Bering Sea,
To higher lands where he may flee,—
Something takes me in thy note,
Quivering wing and bubbling throat,
Something moves me in thy ways,—
Bird, rejoicing in thy days,
In thy upward hovering flight,
In thy suit of black and white,
Chestnut cape and circled crown,
In thy mate a speckled brown ;
Surely I may pause and think
Of my boyhood's Bobolink.

Soaring over meadows wild,—
(Greener pastures never smiled)
Raining music from above,—
Full of rapture, full of love,
Frolic, gay, and debonair,
Yet not all exempt from care,
For thy nest is in the grass,
And thou worried as I pass ;
But no hand nor foot of mine
Shall do harm to thee or thine ;
I, musing, only pause to think
Of my boyhood's bobolink.

But no bobolink of mine
Ever sang o'er mead so fine,—
Starred with flowers of every hue,
Gold and purple, white and blue.
Painted cup, anemone,
Jacob's ladder, fleur-de-lis,
Orchid, harebell, shooting star,
Crane's bill, lupine, seen afar,
Primrose, rubus, saxifrage,
Pictured type on Nature's page,—
These and others, here unnamed,
In northland gardens yet untamed,
Deck the fields where thou dost sing,
Mounting up on trembling wing ;
Yet in wistful mood I think
Of my boyhood's bobolink.

On Unalaska's emerald lea,
On lonely isles in Bering Sea,
On far Siberia's barren shore,
On north Alaska's tundra floor ;
At morn, at noon, in pallid night,
We heard thy song and saw thy flight,
While I, sighing, could not think,
Of my boyhood's bobolink.
                    JOHN BURROUGHS.

THE MYNA-BIRD

THE Indian Myna lightly dozed,
  And dreamt of its old wild life ;
In dreams it still haunted its jungle home,
  Deep in the jungle-strife.
Stirring uneasily on its perch
  It uttered strange, weird calls,
Calls that had struck its listening ear
  In vast, dim forest halls.

Soon it awoke to its present life,
  And gazed round the narrow cage,
Shaking the glossy tho' ruffled plumes,
  A wise black-coated sage !
Few mimics excel the wondrous tongue
  Of the Myna of varied tones ;
In cries of birds and the human voice
  Its fate it now bemoans.
                    R. M. INGERSLEY.

THE STARLING

OF all the birds whose tuneful throats
Do welcome in the verdant spring,
I prefer the starling's notes,
And think she does most sweetly sing.
Nor thrush, nor linnet, nor the bird
Brought from the far Canary's coast,
Nor can the nightingale afford
Such melody as she can boast.
                    ALLAN RAMSAY.

THE STARLINGS

EARLY in springtime, on raw and windy mornings,
Beneath the freezing house-eaves I heard the
    starlings sing—
" Ah, dreary March month, is this then a time for
    building wearily ?
Sad, sad to think that the year is but begun."

Late in the autumn, on still and cloudless evenings,
Among the golden reed-beds I heard the starlings
    sing,
" Ah, that sweet March month, when we and our
    mates were courting merrily ;
Sad, sad to think that the year is all but done."

CHARLES KINGSLEY.

ODE TO A STARLING

SPRING'S pilot, and her nimblest-wingèd darling,
    Despite the arrowy-flighted Swallow
    That in thy wake doth follow,
To rob thee of renown, intrepid Starling !
    Full weary of old Winter, sick of sorrow,
As I lay a-drowsing in the dark at dawn of day,
    Seeking to shut from sight a sunless morrow,
And suing to assist me flitting Sleep, that would not
    stay,
    Out of dim lands remote
    Came a hoarse but happy note ;
And then a scatter'd rustling loud beyond the lattice
    eaves
Of jostled wings, a-riot in the rare and rainy leaves.

Surely, surely, saucy angel
Of the Virgin Spring's evangel,
  'Twas the sound of thee and thine
Singing songs yet somewhat hoarser
  For the sea-wind and the brine
Breathed and braved by each precursor
. Of May's azure and sunshine.

I, at least, thy voice believing,
  And, in responsive mood,
Religiously receiving
  Its prophecies of good,
All the morn long have been roaming
  The wet field and wintry wood,
The burthen of an old song humming :—
" The starlings are come ! and merry May,
And June, and the white thorn, and the hay,
And the violet, and then the rose, and all sweet things
    are coming ! "

But O ill-welcom'd bird !
  Thy most impassion'd lays
  By heedless ears are heard.
Thou comest before thy time, and unattended.
  The sluggard Spring delays
  To justify thy word ;
And rancorous Winter stays
To wreak on thee the wrath of frosts and rains offended;
  Whilst thou of sunny days
  Still singest, undeterr'd
  By scorn or stinted praise,
Befriending thus a land that leaves thee unbefriended.

Envy not thou Cëyx, or Halcyon,
  Their sultry seas, fair-meadow'd lands of fable,
And foamless isles, the tempest strikes not on,
  That sleep in harbours green and hospitable ;
For thou, within thyself, despite foul weather,
  Hast golden calms and glories
Like windless lights where wizards meet together
  On stormy promontories.
Leave to the soft luxurious Nightingale
  Her amorous revels and embower'd delights
Where, over lush rose-leaves the balmy gale
  Is breathing low thro' blue midsummer nights.

Thine is the bardic chant, the battle strain,
  The strenuous impulse thine,
Antagonising wind and sleety rain
  In the tough-headed pine.
Leave to the Lark his lucid chariotings
  And mirth Memnonian, when auroral skies
With shining azure bathe his lyric wings.
  Thy realm beyond to-morrow's orient lies,
Safe from the reach of this anarchic time,
  Where' unreveal'd primroses,
And many a lurking love, and budding rhyme
  Each note of thine discloses.

Thy friends are yet unborn ;
  The earliest violet,
The first bud on the thorn,
  The first wan cowslip, wet
With tears of the first morn
  That doth such joys beget.

Thy foes are yet a-dying ;
Ragged-skirted rains,
Winds at random flying
Fast with cloudy manes,
And the last snows, lying
Lost on chilly plains.
Grief and joy together
Colloquise with thee :
Sad and sunny weather
Shift around the tree
Where, not heeding either,
Thou dost carol free
A music over-winging
On laughter-lifted pinions
Earth's bleakness and despair,
Like old Amphion's singing,
To raise serene dominions
And fashion from void air,
Stirr'd by the nimbly-sounding minions
Of its mysterious mandate, everywhere
Those blossomy battlements,
And florid tents,
Where, in due time, shall dwell
All the delicious sights, and sounds, and scents
Of Spring's green citadel.

EARL OF LYTTON (" Owen Meredith ")

BIRD OF PARADISE

In fair tropic regions
  Thy bright form is seen,
Glancing like a meteor
  O'er the forest green.

Hovering on light pinions
  In far ether blue,
Thy gay feathers showing
  Tints of ev'ry hue.

Like a feathered rainbow
  Soaring to the skies.
Why did Adam name thee
  " Bird of Paradise " ?

Was it that thy dazzling
  Coat of radiant sheen
Faintly shows the colours
  No mortal eyes have seen ?

Or because thy dainty
  Feet scarce touch the earth,
Thee he deemed a creature
  Of a higher birth ?

If God with such splendour
  Clothed thee for a day,
Fancy cannot picture
  Robes that last alway.
                    ADA LOVEGROVE.

THE JAY

From " The Hamlet "

Midst gloomy glades, in warbles clear,
Wild nature's sweetest notes they hear ;
On green untrodden banks they view
The hyacinth's neglected hue :
In their lone haunts, and woodland rounds,
They spy the squirrel's airy bounds,
And startle from her ashen spray
Across the glen, the screaming jay,
Each native charm their steps explore
Of solitude's sequester'd store.

Thomas Warton.

THE JAYS

From " The Battle of the Lake Regillus "

Once the jay sent a message
   Unto the eagle's nest :—
Now yield thou up thine eyrie
   Unto the carrion-kite,
Or come forth valiantly, and face
   The jays in deadly fight.—
Forth looked in wrath the eagle ;
   And carrion-kite and jay,
Soon as they saw his beak and claw,
   Fled screaming far away.

Lord Macaulay.

THE MAGPIE

And he, the loud intrusive Pie
Who plies his quick wings scouring by,
And not content to steal a feast
Voracious from each neighbouring nest,
His plunder on the poultry's hold
Directs, and on the wattled fold
Duckling or chick, or new fall'n lamb,
If haply from the fleecy dam
In life's fresh joy and frolic play,
At distance heedlessly they stray :—
To his voracity we owe,
In common with his brother Crow,
That from their lurking place are dug
Beetle and grub, and noxious slug ;
And safely thus, with unharmed roots,
The grass and spreading corn-blade shoots.
And well it is, if they who hold
His manners selfish, fraudful, bold,
In well-deserved dislike would turn
Their searching eyes at home, and learn
A lesson, and themselves disdain
The faults that in the Pie they blame.
But of his ways however ill.
We deem, and justly, yet for skill
To build his dwelling few can vie,
In talent with the artful Pie.

Bishop Mant.

THE DAW

No, no here lies indeed,
   The bird within the straw,
For each man pleadeth need,
   And he is held a Daw
That gives to such a want
   And thinks himself in luck,
This makes the world to scant,
   And turneth all to wreck.
                THOMAS CHURCHYARD.

THE JACKDAW

THERE is a bird, who by his coat,
And by the hoarseness of his note,
   Might be supposed a crow ;
A great frequenter of the church,
Where, bishop-like, he finds a perch,
   And dormitory too.

Above the steeple shines a plate,
That turns and turns, to indicate
   From what point blows the weather
Look up—your brains begin to swim,
'Tis in the clouds—that pleases him,
   He chooses it the rather.

Fond of the speculative height,
Thither he wings his airy flight,
   And thence securely sees
The bustle and the raree-show,
That occupy mankind below,
   Secure and at his ease.

You think, no doubt, he sits and muses
On future broken bones and bruises,
  If he should chance to fall.
No ; not a single thought like that
Employs his philosophic pate,
  Or troubles it at all.

He sees that this great roundabout,
The world, with all its motley rout,
  Church, army, physic, law,
Its customs and its bus'nesses;
Is no concern at all of his,
  And says—what says he ?—Caw.

Thrice happy bird ! I too have seen
Much of the vanities of men ;
  And, sick of having seen 'em,
Would cheerfully these limbs resign
For such a pair of wings as thine
  And such a head between 'em.
                    WILLIAM COWPER.

THE CARRION CROW

THE carrion crow, that loathsome beast,
  Which cries against the rain,
Both for his hue and for the rest,
  The Devil resembleth plain ;
And as with guns we kill the crow,
  For spoiling our relief,
The Devil so must we overthrow,
  With gunshot of belief.
                    GEORGE GASCOIGNE.

THE CARRION CROW

THE carrion crow is a sexton bold,
He raketh the dead from out the mould,
He delveth the ground like a miser old,
Stealthily hiding his store of gold.
Caw ! caw ! the carrion crow,
Dig ! dig ! in the ground below.

The carrion crow hath a coat of black,
Silky and sleek, like a priest's, to his back ,
Like a lawyer he grubbeth—no matter what way—
The fouler the offal, the richer his prey !
Caw ! caw ! the carrion crow,
Dig ! dig ! in the ground below.

The carrion crow hath a dainty maw,
With savoury pickings, he crammeth his craw ;
Kept meat from the gibbet it pleaseth his whim,
It never can hang too long for him.
Caw ! caw ! the carrion crow,
Dig ! dig ! in the ground below.

The carrion crow smelleth powder, 'tis said,
Like a soldier escheweth the taste of cold lead ;
No jester or mime hath more marvellous wit,
For wherever he lighteth he maketh a hit.
Caw ! caw ! the carrion crow,
Dig ! dig ! in the ground below.
WILLIAM HARRISON AINSWORTH.

THE TWA CORBIES

As I was walking all alane
I heard twa corbies making a mane ;
The tane unto the t'other say,
" Where sall we gang and dine to-day ? "

" —In behint yon auld fail dyke,
I wot there lies a new-slain knight ;
And naebody kens that he lies there,
But his hawk, his hound, and lady fair.

" His hound is to the hunting gane,
His hawk to fetch the wild fowl hame,
His lady's ta'en another mate,
So we may mak our dinner sweet.

" Ye'll sit on his white hause-bane,
And I'll pick out his bonny blue een
Wi' ae lock o' his gowden hair
We'll theek our nest·when it grows bare.

" Mony a one for him makes mane,
But nane sall ken where he is gane ;
O'er his white banes, when they are bare,
The wind sall blaw for evermair."

ANON.

TO THE CROW

Say, weary bird, whose level flight
Thus, at the dusky hour of night,
Tends through the midway air,
Why yet beyond the verge of day
Is lengthen'd out thy dark delay,
Adding another to the hours of care ?

The wren within her mossy nest
Has hush'd the little brood to rest ;
The wild wood-pigeon, rock'd on high,
Has coo'd his last soft note of love,
And fondly nestles by his dove,
To guard their downy young from an inclement sky.

Each twittering bill and busy wing,
That flits through morning's humid Spring,
Is still,—listening perhaps so late,
To Philomel's enchanting lay,
Who now, asham'd to sing by day,
Trills the sweet sorrows of her fate.

Haste, bird, and nurse thy callow brood,
They call on Heaven and thee for food,
Bleak,—on some cliff's neglected tree ;
Haste, weary bird, thy lagging flight—
It is the chilling hour of night,
Fit hour of rest for thee !

ANON.

AN ADDRESS TO A ROOK

From " The Cloisters "

LET me still love thee in thy quietude,
  Sweet sylvan village ! and thou, agèd rook,
  Who sitt'st sole sentinel in ivied nook
Survivor of thy noisy brotherhood !
And I with thee, in thine own pensive mood
  Could linger till the light of ages fall
  Around us, like moonbeams on tap'stried hall,
And saintly forms come forth, and virgins good
  Who gave their days to Heaven.   From that lone
    pile
Avaunt, rude change, thy disenchanting Wand
  And let the holy Cross linger awhile !
  Ah, feather'd Chronicler, would that from thee
Thou couldst forefend Art's all-transforming hand,
  And guard thy hoary haunts of Antiquity.
                              ISAAC WILLIAMS.

ROOKS

From " The Birds "

WHAT means that riot in your citadel ?
Be honest, peaceable, like brethren dwell.
How while we live so near to man can life
Be anything but knavery, noise, and strife ?
                              JAMES MONTGOMERY.

THE ROOK SITS HIGH

THE Rook sits high when the blast sweeps by,
  Right pleased with his wild see-saw ;
And though hollow and bleak be the fierce wind's
  shriek,
  It is mock'd by his loud caw-caw.
What careth he for the bloom-robed tree,
  Or the rose so sweet and fair ;
He loves not the sheen of the spring-time green,
  Any more than the branches bare.
Oh ! the merriest bird the woods e'er saw,
Is the sable Rook with his loud caw-caw.

Winter may fling crystal chains on the wing
  Of the fieldfare, hardy and strong ;
The snow-cloud may fall like a downy pall ;
  Hushing each warbler's song ;
The starved gull may come from his ocean home
  And the poor little robin lie dead ;
The curlew bold may shrink from the cold,
  And the house-dove droop his head ;
But the sable Rook still chatters away,
Through the bitterest frost and the darkest day.

He builds not in bowers, 'mid perfume and flowers,
  But as far from the earth as he can ;
He " weathers the storm," he seeks for the worm,
  And craves not the mercy of man.
Then a health to the bird whose music is heard
  When the ploughboy's whistle is still ;

To the pinions that rise, when the hail-shower flies,
  And the moor-cock broods under the hill
For the merriest fellow the woods e'er saw
Is the sable Rook with his loud caw-caw.

We read in the page of the grey-hair'd sage,
  That misfortune should ne'er bow us down ;
Yet if Care come nigh, the best of us sigh,
  And cower beneath his frown.
But the Rook is content when the summer is sent,
  And as glad when its glories fade ;
Then fill, fill to the brim—here's a bumper to him
  Who sings on through the sun and the shade ;
For the wisest fellow the world e'er saw
Is the sable Rook with his loud caw-caw.

ELIZA COOK.

THE RAVENS

From " The Spirit "

" Is there no road but by those gibbets ? "
" No road," the woman replied.
" But though with the wind each murderer swings
They both of them are harmless things,
  And so are the ravens beside."

" What ! are there ravens there ?—those creatures
  That are so black and blue !
But, are they ravens ? I inquire,
For I have heard by the winter's fire,
  That phantoms the dead pursue."

The woman replied, " They are night-ravens
    That pick the dead men's eyes ;
And they cry qua, with their hollow jaw ;
    Methinks I one this moment saw !
To the banquet at hand he flies."
                            ROBERT SOUTHEY.

THE LAY OF THE LAST RAVEN

UP on the cliffs lies the gallant old raven,
    Waiting the death that is claiming him fast ;
Born of a race that has never turned craven,
    Bravely he faces it—game to the last !

Aristocrat to the tips of his feathers ;
    Back through the years can his pedigree trace,
Summer and winter, through calm and rough
        weathers,
    Up on the Dover Cliffs dwelt the brave race.

Back to the ages that seem to us mystery,
    " We were here then ! " Can the warrior boast ?
Here—when the woad-painted Britons of history
    Beat Julius Cæsar away from the coast !

Here—when 'twixt Ramsgate and Deal—oh ! the
        shame of it !
    Failing at Dover, a footing they gained ;
Came with their legions—ah ! who shall bear blame
        for it ?
    Bringing the Eagles of Rome, and remained !

Here—on the beach when the Norman keels grated.
Here—as the centuries stormily passed ;
The Ravens of Dover have hatched and have mated,
Have died—and now dying, here lies the last !

Bachelor : Wherefore ?   Has love's tender passion
Never disturbed the calm peace of his mind ?
Widower : Needs he our deepest compassion ?
Had he a grief in the years left behind ?

Hush ! he is dying—is dead—nay, but rather,
Whisper instead his brave spirit has flown
Upwards, not downwards, because the All-Father,
Source of all life, gathers back of His own.

Only a bird life, a tiny cord broken,
Into life's greatness a spirit released ;
Question we this that the Psalmist hath spoken,
" Thou, Lord, shall save "—ay *save*—" both man
and beast."

Here's to him !   Last of the Ravens of Dover,
Gallant old warrior, game to the end !   •
Surely the face of the cliffs shadow over,
Grieving with us, for the loss of their friend.

LUCY   R.   HARDY.

THE SKYLARK

Go, tuneful bird ! that gladd'st the skies,
To Daphne's window speed thy way,
And there on quivering pinions rise,
And there thy vocal art display.

And if she deign thy notes to hear,
And if she praise thy matin song,
Tell her the sounds that soothe her ear
To Damon's native plaint belong.

Tell her, in livelier plumes array'd,
The bird from Indian groves may shine ;
But ask the lovely partial maid
What are his notes compared to thine !

Then bid her treat yon witless beau,
And all his flaunting race with scorn,
And lend an ear to Damon's woe,
Who sings her praise, and sings forlorn.
WILLIAM SHENSTONE.

THE SKYLARK

BIRD of the wilderness,
Blithesome and cumberless,
Sweet be thy matin o'er moorland and lea
Emblem of happiness,
Blest is thy dwelling-place—
Oh, to abide in the desert with thee !

Wild is thy lay and loud,
Far in the downy cloud,
Love gives it energy, love gave it birth.
Where, on thy dewy wing,
Where art thou journeying ?
Thy lay is in heaven, thy love is on earth.

O'er fell and fountain sheen,
O'er moor and mountain green,
O'er the red streamer that heralds the day,
Over the cloudlet dim,
Over the rainbow's rim,
Musical cherub, soar, singing, away !

Then, when the gloaming comes,
Low in the heather blooms,
Sweet will thy welcome and bed of love be
Emblem of happiness,
Blest is thy dwelling-place—
Oh, to abide in the desert with thee !

JAMES HOGG.

TO A SKYLARK

ETHEREAL minstrel ! pilgrim of the sky !
Dost thou despise the earth where cares abound ?
Or, while the wings aspire, are heart and eye,
Both with thy nest upon the dewy ground ?
Thy nest which thou canst drop into at will,
Those quivering wings composed, that music still !

To the last point of vision, and beyond
Mount, daring warbler ! that love-prompted strain
('Twixt thee and thine a never-failing bond)
Thrills not the less the bosom of the plain
Yet might'st thou seem, proud privilege ! to sing
All independent of the leafy spring.

Leave to the nightingale her shady wood ;
A privacy of glorious light is thine ;
Whence thou dost pour upon the world a flood
Of harmony, with instinct more divine ;
Type of the wise who soar, but never roam ;
True to the kindred points of heaven and home.

WILLIAM WORDSWORTH.

TO THE LARK

O THOU sweet lark, that in the heaven so high,
Twinkling thy wings dost sing so joyfully,
  I watch thy soaring with no mean delight ;
And when at last I turn mine aching eye
  That lags, how far below that lofty flight,
Still silently receive thy melody..
O thou sweet lark, that I had wings like thee !
  Not for the joy it were in yon blue light
  Upward to plunge, and from my heavenly height
Gaze on the creeping multitude below,
  But that I soon would wing my eager flight
To that lov'd home where fancy even now
Hath fled, and hope looks onward through a tear,
Counting the weary hours that keep her here.

ROBERT SOUTHEY.

THE SKYLARK

WITH fluttering start, in silence, from her nest
The skylark breaks :—then steadier, upwards soars,
And with melodious trill her prelude pours
To earth, in hues of full-flushed summer drest ;
Now, poised on moveless wing, she seems to rest ;
    Careless what bird, beneath the airy height,
    May cross her path with horizontal flight,
The measured lay she breathes :—then, like a guest
    Singing to other spheres, is lost in light :
Till, fondly lured, she turns her faithful breast
Downward through fields of blue. The warbling
    strain
Near and more near she swells ;—then hushed again,
Falls like a shadow from the sunny dome,
And chants her three wild notes to welcome home.

MRS J. CONDER.

THE SKYLARK

HAIL to thee, blithe Spirit !
    Bird thou never wert,
That from heaven, or near it,
    Pourest thy full heart
In profuse strains of unpremeditated art.   '

Higher still and higher,
    From the earth thou springest
Like a cloud of fire ;
    The blue deep thou wingest,
And singing still dost soar, and soaring ever singest.

In the golden lightning
Of the sunken sun,
O'er which clouds are bright'ning,
Thou dost float and run,
Like an unbodied joy whose race is just begun.

The pale purple even
Melts around thy flight ;
Like a star of heaven
In the broad daylight
Thou art unseen, but yet I hear thy shrill delight.

Keen as are the arrows
Of that silver sphere,
Whose intense lamp narrows
In the white dawn clear
Until we hardly see, we feel that it is there.

All the earth and air
With thy voice is loud,
As, when night is bare,
From one lonely cloud
The moon rains out her beams, and heaven is over-
flowed.

What thou art, we know not ;
What is most like thee ;
From rainbow clouds there flow not
Drops so bright to see,
As from thy presence showers a rain of melody.

2 C

Like a poet hidden
    In the light of thought,
Singing hymns unbidden,
    Till the world is wrought
To sympathy with hopes and fears it heeded not.

Like a high-born maiden
    In a palace tower,
Soothing her love-laden
    Soul in secret hour
With music sweet as love, which overflows her
    bower.

Like a glow-worm golden
    In a dell of dew,
Scattering unbeholden
    Its aërial hue
Among the flowers and grass, which screen it from
    the view.

Like a rose embower'd
    In its own green leaves,
By warm winds deflower'd
    Till the scent it gives
Makes faint with too much sweet these heavy-
    winged thieves.

Sound of vernal showers
    On the twinkling grass,
Rain-awaken'd flowers,
    All that ever was
Joyous, and clear, and fresh, thy music doth sur-
    pass.

Teach us, sprite or bird,
  What sweet thoughts are thine ·
I have never heard
  Praise of love or wine
That panted forth a flood of rapture so divine.

Chorus hymeneal,
  Or triumphal chaunt,
Match'd with thine would be all
  But an empty vaunt—
A thing wherein we feel there is some hidden want.

What objects are the fountains
  Of thy happy strain ?
What fields, or waves, or mountains ?
  What shapes of sky or plain ?
What love of thine own kind ? what ignorance of
  pain ?

With thy clear keen joyance
  Languor cannot be :
Shadow of annoyance
  Never come near thee ·
Thou lovest ; but ne'er knew love's sad satiety.

Waking or asleep,
  Thou of death must deem
Things more true and deep
  Than we mortals dream,
Or how could thy notes flow in such a crystal
  stream ?

We look before and after,
And pine for what is not ·
Our sincerest laughter
With some pain is fraught ;
Our sweetest songs are those that tell of saddest
thought.

Yet if we could scorn
Hate, and pride, and fear,
If we were things born
Not to shed a tear,
I know not how thy joy we ever should come near.

Better than all measures
Of delightful sound,
Better than all treasures
That in books are found,
Thy skill to poet were, thou scorner of the ground.

Teach me half the gladness
That thy brain must know,
Such harmonious madness
From my lips would flow,
The world would listen then, as I am listening now.

PERCY BYSSHE SHELLEY.

THE WOUNDED LARK

Written on the Illness of an Eminent Musician

I

LAY low thine ear with kindly care,
    And gently tread the ground ;
Some mourner haunts the grassy lair ;
    What means this plaintive sound ?

II

Here, 'mongst his little nestlings, lies
    A lark, with broken wing,
Gazing aloft into the skies,
    Where once he used to sing.

III

No more upspringing from the lawn,
    To greet the brightening sky,
High-poised, 'mid rosy tints of dawn,
    He'll thrill the world with joy.

IV

No more above the sun-tipt hills
    He'll fan his happy wings ;
His notes have sunk to mournful trills,
    And sorrow's all he sings.

V

So prone lies he, whose genial power
    Once led the tuneful train ;
So fate has changed his joyous dower
    To cadences of pain.

VI

Thus, daily, minstrel tones do creep
In sadness, one by one,
Into the silent land, where sleep
The voices that are gone.

EDWIN WAUGH.

THE SKYLARK

GONE is the speck that was a bird,
And was a voice, until we saw
No more of what we thought **we** heard
In awe,
And strained to see until **we** heard
The thing we dreamed we saw—
A voice for ever and a song
Unbroken,
And through the azure long,
Dear bird, a token
We may not think thee from our sight ;
We do not see yon azure through,
But thee, that thrilling trilling in the height
Art blue of blue,
Art light in light !

WILLIAM RENTON.

TO A LARK

HARP OF A THOUSAND STRINGS

O WINGÈD Love, thou Angel of the sky,
    Who rapturously
Dost rend those quiet spaces with the spray
Of hope in its eternal holiday,
The prophet thou of immortality ;
    In paths untrod
White souls, like thee, but as through burning fire
And altar upon altar, mount to God,
Wafted by wings of infinite desire.

Meanest and grandest of all lives, men go
    Sinful and slow,
With hearts of heaven entombed in walls of dust
That cannot shut us from our native trust,
Yet save for thee they would be bound below ;
    Thou callest us
Unto our kindred freedom, and we rise
Buoyed with thy flaming faith and love, and thus
We learn we walked unconscious Paradise.

Harp of a thousand strings, that still are one
    And jarring none,
In that accord which flows from vision clear
Gleaned out of ages, vaster than all fear,
We catch thy note in all sweet service done ;
    But thou and we
Could never soar to such exceeding height,
Unless our homes were humble and thence free
To clasp with lowly hands the climes of light.

Were we but mortal, yet our faith would wring
    Eternal spring
From God Himself and be immortal thence—
If but a moment of Omnipotence,
By the same power of the same fiery wing ;
    Trust cannot err
Though heaven and earth and many an age go by,
It looks beyond as God's interpreter
And drinks in rapture of Divinity

Grant me, dear Lord, Thy mounting spirit, give
    Whereby to live
The love which dares to venture much and throws
A bridge of light o'er darkness till it glows,
In the proud strength of Thy prerogative ;
    That under it
The chasm or gulf of doubt may prove a stair
Upward to Thee by progress infinite,
And turn to solid ground shades of despair.

                        F. W. ORDE WARDE.

ADDRESS TO THE WOODLARK

OH, stay, sweet warbling woodlark, stay
Nor quit for me the trembling spray ;
A hapless lover courts thy lay,
    Thy soothing, fond complaining.

Again, again that tender part,
That I may catch thy melting art ;
For surely that wad touch her heart
    Wha kills me wi' disdaining.

Say, was thy little mate unkind,
And heard thee as the careless wind ?
Oh, nocht but love and sorrow join'd,
   Sic notes o' wo could wauken.

Thou tells o' never-ending care,
O' speechless grief and dark despair :
For pity's sake, sweet bird, nae mair !
   O*r* my poor heart is broken !
             Robert Burns.

ON THE SWIFT

Of all the feathered tribes that meet
In crowded city, or retreat
Of rural scenes, the British eye,
What pinion with the Swift can vie ?
How passing wonder is the gift
Of fleetness in the unrivalled Swift,
Which ere a double pulse can beat,
Is here and there with motion fleet,
As Ariel's wing could scarce exceed ;
And, full of vigour as of speed,
Forestalls the dayspring's earliest gleam,
Nor fails with evening's latest beam !

How passing wonder is the might
Which, in a bird with powers of flight
So gifted as the Swift can lay
Injunction through the livelong day,
In life, in health, in vig'rous prime,
To watch the lazy-footed time,

As if in indolent repose,
The sweeping breath of wing to close,
Immured, inactive sit ; nor roam
An instant from her lonely home !
But what is each, the state of rest
Or action, but the law impressed
By nature on the obedient kind ?
And what is nature's law, the mind
Instructing, but a silent sign
Perspicuous of the will divine,
The Maker Spirit's high behest,
Who forms the wing, directs the rest ;
By whom the time, the season's given
For every purpose under heaven ?

                              BISHOP MANT.

THE HUMMING-BIRD

THE humming-bird ! the humming-bird
  So fairy-like and bright ;
It lives among the sunny flowers,
  A creature of delight !

In the radiant islands of the East
  Where fragrant spices grow,
A thousand, thousand humming-birds
  Go glancing to and fro.

Like living fires they flit about,
  Scarce larger than a bee,
Among the broad palmetto leaves,
  And through the fan-palm tree.

And in those wild and verdant woods,
  Where stately mosses tower,
Where hangs from branching tree to tree
  The scarlet passion flower ;

Where, on the mighty river banks,
  La Plate and Amazon,
The cayman, like an old tree trunk,
  Lies basking in the sun ;

There builds her nest the humming-bird,
  Within the ancient wood—
Her nest of silky cotton down—
  And rears her tiny brood.

She hangs it to a slender twig,
  Where waves it light and free,
As the campanero tolls his song,
  And rocks the mighty tree.

All crimson is her shining breast,
  Like to the red, red rose ;
Her wing is the changeful green and blue
  That the neck of the peacock shows.

Thou happy, happy humming-bird,
  No winter round thee lours ;
Thou never saw'st a leafless tree,
  Nor land without sweet flowers.

A reign of summer joyfulness
  To thee for life is given ;
Thy food, the honey from the flower,
  Thy drink, the dew from heaven !

How glad the heart of Eve would be,
  In Eden's glorious bowers,
When she saw the first, first humming-bird
  Among the spicy flowers ;

Among the rainbow butterflies,
  Before the rainbow shone—
One moment glancing in her sight
  Another moment gone !

Thou little shining creature,
  God sav'd thee from the Flood,
With eagle of the mountain-land,
  And tiger of the wood !

Who cared to save the elephant,
  He also cared for thee,
And gave those broad lands for thy home,
  Where grows the cedar-tree !

                                MARY HOWITT.

THE NIGHTJAR OR FERN-OWL

FLEET Courser of the feathered hosts,
No halcyon hues thy plumage boasts,
In sober russet garb bedight,
Aërial Huntsman of the night.
Say art thou bird, or spectral shade,
A ghost whose penance is not paid,
Some ancient warrior doomed to flying
Unshriven and uncoffined lying ?
The sun is set, the day is sped,
Thy dusky form appears o'erhead,

To search the park, and skim the ponds,
And glide among the bracken fronds,
Where sleeps the tinted butterfly,
Unconscious of thy hawking cry;
Till in the twilight's deepening gloom,
The insect finds a living tomb.
How weird thy jarring, purring note,
Now close at hand, now far remote !
Eye cannot watch thy rapid race,
The chafers and the moths to chase ;
With gnats the evening air is fraught,
How many, tell me, hast thou caught ?
As over knoll, and wooded height,
Thou wingest thy nocturnal flight ?

ADA LOVEGROVE.

THE WHIP-POOR-WILL

FROM yonder wooded hill
I hear the Whip-poor-will,
  Whose mate or wandering echo answers him
  Athwart the lowlands dim.

He calls not through the day;
But when the shadows gray
  Across the sunset draw their lengthening veil,
  He tells his twilight tale.

What unforgotten wrong
Haunts the ill-omened song ?
  What scourge of Fate has left its loathèd mark
  Upon the cringing dark ?

" Whip ! Whip-poor-will ! "
O sobbing voice be still !
Tell not again, O melancholy bird,
The legend thou hast heard !

                    JOHN B. TABB.

WRYNECK

                    IN sober brown
Drest, but with nature's tenderest pencil touch'd,
The Wryneck her monotonous complaint
Continues ; ·harbinger of her who, doom'd
Never the sympathetic joy to know.
That warms the mother cowering o'er her young,
A stranger robs, and to that stranger's love
Her eggs commits unnatural.

                    THOMAS GISBORNE.

THE WRYNECK

FIRST of the migratory swarm,
His lodging in our woods to form,
The Wryneck comes, a lovely bird
Not oft his gentle voice is heard,
Not oft are spread, retired and shy,
His pinions in the open sky,
Yet when occasion serves, 'tis well,
Where in Hamptonian groves they dwell,
Or Glo'cester's wooded vales remote,
Their habits and their forms to note :
To note the mottled plumes that grace,
As with a robe of tissued lace,

Their russet wings, to see them drill
With sharp and penetrating bill,
Their caverned dwelling, and among
Their insect prey the horn-tipped tongue
Tenacious dart ; and as they pry
Now here, now there, and turn awry
The head and spiral throat, to mark
How from the crown descending dark,
With course aslant, the listed black
Inlays the gray and speckled back,
The embroidery of that vesture gray
Nor pen nor pencil can portray :
But still more wondrous to the mind
Is that sharp tip of horn, designed
The pliant length of tongue to guide
With constant aim unerring, glide
Resistless to the emmet's nest,
The dark mould piercing ; there arrest
And to the expecting bill convey
On gluey point the insect prey.
The pliant tongue's horn-pointed frame,
The adhesive glue, the unerring aim ·
What proofs are here of wise design,
Of nice adjustment, power divine,
Disclosing what the will intends
By means adapted to the ends ;
Nor failing by those means to teach
His works the intended ends to reach.

Bishop Mant.

THE WOODPECKER OR HEWEL

From " Appleton House"

BUT most the hewel's wonders are,
Who here has the holtfelster's care ;
He walks still upright from the root,
Measuring the timber with his foot,
And all the way, to keep it clean,
Doth from the bark the wood-moths glean ;
He, with his beak, examines well
Which fit to stand and which to fell ;
The good he numbers up, and hacks
As if he mark'd them with the axe ;
But where he, tinkling with his beak,
Doth find the hollow oak to speak,
That for his building he designs
And through the tainted side he mines.
Who could have thought the tallest oak
Should fall by such a feeble stroke ?
Nor would it, had the tree not fed
A traitor worm within it bred,
(At first our flesh, corrupt within
Tempts impotent and bashful sin)
And yet that worm triumphs not long,
But serves to feed the Hewel's young,
While the oak seems to fall content
Viewing the treason's punishment.

ANDREW MARVEL.

GREEN WOODPECKER

From " Walks in the Forest "

WITH shrill and oft-repeated cry
Her angular course, alternate rise and fall,
The Woodpecker prolongs ; then to the trunk
Close clinging, with unwearied beak assails
The hollow bark ; through every cell the strokes
Roll the dire echoes that from wintry sleep
Awake her insect prey ; the alarmed tribes
Start from each chink that bores the mouldering stem :
Their scatter'd flight with lengthening tongue the foe
Pursues ; joy glistens on her verdant plumes,
And brighter scarlet sparkles on her crest.

THOMAS GISBORNE.

THE KINGFISHER

WHEN the summer's bright and tender sunbeams fill
    the land with splendour,
In his robes of blue and purple, and his crown of
    burnished green,
Lone the kingfisher sits dreaming, with his dark eyes
    brightly gleaming,
While he peers for chub and minnows in the water's
    limpid sheen.

And he haunts the river's edges, oozy flats, and
    rustling sedges,
Till he sees his prey beneath him in the waters clear
    and cool ;

2 D

Then he quickly dashes nearer, and he breaks the
  polished mirror
That was floating on the surface of ,the creek or
  hidden pool.

Where the nodding reeds are growing, and the yellow
  lilies blowing,
In our little boat we slowly glide along the placid
  stream ;
And we know he's coming after, by the music of his
  laughter,
And the flashing of his vesture in the sun's effulgent
  beam.

Well he knows the alder bushes, and the slender slimy
  rushes,
And the swamp, and pond, and lakelet, and the ice-
  cold crystal spring ;
And the brooklet oft he follows through the meadows
  and the hollows,
Far within the shadowv woodland where the thrush
  and robin sing.

Oh, he well can flutter proudly, and he well can laugh
  so loudly,
For he lives within a castle where he never knows a
  care !
And his realm is on the water, and his wife a monarch's
  daughter ;
And his title undisputed is on earth, or sea, or air !

CHARLES LEE BARNES.

THE SONG OF THE MALTESE TO THE ROLLER

OF a changeful hue, now green, now blue,
　Like the breast of the ocean are thy plumes,
And lands remote have heard thy note
　Break the stillness deep of their forest glooms ;
And year by year thou comest here
　In the gentle spring and the autumn-tide,
A little while in our sunny isle,
　'Mid the citron groves and the vines to bide.

In Italy they look for thee,
　And the isles that wait Sicilia round ;
By the Rhine, the Rhone, and swift Garonne,
　Are watchers for thy coming found ;
And far thy wing goes journeying,
　O'er Suabian forests all of pine ;
And thou dost speed where Dane and Swede
　May list that noisy chant of thine.

When blossoms fair the green boughs bear,
　Of almond and of orange trees,
Thou crossest o'er from Afric's shore,
　To revel and to sport 'mid these ;
And here again thou com'st, when grain
　Is ripe, and clusters load the vine ;
When glistening green are olives seen,
　And laden boughs to earth incline.

We never sing Spring's welcoming,
　But thou dost chant a pæan strong ;
In grove and dell thy loud notes swell
　The harvest and the vintage song ;

Oh ! tarry here the livelong year,
  Wing not thy flight across the sea.
Why should'st thou roam from this fair home,
  Where joy and plenty wait on thee ?

                                   H. G. A.

THE HOOPOE TO THE NIGHTINGALE

From " The Birds" of Aristophanes

WAKEN, dear one, from thy slumbers ;
Pour again those holy numbers,
Which thou warblest there alone
In a heaven-instructed tone,
Mourning from this leafy shrine
Lost—lost Itys, mine and thine,
In the melancholy cry
Of a mother's agony.
Echo, **ere** the murmurs fade,
Bear them from the yew-tree's shade
To the throne of Jove ; and there,
Phœbus with his golden hair
Listens long, and loves to suit
To his ivory-mounted lute
Thy sad music ; at the sound
All the gods come dancing round,
And a sympathetic song
Peals from the immortal throng.

                  WINTHROP MACKWORTH PRAED.

HOOPOE

O HOOPOE, hast thou reached our shore
  From far-off foreign place,
To be a lifeless specimen
  Inside a glass show-case !

Thou wishest naught but sheltered home
  Within some forest aisle,
Why should thy trusting confidence
  Be met with cruel guile ?

Poor lonely exiled wanderer,
  For thee I'll intercede,
Else thou wilt fall a luckless prey
  To man's insatiate greed.

'Twere better far if thou couldst stay
  Our English woods to grace,
And fill our sombre spinneys
  With gay scions of thy race !

Thou shouldst beneath the British flag
  Its boasted freedom claim ;
And naturalised once more attain
  To prestige and to fame.

From wanton waste of happy life
  All manly hearts recoil ;
Why should each bird be slain who seeks
  A homestead on our soil ?

At sight of thee glad rhapsodies
   Overflow the poet's brain,
And nature lovers feel their hearts
   Throb fast with joyous pain.

With outspread wings and crest erect
   Thou fliest to this isle ;
Canst thou not find within its bounds
   A peaceful domicile ?
                              ADA LOVEGROVE.

THE CUCKOO

(Usually attributed to John Logan)

HAIL, beauteous stranger of the grove
   Thou messenger of spring !
Now Heaven repairs thy rural seat,
   And woods thy welcome sing.

What time the daisy decks the green,
   Thy certain voice we hear :—
Hast thou a star to guide thy path
   Or mark the rolling year ?

Delightful visitant ! with thee
   I hail the time of flowers,
And hear the sound of music sweet
   From birds among the bowers.

The school-boy, wandering through the wood
   To pluck the primrose gay,
Starts, thy curious voice to hear,
   And imitates thy lay.

What time the pea puts on the bloom,
  Thou fliest the vocal vale,
An annual guest, in other lands
  Another spring to hail.

Sweet bird ! thy bower is ever green,
  Thy sky is ever clear ;
Thou hast no sorrow in thy song,
  No winter in thy year.

Oh ! could I fly, I'd fly with thee ;
  We'd make, with joyful wing,
Our annual visit o'er the globe,
  Companions of the spring.
                MICHAEL BRUCE.

THE PARROT

THE deep affections of the breast,
  That Heaven to living things imparts,
Are not exclusively possess'd
  By human hearts.

A parrot, from the Spanish Main,
  Full young, and early caged, came o'er
With bright wings, to the bleak domain
  Of Mulla's shore.

To spicy groves, where he had won
  His plumage of resplendent hue,
His native fruits, and skies, and sun,
  He bade adieu.

For these he changed the smoke of turf,
 A heathery land and misty sky,
And turned on rocks and raging surf
  His golden eye.

But fretted, in our climate cold
 He lived and chatter'd many a day ;
Until with age, from green and gold
  His wings grew gray.

At last, when blind and seeming dumb,
 He scolded, laughed, and spoke no more,
A Spanish stranger chanced to come
  To Mulla's shore ;

He hail'd the bird in Spanish speech,
 The bird in Spanish speech replied,
Flapp'd round the cage with joyous screech,
  Dropt down and died !

THOMAS CAMPBELL.

THE BARN OWL

WHILE moonlight, silvering all the walls,
Through every mouldering crevice falls,
Tipping with white his powdery plume,
As shades or shifts the changing gloom ;
The Owl that, watching in the barn,
Sees the mouse creeping in the corn,
Sits still, and shuts his round blue eyes,
As if he slept—until he spies
The little beast within his stretch—
Then starts—and seizes on the wretch !

SAMUEL BUTLER.

TO A SCREECH OWL

THOU shrill proclaimer of the lonely hour !
Thou dusky courier of the sable night !
Come, leave the hollow tree, or ivy'd tow'r,
And to thy vot'ry urge thy flapping flight.

Thy voice than Philomel's appears more sweet,
When thou, companion of the flitting bat,
With echoing screeches leav'st thy rude retreat,
To smooth the discord of the wandering cat.

What, tho' no glaring plumage marks thy wings,
No varied hues bespeak the Peacock kind,
Humble thou shew'st the joys Contentment brings,
Thou stern reformer of the human mind.

Leave thou those haunts where fools thy noise despise,
And seek the shades of academic groves ;
Where men of science thy perfections prize,
And the young Muses woo thee to their loves.

ANON.

THE AZIOLA

" Do you not hear the Aziola cry ?
  Methinks she must be nigh,"
  Said Mary, as we sate
In dusk, ere the stars were lit or candle brought.
  And I, who thought
This Aziola was some tedious woman,

Asked, " Who is Aziola ? "   How elate
I felt to know that it was nothing human,
No mockery of myself to fear and hate !
    And Mary saw my soul,
And laughed and said, " Disquiet yourself not ;
'Tis nothing but a little downy owl."

Sad Aziola ! many an eventide
    Thy music I had heard
By wood and stream, meadow and mountainside,
    And fields and marshes wide,—
Such as nor voice nor lute nor wind nor bird
    The soul ever stirred ;
Unlike and far sweeter than they all.
Sad Aziola ! from that moment I
    Loved thee and thy sad cry.
                    PERCY BYSSHE SHELLEY.

OWL SONG

From " Tumble-down-Dick "

THUS when the wretched owl has found
Her young owls dead as mice,
O'er the sad spoil she hovers round,
And views 'em once or twice,
Then to some hollow tree she flies
To holloo, hoot, and howl,
Till every boy that passes cries
The Devil's in the owl !
                    HENRY FIELDING.

THE OWL AND THE ELVES

From " The Fairies "

FROM the silent heart of a hollow yew,
The Owl sailed forth with a loud haloo ;
And his large yellow eyes looked bright
With wonder, in the wan moonlight,
As hovering white, and still as snow,
He caught a glance of the things below,
All burning on the bridge like fire
In the sea-green glow of their wild attire.
" Haloo !   Haloo ! tu-whit ! tu-whoo ! "
Cried the gleesome Elves, and away they flew,
With mimic shriek, sob, cry, and howl,
In headlong chase of the frightened Owl.
With many a buffet they drove him onward,
Now hoisted him up, now pressed him downward ;
They pulled at his horns, and with many a tweak,
Around and around they screwed his beak ;
On his back they beat with a birch-spray flail,
And they tore the long feathers from his tail ;
Then, like warriors mounted in their pride,
Behind his wings behold them ride !
And shouting, charge unto the war,
Each waving his soft plume-scymitar ;
A war of laughter, not of tears,
The wild-wood's harmless Cuirassiers.

JOHN WILSON ("Christopher North ").

THE HORNED OWL

In the hollow tree in the old grey tower,
    The spectral owl doth dwell ;
Dull, hated, despised, in the sunshine hour ;
    But at dusk he's abroad and well :
Not a bird of the forest e'er mates with him ;
    All mock him outright by day ;
But at night, when the woods grow still and dim,
    The boldest will shrink away.
Oh, when the night falls, and roosts the fowl,
Then, then is the reign of the hornèd owl !

And the owl hath a bride who is fond and bold
    And loveth the wood's deep gloom :
And with eyes like the shine of the moonshine cold
    She awaiteth her ghastly groom !
Not a feather she moves, not a carol she sings,
    As she waits in her tree so still :
But when her heart heareth his flapping wings,
    She hoots out her welcome shrill !
Oh, when the moon shines and dogs do howl,
Then, then is the joy of the hornèd owl.

Mourn not for the owl nor his gloomy plight
    The owl hath his share of good :
If a prisoner he be in the broad daylight,
    He is lord in the dark green wood !

Nor lonely the bird, nor his ghastly mate ;
They are each unto each a pride—
Thrice fonder, perhaps, since a strange dark fate
Hath rent them from all beside !
So when the night falls, and dogs do howl,
Sing ho ! for the reign of the hornèd owl !
We know not alway who are kings by day,
But the king of the night is the bold brown owl.

BARRY CORNWALL.

CONDOR

From " The Voyage of Columbus "

'TWAS the mid-hour, when He, whose accents dread
Still wandered through the regions of the dead,
Merion, commissioned with his host to sweep
From age to age the melancholy deep,
To elude the seraph-guard that watched for man,
And mar, as erst, the Eternal's perfect plan,
Rose-like, the condor, and, at towering height,
In pomp of plumage sailed, deepening the shades of
  night.
Roc of the West ! to him all empire given !
Who bears Axalhua's dragon-folds to heaven ;
His flight a whirlwind, and, when heard afar,
Like thunder, or the distant din of war.

SAMUEL ROGERS.

THE VULTURE

From the " Faerie Queene "

A VULTURE greedie of his pray,
Through hunger long that hart to him doth lend,
Strikes at a Heron with all his bodies sway,
That from his force seemes nought may it defend ;
The warie fowle, that spies him toward bend
His dreadful souse, avoydes it, shunning light,
And maketh him his wing in vaine to spend ;
That with the weight of his owne weeldless might
He falleth nigh to ground, and scarce recovereth
    flight.

EDMUND SPENSER.

THE VULTURE

IN days of yore (my cautious rhymes
Always except the present times)
A greedy Vulture, skill'd in game,
Inur'd to guilt, unaw'd by shame,
Approach'd the throne in evil hour,
And step by step intrudes to pow'r :
When at the royal Eagle's ear,
He longs to ease the monarch's care.
The monarch grants.   With pride elate,
Behold him minister of state !
Around him throng the feather'd rout ;
Friends must be serv'd, and some must out ;

Each thinks his own the best pretension ;
This asks a place, and that a pension.
The Nightingale was set aside
A forward daw his room supplied.
" This bird (says he) for business fit,
Hath both sagacity and wit :
With all his turns, and shifts, and tricks,
He's docile, and at nothing sticks :
Then with his neighbours one so free
At all times will connive at me."
The Hawk had due distinction shown,
For parts and talents like his own.
Thousands of hireling cocks attend him,
As blustering bullies to defend him.
At once the Ravens were discarded,
And Magpies with their posts rewarded.
Those fowls of omen I detest,
That pry into another's nest.
State lies must lose all good intent,
For they foresee and croak the event.
My friends ne'er think, but talk by rote,
Speak what they're taught, and so to vote.
" When rogues like these (a Sparrow cries)
To honours and employments rise,
I court no favour, ask no place,
From such preferment is disgrace.
Within my thatch'd retreat I find
(What these ne'er feel) true peace of mind."

JOHN GAY.

THE GOLDEN EAGLE

The tawny eagle seats his callow brood
High on the cliff, and feasts his young with blood,
On Snowdon's rocks, or Orkney's wide domain,
Whose beetling cliffs o'erhang the western main,
The royal bird his lonely kingdom forms
Amidst the gathering clouds and sullen storms.
Through the wide waste of air he darts his sight,
And holds his sounding pinions poised for flight ;
With cruel eye premeditates the war,
And marks his destined victim from afar ;
Descending in a whirlwind to the ground,
His pinions like the rush of waters sound ;
The fairest of the fold he bears away,
And to his nest compels the struggling prey ;
He scorns the game by meaner hunters tore,
And dips his talons in no vulgar gore.

MRS A. LETITIA BARBAULD.

EAGLES TRAINED

From " Field Sports "

In earlier times monarchs of Eastern race,
In their full blaze of pride, as story tells,
Train'd up the imperial eagle, sacred bird !
Hooded, with jingling bells she perch'd on high ;
Not as when erst on golden wings she led
The Roman legions o'er the conquer'd globe,
Mankind her quarry ; but a docile slave,
Tam'd to the lure, and careful to attend
Her master's voice.

WILLIAM SOMERVILLE.

THE EAGLE AND SERPENT

—— In the air do I behold indeed
An eagle and a serpent wreath'd in fight,
And now, relaxing its impetuous flight,
Before th' aërial rock on which I stood,
The eagle hovering wheel'd to left and right,
And hung with lingering wings over the flood,
And startled with its yells the wide air's solitude.

A shaft of light upon its wings descended,
And every golden feather gleam'd therein,
Feather and scale inextricably blended,
The serpent's mail'd and many-colour'd skin
Shone through the plumes, its coils were twined
    within,
With many a swol'n and knotted fold ; and high,
And far, the neck receding lithe and thin,
Sustain'd a crested head, which warily
Shifted, and glanced before the eagle's steadfast eye.

Around, around, in ceaseless circles wheeling,
With clang of wings and scream the eagle sail'd
Incessantly ; something on high concealing
Its lessening orbs, sometimes as if it fail'd,
Dropp'd through the air, and still it shriek'd and
    wail'd,
And casting back its eager head, with beak
And talon unremittingly assail'd
The wreathèd serpent, who did ever seek
Upon his enemy's heart a mortal wound to wreak.

PERCY BYSSHE SHELLEY.

EAGLE

From " Manfred "

THOU winged and cloud-cleaving minister,
Whose happy flight is highest into heaven,
Well may'st thou swoop so near me—I should be
Thy prey, and gorge thine eaglets : thou art gone
Where the eye cannot follow thee ; but thine
Yet pierces downward, onward, or above,
With a pervading vision.

LORD BYRON.

THE EAGLE

OH, Britain, had we never known
The kindling breath of Freedom's zone,
Or, vanquished, had we still remained
In slavery's deepest dungeon chained,
Without one ray of freedom's sun
To wake our sighs for glories gone,
Such cheerless thraldom we might bear
With the dark meekness of despair ;
But the chained Eagle when he sees
His mates upon the mountain breeze,
And marks their free wing upward soar
To heights his own oft reach'd before,
Again that kindred clime he seeks.
Bold bird, 'tis vain—thy wild heart breaks

J. J. CALLANAN.

THE EAGLE

FRAGMENT

HE clasps the crag with crooked hands ;
Close to the sun in lonely lands,
Ring'd with the azure world, he stands.

The wrinkled sea beneath him crawls ;
He watches from his mountain walls,
And like a thunderbolt he falls.

ALFRED, LORD TENNYSON.

THE EAGLE ON SKIDDAW

HARK to the eagle ! how shrill is his cry,
From the breast of the hill which re-echoes on high
Then, borne on the breezes which softly do play,
Tow'r'd the fells of the Derwent it dieth away.
Again from these rocks it doth suddenly break,
And sounding as shrilly, it sweeps o'er the lake ;
Then echoed again from gigantic Grassmoor,
And sharply rebounding from shore unto shore.
But where is the mountain-bird ?   Where doth he
  spring ?
Where beats the breeze backward the flap of his wing ?
Lo, see where impelled by his tempest-like force,
In cloud-hidden circles he wheels on his course ;
O'er the rock-beating torrent he fearless is soaring ;
Scarce hearing its thunders eternally roaring !

JOHN RUSKIN.

HYMN OF THE EAGLE

UPON a sheer-sloped mountain height
My eyrie is ; from thence my sight
Looks down o'er the wide lands below
I watch the wild winds swoop and blow
In savage violence—but here
They howl in vain ; I have no fear
Who am the lord of this high sphere.

At sunrise on this peak I stand,
And watch the glory flood the land ;
And then on mighty wings I speed
Far hence for lowland prey to feed
My clamorous young—though when night falls
Still echo loud their fledgling calls
About these gloomy mountain walls.

I watch the moon rise o'er the sea
And inland sail mysteriously,
A globe of silver fire on high ;
Then pulse the planets in the sky,
And flash the stars, and meteors stream
And then I drowse, to wake with dream
Of prey, and thro' the stillness scream.

WILLIAM SHARP.

TO A HAWK

How gallantly thy soaring wing
Hath won yon place on high !
And there remains, unwavering,
As if its home were in the sky !
Usurper ! thence thou spread'st afar
Terror—like some portentous star !
The birds that skim the lower air
To covert dark, with shrieks repair ;
For well thy sudden swoop they know,
Thy lightning glance, and deadly blow.
The leveret crouches close and still,
On rushy brake and sheltering hill ;
With rustling wing, and fearful wail,
Slow round their young the plovers sail ;
And Man's dim eye and giddy brain
Up to that dazzling height strain after thee in vain.

E. W. BARNARD.

THE FALCON'S AND HERON'S COMBAT

FAIR Princesse of the spacious air,
That hast vouchsaf'd acquaintance here,
With us are quarter'd below stairs,
That can reach heav'n with nought but pray'rs ;
Who, when our activ'st wings we try,
Advance a foot into the sky.

Bright heir t' th' bird imperial,
From whose avenging penons fall
Thunder and lightning twisted spun !
Brave cousin-german to the Sun !

That didst forsake thy throne and sphere,
To be an humble pris'ner here ;
And for a pirch of her soft hand,
Resign the royal woods' command.

How often would'st thou shoot heav'ns ark,
Then mount thyself into a lark ;
And after our short faint eyes call,
When now a fly, now nought at all !
Then stoop so swift under our sence,
As thou wert sent intelligence !

Free beauteous slave, thy happy feet
In silver fetters vervails meet,
And trample on that noble wrist,
The gods have kneel'd in vain t' have kist.
But gaze not, bold deceived spye,
Too much oth' lustre of her eye ;
The Sun thou dost outstare, alas !
Winks at the glory of her face.

But now a quill from thine own wing
I pluck, thy lofty fate to sing;
Whilst we behold the various fight
With mingled pleasure and affright ;
The humbler hinds do fall to pray'r,
As when an army's seen i' th' air,
And the prophetick spannels run,
And howle thy epicedium.

The heron mounted doth appear
On his own Peg'sus a lanceer,
And seems, on earth when he doth hut,
A proper halberdier on foot ;
Secure i' th' moore, about to sup,
The dogs have beat his quarters up.

And now he takes the open air,
Drawes up his wings with tactick care ;
Whilst th' expert falcon swift doth climbe
In subtle mazes serpentine ;
And to advantage closely twin'd
She gets the upper sky and wind,
Where she dissembles to invade,
And lies a pol'tick ambuscade.

The hedg'd-in heron, whom the foe
Awaits above, and dogs below,
In his fortification lies,
And makes him ready for surprize ;
When roused with a shrill alarm,
Was shouted from beneath : they arm.

The falcon charges at first view
With her brigade of talons, through
Whose shoots, the wary heron beat
With a well counterwheel'd retreat.
But the bold gen'ral, never lost,
Hath won again her airy post ;
Who, wild in this affront, now fryes,
Then gives a volley of her eyes.

The desp'rate heron now contracts
In one design all former facts ;
Noble, he is resolv'd to fall,
His and his en'mies' funerall,
And (to be rid of her) to dy,
A publick martyr of the sky.

When now he turns his last to wreak
The palizadoes of his beak,
The raging foe impatient,
Wrack'd with revenge, and fury rent,
Swift as the thunderbolt he strikes
Too sure upon the stand of pikes ;
There she his naked breast doth hit,
And on the case of rapiers's split.

But ev'n in her expiring pangs
The heron's pounc'd within her phangs,
And so above she stoops to rise,
A trophee and a sacrifice ;
Whilst her own bells in the sad fall
Ring out the double funerall.

Ah, victory, unhap'ly wonne !
Weeping and red is set the Sun ;
Whilst the whole field floats in one tear,
And all the air doth mourning wear.
Close-hooded all thy kindred come
To pay their vows upon thy tombe ;
The hobby and the musket too
Do march to take their last adieu.

The lanner and the lanneret
Thy colours bear as banneret ;
The goshawk and her tercel rows'd
With tears attend thee as new bows'd,
All these are in their dark array,
Led by the various herald-jay.

But thy eternal name shall live
Whilst quills from ashes fame reprieve,
Whilst open stands renown's wide dore
And wings are left on which to soar ;
Doctor robbin the prelate pye,
And the poetick swan, shall dye,
Only to sing thy elegie.

RICHARD LOVELACE.

THE FISH-HAWK, OR OSPREY

SOON as the Sun, great ruler of the year,
Bends to our northern climes his bright career,
And from the caves of ocean calls from sleep
The finny shoals and myriads of the deep ;
When freezing tempests back to Greenland ride,
And day and night the equal hours divide ;
True to the season, o'er our sea-beat shore,
The sailing Osprey high is seen to soar,
With broad unmoving wing ; and circling slow,
Marks each loose straggler in the deep below ;
Sweeps down like lightning ! plunges with a roar
And bears his struggling victim to the shore.

The long-housed fisherman beholds with joy,
The well-known signals of his rough employ,

And, as he bears his nets and oars along,
Thus hails the welcome season with a song :—

THE FISHERMAN'S HYMN

The osprey sails above the sound,
    The geese are gone, the gulls are flying ;
The herring shoals swarm thick around,
    The nets are launch'd, the boats are plying ;
        Yo ho, my hearts ! let's seek the deep,
            Raise high the song, and cheerly wish her,
        Still as the bending net we sweep,
            " God bless the Fish-hawk and the Fisher "

She brings us fish,—she brings us Spring,
    Good times, fair weather, warmth and plenty,
Fine store of shad, trout, herring, ling,
    Sheepshead, and drum, and old wives' dainty.
        Yo ho, my hearts ! let's seek the deep,
            Ply every oar, and cheerly wish her,
        Still as the bending net we sweep,
            " God bless the Fish-hawk and the Fisher "

She rears her young on yonder tree,
    She leaves her faithful mate to mind 'em ;
Like us, for fish, she sails to sea,
    And plunging, shows us where to find 'em.
        Yo ho, my hearts ! let's seek the deep,
            Ply every oar, and cheerly wish her,
        While the slow-bending net we sweep,
            " God bless the Fish-hawk and the Fisher "
                                    ALEXANDER WILSON.

MEDRAKE AND OSPREY

MEDRAKE, waving wide wings low over the breeze-
rippled bight !
Osprey, soaring superb overhead in the fathomless
blue,
Graceful, and fearless, and strong ! do you thrill with
the morning's delight
Even as I ? Brings the sunshine a message of
beauty for you ?

O the blithe breeze of the west, blowing sweet from
the far away land,
Bowing the grass heavy-headed, thick crowding, so
slender and proud !
O the warm sea sparkling over with waves by the
swift wind fann'd !
O the wide sky crystal clear, with bright islands of
delicate cloud !

Feel you the waking of life in the world lock'd so long
in the frost,
Beautiful birds, with the light flashing bright from
your banner-like wings ?
Osprey, soaring so high, in the deeps of the sky half
lost !
Medrake, hovering low where the sandpiper's sweet
note rings !

Nothing am I to you, a blot, perhaps, on the day ;
Naught do I add to your joy, but precious you are
in my sight ;

And you seem on your glad wings to lift me up into
   the ether away,
And the morning divine is more radiant because of
   your glorious flight.

CELIA LEIGHTON THAXTER.

THE CORMORANT

ON distant waves, the raven of the sea,
The cormorant, devours her carrion food ;
Along the blood-stained coast of Senegal,
Prowling she scents the cassia-perfumed breeze,
Tainted with death, and keener forward flies ;
And now she nears the carnage-freighted keel,
Unscared by rattling fetters, or the shriek
Of mothers o'er their ocean-buried babes ;
Lured by the scent unweariedly she flies,
And at the foamy dimples of the track,
Darts sportively, or perches on a corpse.

· JAMES GRAHAME.

SOLAN GOOSE AND EIDER DUCK

THE voice of waters, hark ! the solemn swell
   And sullen roar of the far-surging waves ;
The dash of waters in the sparry cell,
   And wind's shrill music in the rocky caves
Through chink and cranny stream the golden rays ;
   The Wild Swan whiter than the glistening foam,
Amid the flashing billows sports and plays ;
   There for awhile the Solan Goose her home
Hath made, and there the Eider Duck is seen,
With glossy back, and head of burnished green.

H. G. A.

THE GANNET

A FEATHER from a gannet's tail,
   Dropp'd in the middle of the ocean,
Well drench'd and tumbled by the gale,
   He did not much admire his motion :
" Where am I ? " quoth the feather with a whine ;
" Oons ! on the ocean's nasty stinking brine ! "

" Sir Plume," quoth ocean to the feather,
" It seems you don't much like foul weather ·
   But pray be grateful, if you please ;
For, pert young gentleman, d'ye see,
Your lofty parent, but for me,
   Had never earn'd his bread and cheese."

DR WOLCOT (" Peter Pindar ")

THE PELICAN

Extracted from " Nature," by Madame Michelet

WHEN weary with her day-long wanderings,
Through evening mists the pelican returns
Home to the reedy nest, and all her young
Gaping with hunger hasten to the shore,
What time they see her o'er the waters swoop.
She with slow steps a rock projecting gains,
And with her drooping wing protects her brood,
While with a wistful gaze she notes the skies.
Fast from her open breast the blood-drops fall ;
In vain has she close searched the watery depths,
Ocean was empty, desolate the shore,
And for her young she brings them but her heart.

Silent and sad, and stretched upon the rock,
She 'mong her sons her very self divides,
Stilling her anguish in her love sublime ;
As from her breast the life-blood swiftly flows,
She with the death-feast totters and grows faint,
With joy, and tenderness, and horror drunk.
But sometimes in the midst of her divine
Self-sacrifice, and weary with the long,
Slow punishment, she fears that death may be
The outcome of that hunger of her brood.
Then quick she rises—opening wide her wings,
Striking her bosom with a wild sharp cry,
And breathing on the night a sad farewell !
So sad that all the sea-birds quit the shore,
And the lone traveller lingering on the strand,
Feels death pass by, and softly recommends
His soul to God !

PAUL HUET.

THE BITTERN AND LAPWING

From " The Deserted Village "

SWEET smiling village, loveliest of the lawn,
Thy sports are fled, and all thy charms withdrawn ;

No more thy glassy brook reflects the day,
But choked with sedges, works its weedy way ;
Along thy glades a solitary guest,
The hollow-sounding bittern guards its nest ;
Amidst thy desert walks the lapwing flies,
And tires their echoes with unvaried cries.

OLIVER GOLDSMITH.

THE HERON

SONNET

I STOOD beside a pool, from whence ascended,
Mounting the cloudy platforms of the wind,
A stately heron ; its soaring I attended,
Till it grew dim, and I with watching blind—
When lo ! a shaft of arrowy light descended
Upon its darkness and its dim attire ;
It straightway kindled then, and was afire,
And with the unconsuming radiance blended.
And bird, a cloud, flecking the sunny air,
It had its golden dwelling 'mid the lightning
Of those empyreal domes, and it might there
Have dwelt for ever, glorified and bright'ning,
But that its wings were weak—so it became
A dusky speck again, that *was* a wingèd flame.

ARCHBISHOP TRENCH.

THE EGRET'S ROYAL CHARTER

HENCEFORTH the milk-white heron shall have rest,
  No more the innocent cloud of wings need fly—
  Too brave to leave their children tho' they die,
Too weak to plead with hands by greed possessed ;
No more the brides by love and beauty dressed,
  'Reft of their plumes, in agony shall lie
  Helpless, and hear the unmothered nestlings cry.
And know they faint, sun-smitten on the nest.

For she, our Queen of tenderness and grace,
  Takes with her royal will the poor bird's part.
  Pride now, before her hecatombs of dead
For murder's millinery, veils her face,
  Nor dares to deck with doom her wanton head,
And heartless fashion finds at last a heart.

H. D. RAWNSLEY.

TO THE STORK

*Armenian popular Song, from the prose Version of
Alishan*

WELCOME, O Stork ! that dost wing
  Thy flight from the far-away !
Thou hast brought us the signs of Spring,
  Thou hast made our sad hearts gay.

Descend, O Stork ! descend
  Upon our roof to rest ;
In our ash-tree, O my friend,
  My darling, make thy nest.

To thee, O Stork ! I complain,
  O Stork, to thee I impart
The thousand sorrows, the pain
  And aching of my heart.

When thou away didst go,
  Away from this tree of ours,
Th· withering winds did blow,
  And dried up all the flowers.

Dark grew the brilliant sky,
  Cloudy and dark and drear ;
They were breaking the snow on high,
  And winter was drawing near.

From Varaca's rocky wall,
  From the rock of Varaca unrolled,
The snow came and covered all,
  And the green meadow was cold.

O Stork, our garden with snow
  Was hidden away and lost,
And the rose-trees that in it grow
  Were withered by snow and frost.
        HENRY W. LONGFELLOW.

THE STATELY FLAMINGOES

FLAMINGOES rare that haunt the shimmering strand,
When slow, on stately wings, they wheel in flight,
Seem everchanging clouds of pink and white
And flashing scarlet, far above the land.

The sun's strong rays the long-legged flock espies
And darts upon them ; see, a moving tone
Of roseate tint is on the waters thrown,
As over them they pass with noisy cries.

Anon, the flock lights on the dreary bank
Of some great pestilential swamp, to feed,
Curving their necks amongst the tangled weed
They search, and not in vain, the herbage rank ;

But ply their curious beaks, of bowlike form.—
How sure their skill ! quick-plunging here and there ·
Incongruous place, for birds so passing fair,
Where none but slimy, loathsome reptiles swarm !

Now, when the feast is brought unto its end,
Or sentries warn with signals loud and harsh,
Echoing throughout the vastness of the marsh,
They mount in chainlike flight, and homeward wend,

To seek their piled-up nests, of mud and sand,
Rising high up above the watery base
That soon shall dry, ere hatched an infant race
Of these strange birds, with brilliant plumage grand.

R. M. INGERSLEY.

A PANEGYRIC ON GEESE

I HATE to sing your hackney'd birds—
  So, doves and swans, a truce !
Your nests have been too often stirred ;
My hero shall be—in a word—
      A goose !

The nightingale, or else " bulbul,"
  By Tommy Moore let loose,
Is grown intolerably dull—
I from the feathered nation cull
      A goose !

Can roasted Philomel a liver
  Fit for a pie produce ?
Fat pies that on the Rhine's sweet river
Fair Strasburg bakes.   Pray who's the giver ?
      A goose !

An ortolan is good to eat,
  A partridge is of use ;
But they are scarce—whereas you meet
At Paris, ay, in every street,
      A goose !

When tired of war the Greeks became,
  They pitched Troy to the deuce,
Ulysses, then, was not to blame
For teaching them the noble " game
      Of goose ''

May Jupiter and Buonaparte
  Of thunder less profuse,
Suffer their eagles to depart,
Encourage peace, and take to heart
      A goose
      FRANCIS MAHONY (" Father Prout ")

A SWAN AT MIDNIGHT

From " The Two Swans "

A SOLITARY Swan her breast of snow
Launches against the wave that seems to freeze
Into a chaste reflection, still below,
Twin-shadow of herself wherever she may go.

And forth she paddles in the very noon
Of solemn midnight, like an elfin thing
Charmed into being by the argent moon—
Whose silver light for love of her fair wing
Goes with her in the shade, still worshipping
Her dainty plumage :—all around her grew
A radiant circlet, like a fairy ring ;
And all behind, a tiny little clue
Of light, to guide her back across the waters blue.

THOMAS HOOD.

TWO SWANS

Translated from " Evening Songs " by Edgar A. Bowring

AND over the pond are sailing
    Two swans all white as snow ;
Sweet voices mysteriously wailing
    Pierce through me as onward they go.

They sail along, and a ringing
    Sweet melody rises on high ;
And when the swans begin singing
    They presently must die.

When in sorrow, they dare not show it,
    However mournful their mood,
For the swan, like the soul of the poet,
    By the dull world is ill understood.

And in their death-hour they waken
    The air, and break into song ;
And, unless my ears are mistaken,
    They sing now, while sailing along.

HEINRICH HEINE.

THE SWAN

From " The Disciples "

AND now I speak . . .
But as the Swan (who has pass'd through the spring,
And found it snow still in the white North land,
And over perilous wilds of Northern seas,
White wings above the white and wintry waves,
Has won, through night and battle of the blasts,
Breathless, alone, without one note or cry)
Sinks into summer by a land at last ;
And knows his wings are broken, and the floods
Will bear him with them whither God shall will ;—
And knows he has one hour between the tides ;—
And sees the salt and silent marshes spread
Before him outward to the shining sea,
Whereon was never any music heard.

HARRIET E. HAMILTON KING.

TO A WATERFOWL

WHITHER, 'midst falling dew,
While glow the heavens with the last steps of day,
Far through their rosy depths, dost thou pursue
    Thy solitary way ?

    Vainly the fowler's eye
Might mark thy distant flight to do thee wrong,
As, darkly painted on the crimson sky,
    Thy figure floats along.

Seek'st thou the plashy brink
Of weedy lake, or marge of river wide,
O*r* where the rocking billows rise and sink
    On the chafed ocean-side ?

There is a Power whose care
Teaches that way along thy pathless coast,—
The desert and illimitable air,—
    Lone wandering, but not lost.

All day thy wings have fanned,
At that far height, the cold, thin atmosphere ;
Yet stoop not, weary, to the welcome land,
    Though the dark night is near.

And soon that toil shall end ;
Soon shalt thou find a summer home, and rest
And scream among thy fellows ; reeds shall bend
    Soon o'er thy sheltered nest.

Thou'rt gone, the abyss of heaven
Hath swallowed up thy form : yet on my heart
Deeply hath sunk the lesson thou hast given,
    And shall not soon depart.

He who from zone to zone
Guides through the boundless sky thy certain flight
In the long way that I must tread alone,
    Will lead my steps aright.
                    WILLIAM CULLEN BRYANT.

ON SCARING SOME WATER-FOWL IN LOCH TURFIT

WHY, ye tenants of the lake,
For me your watery haunts forsake ?
Tell me, fellow-creatures, why
At my presence thus you fly ?
Why disturb your social joys,
Parent, filial, kindred ties ?—
Common friend to you and me,
Nature's gifts to all are free :
Peaceful keep your dimpling wave,
Busy feed, or wanton lave ;
Or, beneath the sheltering rock,
Bide the surging billow's shock.

Conscious, blushing for our race,
Soon, too soon, your fears I trace.
Man, your proud usurping foe,
Would be lord of all below :
Plumes himself in freedom's pride,
Tyrant stern to all beside.
The eagle, from the cliffy brow,
Marking you his prey below,
In his breast no pity dwells,
Strong necessity compels :
But man, to whom alone is given
A ray direct from pitying Heaven,
Glories in his heart humane—
And creatures for his pleasure slain.

In these savage, liquid plains,
Only known to wand'ring swains,
Where the mossy rivulet strays,
Far from human haunts and ways ;
All on nature you depend,
And life's poor season peaceful spend.
Or, if man's superior might
Dare invade your native right,
On the lofty ether borne,
Man with all his powers you scorn ·
Swiftly seek, on clanging wings,
Other lakes and other springs ;
And the foe you cannot brave,
Scorn at least to be his slave.

ROBERT BURNS.

TO A WOOD-PIGEON

HAVE I sear'd thee from thy bough,
Tenant of the lonely wild,
Where, from human face exil'd,
'Tis thine the sky to plough ;
Hearing but the wailing breeze,
Or the cataracts sullen roaring,
Where, 'mid clumps of ancient trees,
O'er its rocks the stream is pouring ?—
Up on ready wing thou rushest
To the gloom of woods profound,
And through silent ether brushest
With a whirring sound.

Ring-dove beauteous ! is the face
Of man so hateful, that his sight
Startles thee in wild affright,
From beechen resting-place ?—

Surely pleasant life is thine,
Underneath the shining day ;
Thus, from sorrow far away,
'Mid bowering groves to pine—
To pine with wild, luxurious love,
While coos thy timid partner near thee ;
Flowers below, and boughs above ;
And nought around to fear thee ;
While thy bill so gently carries
To thy young, from field or wood,
Seeds, or fruits, or purple berries,
For their slender food.

Rapidly thou wing'st away—
I saw thee now, a tiny spot—
Again—and now I see thee not—
Nought save the skies of day.—
The Psalmist once his prayer address'd—
" Dove, could I thy pinions borrow,
My soul would flee, and be at rest,
Far from the earth's oppressing sorrow ''
Alas ! we turn to brave the billows
Of the world's tempestuous sway,
Where Life's stream, beneath care's willows,
Murmurs night and day !

DAVID MACBETH MOIR.

THE PLAINT OF THE WOOD-QUEST

IN the lovely, lonely places that are thine, Eirinn dear—
Beneath thy skies of chrysoprase, amber and jasper seas ;
Over thy emerald mosses, 'neath thy ruby-budding trees—
Beeches showing the spring-time, while winter yet is here ;
I wander, lonely stranger, come to thee for peace and calm,
Grief-broken, desolate, alone—a pilgrim from afar ;
While I muse and mourn, and ponder where my lost belovèd are—
In the deep woods there sounds the wild doves' ceaseless psalm.

I hear it in my heart, where it echoes all the day,
That soft, low chanting monotone of pleading dove-like prayer ;
It breathes in all my thoughts and hopes, it sounds on every air,
The Requiem Æternam, that the dear wild wood-doves say

Have other sorrowing hearts, I wonder, heard it as I hear ?
The low refrain—" Take two souls, Lady, Lady—take two ! "
The wood-doves' plaint, the cry of love, the call her ear to woo—
It seems to plead for my beloved in the sweet Mother's ear.

ROSE ARRESTI.

TO THE TURTLE-DOVE

DEEP in the wood, thy voice I list, and love
Thy soft complaining song,—thy tender cooing ;
O what a winning way thou hast of wooing !
Gentlest of all thy race—sweet Turtle-dove.
Thine is a note that doth not pass away,
Like the light music of a Summer's day !
The merle may trill his richest song in vain—
Scarce do we say, " List, for he pipes again,"—
But thou ! that low plaint oft and oft repeating
To the coy mate that needs so much entreating—
Fillest the woods with a discursive song
Of love, that sinketh deep, and resteth long,—
Hushing the voice of mirth and staying folly,—
And waking in the heart a gentle melancholy.

D. CONWAY.

CARRIER-PIGEON

From " Sacred Songs "

The bird let loose in eastern skies,
    When hast'ning fondly home,
Ne'er stoops to earth her wing, nor flies
    Where idle warblers roam.

But high she shoots through air and light,
    Above all low delay,
Where nothing earthly bounds her flight,
    Nor shadow dims her way.

So grant me, God, from every care,
And stain of passion free,
Aloft, through virtue's purer air,
To hold my course to Thee !

No sin to cloud, no lure to stay
My soul, as home she springs ;
Thy sunshine on her joyful way,
Thy freedom on her wings !
                    THOMAS MOORE.

A WHITE DOVE

From the Swedish

THERE sitteth a Dove so white and fair,
All on the lily spray,
And she listeneth when to our Saviour dear
The little children pray.

Lightly she spreads her friendly wings,
And to heaven's gate hath sped ;
And unto the Father in heaven she bears
The prayers that the children have said.

And back she comes from heaven's gate,
And brings—that dove so mild—
From the Father in heaven who hears her speak,
A blessing for every child.

Then, children, lift up a pious prayer ;
It hears whatever you say,
That heavenly Dove so white and fair,
That sits on the lily spray.
                    FREDERIKA BREMER.

ON STARTLING SOME PIGEONS

A HUNDRED wings are dropt as soft as one,
    Now ye are lighted !   Pleasing to my sight
The fearful circle of your wondering flight,
Rapid and loud, and drawing homeward soon ;
And then, the sober chiding of your tone,
    As there ye sit, from your own roofs arraigning
My trespass on your haunts, so boldly done,
    Sounds like a solemn and a just complaining :
O happy, happy race ! for though there clings
    A feeble fear about your timid clan,
Yet ye are blest ! with not a thought that brings
    Disquietude,—while proud and sorrowing man,
An eagle, weary of his mighty wings,
    With anxious inquest fills his mortal span !
                          CHARLES TENNYSON-TURNER.

CAPERCAILLIE

HIE thee away, my bonny moor-hen !
Keep to the south of the Skelf-hill Pen ;
Blithe be thy heart, and soft thy bed
Amang the blooms of the heather so red.
When the weird is sped that I must dree,
I'll come and dwell in the wild with thee.
Keep thee afar from the fowler's ken—
Hie thee away, my bonny moor-hen.

Cock of the mountain, and king of the moor,
A maiden's benison be thy dower ;
For gentle and kind hath been thy life
Free from malice and free from strife.

Light be thy heart on the mountain gray,
And loud thy note at the break of day.
When five times fifty years are gone,
I'll seek thee again 'mang the heath alone,
And change thy form, if that age shall prove
An age that virtue and truth can love ;
True be thy love and far thy reign,
On the Border dale till I see thee again.

JAMES HOGG.

THE HEATH COCK

GOOD-MORROW to thy sable beak
And glossy plumage dark and sleek,
Thy crimson moon and azure eye,
Cock of the Heath, so wildly shy :
I see thee slyly cowering through
That wiry web of silver dew,
That twinkles in the morning air,
Like casements of my lady fair.

A maid there is in yonder tower,
Who peeping from her early bower,
Half shows, like thee, her simple wile,
Her braided hair and morning smile.
The rarest things with wayward will
Beneath the covert hide them still ;
The rarest thing to break of day
Look shortly forth and shrink away.

A fleeting moment of delight
I sunn'd me in her cheering sight,
As short I ween the time will be
That I shall parley hold with thee.
Through Snowdon's mist red beams the day,
The climbing herdboy chants his lay,
The gnat-flies dance their sunny ring,—
Thou art already on the wing.

JOANNA BAILLIE.

GROUSE

From " Fowling "

THEIR eyes, so bright of late,
Surmounted by a brow of scarlet fringe,
How dull and heavy now ! Yet still their plumes
Retain their colour, red and white immixed
With transverse bars and spots of sable hue.
Most common those—yet grouse of other kind
The fowler often finds, of larger growth
And glossy jet, Black-game or Heath-cock term'd.
Nor are the red on every heathy moor
Or rocky mountain found ; full many a waste
Wash'd by the southern or the western main,
Has ne'er received them, though abundant else
In store of footed or of feathered game.
But in the north the race is found
More frequent, chief where Scotia spreads at large
Her heaths, her mountains, and her glittering lochs,
With piny forests intersected oft,

Primeval nature, simple and august.
Beneath those deep and·solitary shades,
With native freedom blest, the wild deer roves ;
The Ptarmacan and Capperthaily there,
Jealous and shy glide through the verdant gloom.
H. G. A.

CHAUNTECLERE

A PORE wydow, somewhat stooped with age,
Was whilom dwellyng in a narrow cotáge,

A yerd she had, enclosèd al·aboute,
With stikkes, and a drye ditch withoute,
In which she had a cok, hight Chaunteclere,
In al the lond of crowyng was none his peere.
His vois was merier than the mery orgon,
On masse dayes that in the chirche drone ;
Wel surer was his crowyng in his cell,
Than is a clok, or yet an abbay bell,
By nature knew he ech ascension
Of all the houres that struck in thilke toun ;
For when degrees fyftene were ascendid,
Thanne crew he wel, it might not be amendid.
His comb was redder than the fyn coral,
Embattled, as it were a castel wal.
His bill was blak, and lyke jet it shon ;
Like azure were his legges, and his tone ;
　H nisayles whitter than the lily flour,
　And lik the burnisht gold was his colour.
GEOFFRY CHAUCER.

(This has been modernised by J. DRYDEN. It is from CHAUCER'S Nun's Priest Tale of the Cock and the Fox.)

THERE lived, as authors tell, in days of yore,
A widow somewhat old, and very poor :
Deep in a cell her cottage lonely stood,
Well thatch'd, and under covert of a wood.
    .   .   .   .   .
A yard she had with pales inclos'd about,
Some high, some low, and a dry ditch without.
Within the homestead liv'd, without a peer
For crowing loud, the noble Chanticleer ;
So hight her cock, whose singing did surpass
The merry notes of organs at the mass.
More certain was the crowing of the cock
To number hours, than is an abbey clock ;
And sooner than the matin bell was rung,
He clapt his wings upon his roost, and sung
For when degrees fifteen ascended right,
By sure instinct he knew 'twas one at night.
High was his comb, and coral-red withal,
In dents embattled like a castle wall ;
His bill was raven-black, and shone like jet ;
Blue were his legs, and orient were his feet :
White were his nails, like silver to behold ;
His body glittering like the burnish'd gold.

JOHN DRYDEN.

CHANTICLEER

From " The Bristowe Tragedy "

THE feather'd songster, Chanticleer,
Had wound his bugle-horn,
And told the early villager
The coming of the morn.
King Edward saw the ruddy streaks
Of light eclipse the grey,
And heard the raven's croaking throat
Proclaim the fated day.
" Thou'rt right," he said, " for, by the God
That sits enthroned on high,
Charles Bawdin, and his fellows twain,
This day shall surely die."

THOMAS CHATTERTON.

THE COCK

O WAKEFUL bird ! proclaimer of the day,
  Whose piercing note doth daunt the lion's rage ;
Thy crowing did myself to me bewray,
  My frights and brutish heats it did assuage.
But oh ! in this alone, unhappy cock,
That thou to count my foils wert made the clock !

O bird ! the just rebuker of my crime,
  The faithful waker of my sleeping fears,
Be thou the daily clock to strike the time,
  When stinted eyes shall pay their task of tears ;
Upbraid mine ears with thine accusing crow,
To make me rue what first it made me know.

O mild revenger of aspiring pride !
Thou canst dismount high thoughts to low effects ;
Thou mad'st a cock me for my fault to chide,
My lofty boasts this lowly bird corrects.
Well might a cock correct me with a crow,
Whom hennish cackling first did overthrow.

ROBERT SOUTHWELL.

THE TURKEY

From " The Dumb Orators "

As a male turkey straggling on the green,
When by fierce harriers, terriers, mongrels seen,
He feels the insult of the noisy train
And skulks aside, though moved by much disdain ;
But when that turkey, at his own barn-door,
Sees one poor straying puppy and no more,
(A foolish puppy who had left the pack,
Thoughtless that foe was threatening at his back,)
He moves about, as ship prepared to sail,
He hoists his proud rotundity of tail,
The half-seal'd eyes and changeful neck he shows,
Where, in its quick'ning colours, vengeance glows ;
From red to blue the pendant wattles turn,
Blue mix'd with red, as matches when they burn ;
And thus th' intruding snarler to oppose,
Urged by enkindling wrath, he gobbling goes.

GEORGE CRABBE.

A PHEASANT OF " WINDSOR FOREST "

See ! from the brake the whirring pheasant springs,
And mounts exulting on triumphant wings
Short is his joy ; he feels the fiery wound,
Flutters in blood, and panting beats the ground.
Ah ! what avail his glossy, varying dyes,
His purple crest, and scarlet-circled eyes,
The vivid green his shining plumes unfold,
His painted wings, and breast that flames with gold ?
.
With slaughtering guns the unwearied fowler roves
When frosts have whiten'd all the naked groves,
Where doves in flocks the leafless trees o'ershade,
And lonely woodcocks haunt the watery glade.
He lifts the tube, and levels with his eye ;
Straight a short thunder breaks the frozen sky ·
Oft, as in airy rings they skim the heath,
The clamorous lapwings feel the leaden death :
Oft, as the mounting larks their notes prepare,
They fall, and leave their little lives in air.

ALEXANDER POPE.

THE PHEASANT

CLOSE by the borders of the fringèd lake,
And on the oak's expanding bough, is seen,
What time the leaves the passing zephyrs shake,
And gently murmur through the sylvan scene :
The gaudy Pheasant, rich with varying dyes,
That fade alternate, and alternate glow,
Receiving now his colours from the skies,
And now reflecting back the watery bow.
He flaps his wings, erects his spotted crest ;
His flaming eyes dart forth a piercing ray ;
He swells the lovely plumage of his breast,
And glares a wonder of the orient day.
Ah ! what avail such heavenly plumes as thine,
When dogs and sportsmen in thy ruin join !

ANON.

PARTRIDGE AND TIERCEL 'GENTLE

THEN for an evening flight
A Tiercel Gentle, which I call my Master's,
As he were sent a message to the moon,
In such a place flies, as he seems to say,
See me, or see me not ! The Partridge springs,
He makes his stoop ; but wanting breath is forced
To chanceler ; then with such speed, as if
He carried lightning in his wings, he strikes
The trembling bird, who even in death appears
Proud to be made his quarry.

PHILIP MASSINGER.

THE PEACOCK

From " Truth "

THE self-applauding bird, the peacock, see—
Mark what a sumptuous pharisee is he !
Meridian sunbeams tempt him to unfold
His radiant glories, azure, green, and gold ·
He treads as if, some solemn music near,
His measur'd step were govern'd by his ear ·
And seems to say—Ye meaner fowl, give place,
I am all splendour, dignity, and grace !
                              WILLIAM COWPER.

THE PEACOCK COMPLAINING TO JUNO

THE Peacock to the queen of heaven
Complained in some such words
" Great goddess, you have given
To me, the laughing-stock of birds,
A voice which fills, by taste quite just,
All nature with disgust ;
Whereas that little paltry thing,
The nightingale, pours from her throat
So sweet and ravishing a note,
She bears alone the honours of the spring."

In anger Juno heard,
And cried, " Shame on you, jealous bird !
Grudge you the nightingale her voice,
Who in the rainbow-neck rejoice,
Than costliest silks more richly tinted,
In charms of grace and form unstinted,—

Who strut in kingly pride,
Your glorious tail spread wide
With brilliants which in sheen do
Outshine the jeweller's bow window ?

Is there a bird beneath the blue
That has more charms than you ?
No animal in everything can shine.
By just partition of our gifts divine,
Each has its full and proper share ;
Among the birds that cleave the air,
The hawk's a swift, the eagle is a brave one,
For omens serves the hoarse old raven,
The rook's of coming ills the prophet ;
  And if there's any discontent,
  I've heard not of it.
    Cease, then, your envious complaint ;
  Or I, instead of making up your lack,
Will take your boasted plumage from your back."
JEAN DE LA FONTAINE.

THE DOTTEREL

From " Polyolbion "

THE Dotterell, which we think a very dainty dish,
Whose taking makes more sport, as man no more can
    wish,
For as you creepe, or coure, or lye, or stoupe, or goe,
So marking you (with care) the apish bird doth soe,
And acting everything, doth never mark the net,
Till he be in the snare, which men for him have set.
MICHAEL DRAYTON.

THE LAPWING

THE desert's heart is thine, wild bird,
      The wilderness !
There in the solitude is heard
      God's tenderness.

Thy plaintive scream uplift on high,
      Wilder, more free ;
My soul bounds forward with the cry,
      God's liberty !

With autumn flocks seek clustering grey
      The fallow downs,
With a shiver of silver breasts—away,
      And darkling crowns !

A dusky vapour floats on high—
      It breaks, it breathes !
Bright rippling ranks unfold and fly
      In wavering wreaths.

Diving in airy circles, play
      On dark-edged wing ;
O'er peaty turf now pick thy way,
      Dim, crested thing !

Then like the bird on ocean's coast
      Feathered with foam,
Behind the moor's rock billows lost,
      Thou droppest home !

Life's borders are vast mysteries—
Depths all unknown ;
Wings that in pride of strength uprise
Are backward blown !

C. A. FOX.

THE PLOVER

THE plover safe her airy scream
Circling repeats, then to a distance flies,
And querulous still returns importunate,
Yet still escapes, unworthy of our aim.
Amid the marsh's rushy skirts her nest
Is slightly strewn ; four eggs of olive hue
Spotted with black she broods upon.

She, if or dog
Or man intrude upon her bleak domain,
Skims, clamouring loud, close at their feet, with wing
Stooping, as if impeded by a wound.

JAMES GRAHAME.

THE CORN-CRAKE

AGAIN the ruthless weapon sweeps the ground,
And the grey Corn-crake trembles at the sound ;
Her callow brood around her cowering cling,—
She braves its edge—she mourns her severed wing ;
Oft had she taught them with a mother's love,
To note the pouncing merlin from the dove ;
The slowly floating buzzard's eye to shun,
As o'er the meads he hovers in the sun ;

The weazel's sly imposture to prevent ;
And mark the marten by his musky scent ;—
Ah ! fruitless skill, which taught her not to scan
The scythe afar, and ruthless arm of man !
In vain her mate, as evening-shadows fall,
Still lingering wait for her accustomed call :
The shepherd-boys shall oft her loss deplore
That mocked her notes beside the cottage door.
                                     JOHN LEYDEN.

THE CRY OF THE CORNCRAKE

ON mellow eves as daylight slips away
And darkness creeps above the slumbrous folds,
From sight withdrawn, the corncrake wends his way,
His solemn music ringing o'er the wolds.

The landrail loves the clover-meadows wide,
From whence resounds his weird and rasping cry ;
O'er many a fair and blooming country-side,
His harsh note eddies 'neath the silent sky.

And who that hears this watchman of the night,
Awake the birds with quaint, insistent call,
Can cease to pray for grace to live aright ?
Can quite forget God's presence over all ?
                                     ADA LOVEGROVE.

THE COOT ON THE CHERWELL

Sweet Cherwell ! are thy hawthorn tents
Fit havens for my summer boat,
And fair the lily-isles which float,
The stream's most touching incidents.
There have I watched the downy coot
Pacing with safe and steady foot
The surface of the floating field,
And though the elastic floor might yield
In chinks, and let the water flow
In beads of crystal from below,
Yet was the tremulous region true
To that rough traveller passing through.

F. W. Faber.

THE LITTLE BEACH BIRD

Thou little bird, thou dweller by the sea,
Why takest thou its melancholy voice ?
    Why with that boding cry
    O'er the waves dost thou fly ?
    Oh, rather, bird, with me,
    Through the fair land rejoice !
Thy flitting form comes ghostly dim, and pale,
As driven by a beating storm at sea ;
    Thy cry is weak and scared,
    As if thy mates had shared
The doom of us. Thy wail—
What does it bring to me ?

Of thousands thou, both sepulchre and pall,
Old Ocean, art ! A requiem on the dead,
    From out thy gloomy cells,
    A tale of mourning tells—
Tells of man's woe and fall,
His sinless glory fled.

Then turn thee, little bird, and take thy flight
Where the complaining sea shall sadness bring
    Thy spirit never more :
    Come, quit with me the shore,
For gladness and the light,
Where birds of summer sing.

RICHARD H. DANA.

THE SANDPIPER

ACROSS the narrow beach we flit,
One little sandpiper and I ;
And fast I gather, bit by bit,
The scattered driftwood, bleached and dry.
The wild waves reach their hands for it,
The wild wind raves, the tide runs high,
As up and down the beach we flit—
One little sandpiper and I.

Above our heads the sullen clouds
Scud black and swift across the sky ;
Like silent ghosts in misty shrouds
Stand out the white lighthouses high.

Almost as far as eye can reach
I see the close-reefed vessels fly,
As fast we flit along the beach—
One little sandpiper and I.

I watch him as he skims along,
Uttering his sweet and mournful cry.
He starts not at my fitful song,
Or flash of fluttering drapery.
He has no thought of any wrong ;
He scans me with a fearless eye.
Staunch friends are we, well tried and strong,
The little sandpiper and I.

Comrade, where wilt thou be to-night
When the loosed storm breaks furiously ?
My driftwood fire will burn so bright !
To what warm shelter canst thou fly ?
I do not fear for thee, though wroth
The tempest rushes through the sky ·
For are we not God's children both,
Thou, little sandpiper and I ?

CELIA LEIGHTON THAXTER.

THE SNIPE'S EXPLOIT

A SONG, or dirge for a bird we raise,
(*A man is brooding by the fire*) ·
The snipe tracks out his airy ways ,
Marsh, heath, and home his fond desire.

Chip, chip ! with bill unto his mate,
  (*The man has left the waning fire*) ·
The evening falls, on wing elate,
  The restless pinions never tire.

The sun has gone, the air is cold
  (*The man's heart is a wakened fire*) :
Of night, nor foe with gun all bold,
  Recks not the heedless, happy flier.

His beak—the lance of this brown knight
  (*A hand holds forth a tube of fire*),
Horsed on the night-winds rising light—
  A flash ! Is that his funeral pyre ?

Dame Nature guides her willing child,
  (*No snipe shall glut that man's desire*) ·
Upwing—zigzag ! the shot flies wild—
  Sound for the Snipe a victor's lyre !

                                C. L. BRAIN.

THE CURLEW'S CAMP

THE wilderness receives me deep in its rugged breast ;
Smooth worldly ways delude me, I am wearying for
    rest :
There is a toll of welcome in the Curlew's distant call,
Here buried be my sorrows, with the brown grass for
    a pall.
    I do not come, O warning bird ! to steal thy
    hidden young,
  Curlee to them ;—*Tutuo* to me sounds harshly
    from thy tongue.

There is a quaint obsequience in the drooping of thy
beak,
A sigh of resignation in thine accents as they speak ;
Hast thou caught that strain of sadness from this
wind-swept moorland plain,
Or where thou seek'st God's guerdon near the wave-
. unfolding main ?

Thy bill is but a bugle to breathe the first alarm
For all the feathered regiments to manœuvre out of
harm ;
Grey-uniformed and stalwart, birds' sentry ! Thou
shouldst be,
Since I have fled the haunts of men, a sentinel for me ;
I do not come, O warning bird ! to steal thy
hidden young,
Curlee to them,—curlee to me sound sweetly
from thy tongue !

C. L. BRAIN.

THE SEA GULL

THE white sea-gull, the wild sea-gull,
A joyful bird is he,
As he lies like a cradled thing at rest
In the arms of a sunny sea !
The little waves rock to and fro,
And the white gull lies asleep,
As the fisher's bark, with breeze and tide,
Goes merrily over the deep.

The ship, with her fair sails set, goes by,
  And her people stand to note
How the sea-gull sits on the rocking waves,
  As still as an anchored boat.
The sea is fresh, and the sea is fair,
  And the sky calm overhead
And the sea-gull lies on the deep deep sea,
  Live a king in his royal bed !

The white sea-gull, the bold sea-gull,
  A joyful bird is he,
Sitting, like a king, in calm repose,
  On the breast of the heaving sea ! •
The waves leap up, the wild wind blows,
  And the gulls together crowd,
And wheel about, and madly scream
  To the sea that is roaring loud :

And let the sea roar ever so loud,
  And the wind pipe ever so high,
With a wilder joy the bold sea-gull
  Sendeth forth a wilder cry ;—
For the sea-gull he is a daring bird,
  And he loves with the storm to sail ;
To ride in the strength of the billowy sea,
  And to breast the driving gale !

The little boat she is tossed about
  Like a sea-weed, to and fro ;
The tall ship reels like a drunken man,
  As the gusty tempests blow ;

But the sea-gull laughs at the pride of man,
And sails, in a wild delight,
On the torn-up breast of the night-black sea,
Like a foam-cloud, calm and white.

The waves may rage, and the winds may roar,
But he fears not wreck, nor need ;
For he rides the sea, in its stormy strength,
As a strong man rides his steed.
The white sea-gull, the bold sea-gull,
He makes on the shore his nest,
And he tries what the inland fields may be ;
But he loveth the sea the best !

And away from land, a thousand leagues,
He goes 'mid the surging foam ;—
What matters to him or land or shore,
For the sea is his truest home !
And away to the North among ice-rocks stern,
And among the frozen snow,
To a sea that is lone and desolate,
Will the wanton sea-gull go.

For he careth not for the winter wild,
Nor those desert regions chill ;
In the midst of the cold, as on calm blue seas,
The sea-gull hath his will !
And the dead whale lies on the northern shores,
And the seal, and the sea-horse grim ;
And the death of the great sea-creatures makes
A full merry feast for him.

The wild sea-gull, the bold sea-gull,
  As he screams in his wheeling flight,
As he sits on the waves in storm or calm,
  All cometh to him aright !
All cometh to him as he liketh best,
  Nor any his will gainsay !
And he rides on the waves like a bold young king
  That was crowned but yesterday !

                              MARY HOWITT.

• TO A SEA-GULL

WHITE bird of the tempest !   O beautiful thing !
With the bosom of snow, and the motionless wing ;
Now sweeping the billow, now floating on high,
Now bathing thy plumes in the light of the sky ;
Now poising o'er ocean thy delicate form,
Now breasting the surge with thy bosom so warm ;
Now darting aloft, with a heavenly scorn,
Now shooting along like a ray of the morn ;
Now lost in the folds of the cloud-curtain'd dome,
Now floating abroad like a flake of the foam ;
Now silently poised o'er the war of the main,
Like the spirit of Charity brooding o'er pain ;
Now gliding with pinion all silently furl'd,
Like an angel descending to comfort the world,
Thou seem'st to my spirit, as upward I gaze,
And see thee, now cloth'd in mellowest rays,
Now lost in the storm-driven vapours, that fly
Like hosts that are routed across the broad sky,
Like a pure spirit, true to its virtue and faith,
'Mid the tempest of nature, of passion, and death.

Rise ! beautiful emblem of purity ! rise
On the sweet winds of heaven, to thine own brilliant
    skies ;
Still higher ! still higher ! till lost to our sight,
Thou hidest thy wings in a mantle of light ;
And I think how a pure spirit gazing on thee,
Must long for that moment—the joyous and free,
When the soul disembodied from nature, shall spring
Unfetter'd, at once to her Maker and King ;
When the bright day of service and suffering past,
Shapes, fairer than thine, shall shine round her at last,
While the standard of battle triumphantly furl'd,
She smiles like a victor, serene on the world !

GERALD GRIFFIN.

THE KITTIWAKE

. LIKE white feathers blown about the rocks,
    Like soft snowflakes wavering in the air,
Wheel the Kittiwakes in scattered flocks,
    Crying, floating, fluttering, everywhere.

Shapes of snow and cloud, they soar and whirl
    Downy breasts that shine like lilies white ;
Delicate vaporous tints of grey and pearl
    Laid upon their arching wings so light.

Eyes of jet and beaks and feet of gold,—
    Lovelier creatures never sailed in air ;
Innocent, inquisitive, and bold,
    Knowing not the dangers that they dare.

Stooping now above a beckoning hand,
  Following gleams of waving kerchiefs white,
What should they of evil understand,
  Though the gun awaits them full in sight ?

Though their blood the quiet wave makes red,
  Though their broken plumes float far and wide,
Still they linger, hovering overhead,
  Still the gun deals death on every side.

Oh, begone, sweet birds, or higher soar,
  See you not your comrades low are laid ?
But they only flit and call the more,—
  Ignorant, unconscious, undismayed.

Nay, then, boatman, spare them ! Must they bear
  Pangs like these for human vanity ?
That their lovely plumage we may wear
  Must these fair, pathetic creatures die ?

Let the tawny squaws themselves admire,
  Decked with feathers—we can wiser be.
Ah, beseech you, boatman, do not fire !
  Stain no more with blood the tranquil sea.
                    CELIA LEIGHTON THAXTER.

THE SEA-MEW

How joyously the young sea-mew
Lay dreaming on the waters blue,
Whereon our little bark had thrown
A forward shade—the only one—
But shadows aye will man pursue !

Familiar with the waves, and free,
As if their own white foam were he ·
His heart upon the heart of ocean,
Learning all its mystic motion,
And throbbing to the throbbing sea

And such a brightness in his eye,
As if the ocean and the sky,
Within him had lit up and nurst
A soul God gave him not at first,
To comprehend their majesty.

We were not cruel, yet did sunder
His white wing from the blue waves under,
And bound it—while his fearless eyes
Shone up to ours in calm surprise,
As deeming us some ocean wonder !

We bore our ocean bird unto
A grassy place where he might view
The flowers bending to the bees,
The waving of the tall green trees,
The falling of the silver dew.

But flowers of earth were pale to him
Who had seen the rainbow fishes swim ;
And when earth's dew around him lay,
He thought of ocean's wingèd spray,
And his eye waxèd sad and dim.

The green trees round him only made
A prison, with their darksome shade :
And drooped his wing, and mournèd he
For his own boundless glittering sea—
Albeit he knew not they could fade !

Then one her gladsome face did bring,
Her gentle voice's murmuring,
In ocean's stead his heart to move,
And teach him what was human love
He thought it a strange, mournful thing

He lay down in his grief to die,
(First looking to the sea-like sky,
That hath no waves !) because, alas !
Our human touch did on him pass,
And with our touch, our agony.

ELIZABETH BARRETT BROWNING.

THE SEA-DIVER

MY way is on the bright blue sea,
  My sleep upon its rocking tide ;
And many an eye has followed me
  Where billows clasp the worn seaside.

My plumage bears the crimson blush,
  When ocean by the sun is kissed ;
When fades the evening's purple flush,
  My dark wing cleaves the silver mist.

Full many a fathom down beneath
  The bright arch of the splendid deep,
My ear has heard the sea-shell breathe
  O'er living myriads in their sleep.

They rested by the coral throne,
  And by the pearly diadem,
Where the pale sea-grape had o'er-grown
  The glorious dwellings made for them.

At night, upon my storm-drenched wing,
  I poised above a helmless bark,
And soon I saw the shattered thing
  Had passed away and left no mark.

And when the wind and storm had done,
  A ship, that had rode out the gale,
Sank down without a signal-gun,
  And none was left to tell the tale.

I saw the pomp of day depart—
  The cloud resign its golden crown,
When to the ocean's beating heart
  The sailor's wasted corse went down.

Peace be to those whose graves are made
  Beneath the bright and silver sea !
Peace that their relics there were laid,
  With no vain pride and pageantry.
             Henry W. Longfellow.

THE PENGUIN

From " Pelican Island "

THE heavy penguin, neither fish nor fowl,
With scaly feathers and with finny wings,
Plumped stone-like from the rock into the gulf,
Rebounding upward, swift as from a sling,
Through yielding water as through limpid air.
                                    JAMES MONTGOMERY.

THE STORMY PETREL

HARBINGER of death and danger, o'er the darkling
    furrowed sea
Rides the Stormy Petrel telling where the gathered
    whirlwinds be.
Bird of Fate, whom we should welcome, counting thee
    as truly blest
For thy tidings and thy warnings timely brought
    from east or west,
Know'st not that an ill-tongued prophet is by all men
    deemed accurst—
He that soonest cries disaster, he that sees far doom
    the first ?

Thou and thy weird web-foot brethren, sable-featured,
    tempest-toss'd,
Ye are held for souls of pirates, errant-drifting, sen-
    tenced, lost,

Spirits of such crafty Norsemen as in rapine ruled the
main,
Shedding blood for very fierceness, lust of treasure
and of gain,
Now condemned to wander ever, evermore to dip and
lave
Black-stained sins, black deeds of old time, in the
crystal-crested wave.

Say, ye wraiths of Viking rovers, grim and dreaded
buccaneers,
Whose vindictive quest of white sails still across mid-
ocean steers,
Tracking wreck and bringing wreckage—say, in
mystic demon form
Do ye plan and tread, commanding, every footprint
of the storm ?

Nay, poor Petrel, here's a story writ for thee through
gentler lore :
Named wert thou, that walk'st the water, from the
impetuous saint of yore—
Peter—who by faith would gladly step with trembling
human feet
On the Lord's own shining pathway, there his graci-
ous Lord to greet.
Fear not. He whose touch upheld the apostle's life
on Galilee,
Gave thy wings strong and sustaining, O thou wander-
ing bird, to thee !

LADY LINDSAY.

AN ADDRESS TO AN ALBATROSS

GREAT albatross !—the meanest birds
 Spring up and flit away,
While thou must toil to gain a flight,
 And spread these pinions grey ;
But when thou once art fairly poised
 Far o'er each chirping thing
Thou sailest wide to other lands,
 E'en sleeping on the wing.
CHARLES GODFREY LELAND.

ALBATROSS

Now upon Australian seas,
Wafted by the tropic breeze,
We salute the southern cross,
Watch the wondrous albatross—
Circling round in orbits vast,
Pausing now above the mast,
Leaking now his snowy breast
Where the willows sleeping rest.

Now he skims the surface o'er,
Rising, falling evermore :
Floating high on stillest wing,
Now he seems a guardian thing,
Now a message of wrath,
Cleaving swift his airy path ;
Bearing o'er the liquid plain
Warning of the hurricane.

Oh, thou wild and wondrous bird,
Viewing thee, my thought is stirred.
Round and round the world thou goest,
Ocean solitude thou knowest—
Into trackless wastes hast flown,
Which no eyes save thine hath known
Ever tireless—day or night ;
Calm or tempest—ceaseless flight.

Albatross, I envy thee
Oft thy soaring-pinions free ;
For we deem the realms of air
Too ethereal for care.
Gladness as of endless springs
Seems to me is born with wings.
Thou canst rise and see the sun,
When his course to us is done
A moral here may us engross,
Thou the teacher—albatross !

ANON.

TO THE MAN OF-WAR BIRD

THOU who hast slept all night upon the storm,
Waking renew'd on thy prodigious pinions,
(Burst the wild storm ! above it thou ascended'st,
And rested on the sky, thy slave that cradled thee,)
Now a blue point, far, far in heaven floating,
As to the light emerging here on deck I watch thee,
(Myself a speck, a point on the world's floating vast).

Far, far at sea,
After the night's fierce drifts have strewn the shore
    with wrecks,
With reappearing day as now so happy and serene,
The rosy and elastic dawn, the flashing sun,
The limpid spread of air cerulean,
Thou also reappearest.

Thou born to match the gale (thou art all wings),
To cope with heaven and earth and sea and hurricane,
Thou ship of air that never furl'st thy sails,
Days, even weeks, untired and onward, through
    spaces, realms, gyrating,
At dusk that look'st on Senegal, at morn America,
That sport'st amid the lightning-flash and thunder-
    cloud,
In them, in thy experiences, had'st thou my soul,
What joys ! what joys were thine !
                                        WALT WHITMAN.

SONG OF THE OSTRICH

THE minstrel ever loves to sing
Of the beautiful gloss of the raven's wing ;
He tells of beauty, and seeks to compare
The pinion of jet with the maiden's hair.
The swan has a bright and goodly place
For its spotless down and stately grace ;
And bards unnumber'd have praised the dove,
For its gentle faith and eye of love.

The carolling lark oft wakes a tone.
As rich, as sweet, and fresh as its own ;
Lyres are strung for the wild sea-mew,
And the tawny night-owl hath its due.
The eagle on dark broadwing goes by,
While we hail him and laud him as king of the sky ;
And the poet's responding echoes float
Round the nightingale's lay and the cuckoo's note.

But, forget not, when praising the tribes of the air,
To give to the bird of the desert his share :
Though I warble not in a verdant land,
And am never leash'd to a lady's hand.
Yet many a league does the traveller come,
Seeking me far in my torrid home ;
To gain my plumage " rich and rare "
For the nightly train and courteous fair.

The wished-for heir to the titled line
Is worshipp'd and deck'd as a thing divine ;
The helpless form and tiny face
Are swathed in purple and shaded with lace ;
The mantle of velvet is richly bright,
The robe of fine lawn soft and white ;
But mine are the feathers that nod and bow
Over the first-born's baby brow.

Away on their steeds to the hostile horde
Go the warrior knight and the soldier lord ;
The corselet sparkles, the baldric is gay,
And bravely they bound in their battle array.

The scarf may flutter, the steel may shine,
But a prouder and nobler place is mine :
For the gem-wrought star that may gleam on the
    breast
Dazzles not like the dancing plume on the crest.

The envied daughters of rank are seen
In costly garbs of lustrous sheen ;
And I must be had to grace and crown
Foreheads as fair as my own soft down.
Glad and light such foreheads may seem,
And all look bright as a fairy dream ;
But I have dwelt in halls of state,
While temples have throbb'd beneath my weight.

Man dies and is coffined—but yet I am found
Swelling the train on the bone-strewn ground :
His race is run—his glory is past,
But I come in my pomp to mock him at last.
Then a song for the bird whose feathers wave
O'er the christening font and the fresh-made grave—
A song for the bird of the desert, whose plume
Is seen by the cradle and met at the tomb !

ELIZA COOK.

THE EMU

'NEATH Southern skies the Emu dwells,
In lonely plains, or forests wide,
Its deep note booms amid the bush
In weird loud tones at eventide ;
With strong swift feet, though powerless wings,
All day it roams the grassy plain,
Or hides amid the tangled growth,
When dark clouds burst in tropic rain.

In some slight hollow in the shade
It lays its eggs and rears its brood,
Though oft, alas ! it falls a prey
To some rough settler's onslaught rude ;
Ere long, perchance, this giant bird
Will cease to haunt the grassy land,
And vanish quite from mortal gaze,
A victim to man's ruthless hand !

MAUD E. SARGENT.

THE LAST WISH

The celebrated Alexander Wilson, the ornithologist and poet, requested that he might be buried near some sunny spot. This wish is expressed in the following lines.

IN some wild forest shade,
Under some spreading oak, or waving pine,
Or old elm, festooned with the gadding vine,
Let me be laid.

In this dim lonely grot,
No foot intrusive will disturb my dust ;
But o'er me songs of the wild birds shall burst,
Cheering the spot.

Not amid charnel stones,
Or coffins dark, and thick with ancient mould,
With tattered pall, and fringe of cankered gold,
   May rest my bones ;

But let the dewy rose,
The snowdrop and the violet, lend perfume
Above the spot where, in my grassy tomb,
   I take repose.

Year after year,
Within the silver-birch tree o'er me hung,
The chirping wren shall rear her callow young,
   Shall build her dwelling near.

And ever at the purple dawn of day
The lark shall chant a pealing song above,
And the shrill quail shall pipe her hymn of love,
   When eve grows dim and gray.

The blackbird and the thrush,
The golden oriole, shall flit around,
And waken, with a mellow gust of sound,
   The forest's solemn hush.

Birds from the distant sea
Shall sometimes hither flock on snowy wings,
And soar above my dust in airy rings,
   Singing a dirge to me.

                                        ANON.

EPILOGUE

THE POET AND THE BIRD

A FABLE

SAID a people to a poet " Go out from among us
straightway !
While we are thinking earthly things, thou singest
of divine.
There's a little fair brown nightingale, who, sitting in
the gateway,
Makes fitter music to our ear, than any song of
thine ! "
The poet went out weeping—the nightingale ceased
chanting ;
" Now, wherefore, O thou nightingale, is all thy
sweetness done ? "
" I cannot sing my earthly things, the heavenly poet
wanting,
Whose highest harmony includes the lowest under
sun."
The poet went out weeping—and died abroad, bereft
there—
The bird flew to his grave and died amid a thousand
wails !—
Yet when I last came by the place, I swear the music
left there
Was only of the poet's song, and not the night-
ingale's !

ELIZABETH BARRETT BROWNING.

2 I

L'ENVOI

Go, little booke, God send thee good passage
And specially let this be thy prayere,
Unto them all that thee will read or hear,
Where thou art wrong, after their help to call
Thee to correct in any part or all.

CHAUCER.

INDEX OF BIRDS

INDEX OF AUTHORS

N.B.—Dateless names are those of living Authors

508 INDEX OF AUTHORS

INDEX OF AUTHORS 511

THE RIVERSIDE PRESS LIMITED. EDINBURGH.

GENERAL LIBRARY
UNIVERSITY OF CALIFORNIA—BERKELEY
RETURN TO DESK FROM WHICH BORROWED
This book is due on the last date stamped below, or on the
date to which renewed.
Renewed books are subject to immediate recall.

21–100m-1,'54(1887s16)476

Lightning Source UK Ltd.
Milton Keynes UK
UKOW06f1845281215

265449UK00012B/240/P

9 781330 952580